American Government in Action Series

PHILLIPS BRADLEY, *Editor*

★　　★　　★　　★　　★　　★

The Supreme Court and Judicial Review

American Government in Action

The
Supreme Court
and
Judicial Review

ROBERT K. CARR
Dartmouth College

GREENWOOD PRESS, PUBLISHERS
WESTPORT, CONNECTICUT

1970

To Bill

★　　★　　★　　★　　★　　★

Editor's Foreword

THE LITERATURE of politics has been one of the major forces in our national life. Much of it, especially before the 1860's, although polemic in purpose and form, contributed significantly to the shaping of governmental institutions and policies. Another main current in the literature of politics emerged just over a century ago. We had by the 1820's matured sufficiently to begin to review our own development as a nation. Scholars and lawyers became interested in the observation and appraisal of the institutional patterns of our political order. The new approach was reflected first in formal expositions of the Constitution and later in hardly less formal analyses of the workings of government. As the state became more complex in its organization and more comprehensive in its activities, observation and appraisal of government were, however, too often channeled into rather rigid —and frequently narrow—categories of analysis. The influence of cultural, economic, and social forces on political organization and procedure, the concept of government as the nexus of reconciliation or adjustment of conflicting ideas, interest, and institutions within a dynamic society such as ours, only incidentally affected the scholarly "disciplines." The attempt to apply to the American political scene the catholicity of outlook of an Aristotle or a Montesquieu is indeed yet to be made. "The art of governance" is all too frequently identified with the minutiae of the government's structure or procedure.

There is one brilliant exception. Just a century ago, there appeared the second volume of Alexis de Tocqueville's *Democracy in America.* His unique contribution to our understanding of America—today no less than in the 1830's—was that he saw government in action as a focus of the desires and purposes of the people in all their daily manifestations, as an agency for the democratic accommodation of cultural, economic, and social tensions within society.

It is in this tradition that we who are co-operating in this series have thought it worth while to add to the already voluminous literature about American government. Current discussion of a "functional" approach to its study is in fact a return to the course which De Tocqueville charted as to how and with what tools government should be observed and appraised.

No single refracting lens can, however, today catch all the variables in a political spectrum, the "invisible radiations" of which filter into every aspect of the hopes, desires, and purposes of a people bent on making the ideals and practices of democracy effective. We have sought to bring together, therefore, in this series the special competence and the varied outlook of some of those who in recent years have been responsible in significant ways for setting government in action or of observing and appraising it as it functions in the many aspects of the nation's life. The series as a whole should give citizens and students alike an adequate view of how our national government functions. The individual volumes analyze the institutional forms—constitutional, legislative, executive, administrative, and judicial—at the critical points where they affect, often determine, the workings of a democratic system.

The problems selected for discussion in the series are today, as they have been in the past, foci of public debate and political pressure. They are areas in which emergent ideas and forces are molding the future of American democracy.

Professor Carr treats a highly technical—and, at the same time, a profoundly significant—question with forthright vigor and candor. The nature of judicial review is technical; its use as an instrument of policy is one of the most significant elements in both government and politics in this country. Those who read Professor Carr's analysis and appraisal of the ways in which judicial review has been exercised by the Supreme Court in molding public policy may not always agree with his judgments. They cannot fail to be stimulated to examine afresh the influence of the Court on our national life at many critical junctures in our history.

PHILLIPS BRADLEY

Queens College
January, 1942

★　　★　　★　　★　　★　　★

Preface

THIS VOLUME is in no sense a treatise on constitutional law or a history of judicial review. Instead, its one purpose is to view the exercise of power by the Supreme Court of the United States as a part of the American governmental process. What is the nature of this power? Why was it granted to the judiciary? In what manner has it been exercised? What influences, legal and nonlegal, have helped shape the Court's decisions? How have these decisions contributed to the nation's political development? It is questions such as these that this book endeavors to answer. And it is only in seeking the answers to such questions that technical aspects of constitutional law or episodes in constitutional history are introduced for illustrative purposes.

My thesis is that the Supreme Court is more readily studied and understood as a political agency, sharing with the President and Congress the power to govern, than it is as a judicial body applying strictly legal rules to constitutional questions. Acceptance of such a thesis does not necessarily involve condemnation of the Court or opposition to the practice of judicial review. More than one criticism of the use which the Court has made of its power of judicial review will be found in this essay. Nevertheless my desire

~~is~~ to explain the work of the Supreme Court, not to condemn it.

The Supreme Court has exercised the power of judicial review for nearly a century and a half. All attempts to abolish it or to curtail its powers have ended in failure. But it is entirely possible that a wider public understanding of the true nature of judicial review may influence the way in which this power is exercised in the future.

No author ever had greater obligations to acknowledge. My debt to the great students of the Supreme Court, such men as Charles Beard, Edward Corwin, Robert Cushman, Charles Haines, Thomas Reed Powell, and Charles Warren, will be apparent to the reader. At various stages in its preparation the manuscript has been read by Professor John Leek of the University of Oklahoma and by Professors James P. Richardson, Hugh Elsbree, and Elmer Smead of Dartmouth College. To say merely that all these friends have given valuable assistance is most inadequate in view of the extent to which I have utilized their suggestions. Mention must also be made of Phillips Bradley, editor of this series, whose criticisms and advice have helped this material to assume its present shape. My wife, Olive Carr, has not only assisted with such mechanical matters as spelling and style but has made a material contribution to the substance of the volume. Needless to say, I accept full responsibility for factual errors and controversial points of interpretation.

R. K. C.

Hanover, N.H.
January, 1942

Contents

I
The Quest for Certainty

1

II
The Struggle for Power

26

III
The Genesis of Judicial Supremacy: The Federal and
State Conventions

37

IV
The Genesis of Judicial Supremacy: *Marbury* v. *Madison*

57

V
The Meaning of the Constitution: Instrument and
Symbol

72

VI
The Supreme Court in Action: Interstate Commerce

99

VII
The Supreme Court in Action: Due Process of Law

139

CONTENTS

VIII

The Scope of Judicial Review: Limitations 184

IX

The Scope of Judicial Review: Judicial Interpretation
of Statutes and Review of Administrative Rulings 204

X

Personality and Judicial Review 231

XI

Judicial Review under Fire 257

XII

The Power to Govern 278

Selected Bibliography 293

Index 299

★　　★　　★　　★　　★　　★

Chapter I

The Quest for Certainty

N<small>ON</small> *sub Homine sed sub Deo et Lege*—Not under Man, but under God and Law. So reads the inscription over the entrance to the magnificent library of one of the oldest and greatest law schools in America. The imposing presence, in such a place, of this ancient aphorism of the English common law is symptomatic of one of the strongest traits in the character of man—the quest for certainty. It finds its counterpart in the more modern phrase, so often repeated, that ours is a government of laws, and not of men. Man, himself, is apparently not to be trusted. He is an undependable being, given to capricious and arbitrary thought and deed. Accordingly, to place man under the rule of man is to give him no certainty or security but to subject him to the selfish whims of a potential tyrant or despot. One need take but a hasty glance about the world today to realize that such an outcome of government by man is at least a possibility.

So it is that man seeks to assure himself that he lives under a government of laws. *Equal Justice under Law,* we read as we enter the gleaming, marbled home of the United States Supreme Court in the city of Washington. In our minds takes shape a picture of impartial, impersonal judges applying traditional and immutable principles of law so as

to render absolute justice to all men. Here there is no uncertainty, no mere whim or caprice, no arbitrary edict by
man over man. Instead, here is unchanging, beneficent rule
of law, whereby a "judge as a seeker of the truth . . . dis-
covers the principles on which his conclusions bearing on a
case may be based and from which a judgment follows, subject to no variance or turning."[1]

Such is a traditional and widely accepted conception
of the nature of law and the role of the judge. This concept
is admittedly a noble one. But whether it is a sound one
remains to be seen. What is the true character of law?
Under what circumstances is it born? How does it grow?
What are the respective roles of the judge, the legislator,
and executive in its origin and development? And back of
all these questions lies the basic query: to what extent
does our rule of law actually eliminate the capriciousness
of the human factor and give reality to the dream of certainty?

The Function of Law in Society

Society is essentially a matter of diverse human relationships. One of the most important and often the most difficult and troublesome of these is the relationship between
an employer and his employees. Not infrequently problems
arise which cannot be settled by the parties themselves, but
require intervention by government. Moreover, this intervention, through the agency of the courts, is usually wel-
comed, and often even actively sought, by the quarreling
parties.

Let us make use of a specific illustration. In the spring of
1937 there occurred a particularly violent labor dispute in

[1]Charles G. Haines, *The American Doctrine of Judicial Supremacy* (2nd
ed.; Berkeley: University of California Press, 1932) 500. Haines does not
advocate this thesis. Reprinted by permission of the University of California
Press.

the city of Philadelphia. There the Apex Hosiery Company had been operating an "open shop" in its mills which gave employment to some twenty-five hundred workers in the manufacture of stockings. But in April of that year the local branch of the American Federation of Full Fashioned Hosiery Workers had demanded that the company operate a "closed shop." The demand was refused. Thereupon, at a time when only eight of the company's workers were actually members of the union, the latter ordered a strike. Members of the union who were employees of other hosiery factories in Philadelphia assembled at the mill. "Immediately, acts of violence against . . . [the] plant and the employees in charge of it were committed by the assembled mob. It forcibly seized the plant, whereupon, under union leadership, its members were organized to maintain themselves as sit-down strikers in possession of the plant. . . . While occupying the factory, the strikers wilfully wrecked machinery of great value, and did extensive damage to other property and equipment of the company." In short, the strikers used "force and violence of the most brutal and wanton character."[2] At the time of the strike there were in the plant one and one half million pairs of finished stockings valued at about $800,000, eighty per cent of which were ready to be shipped on order to customers outside the state. Three times the company asked the strikers to let it make shipment of these finished stockings, and three times it was refused.

Under these circumstances, it is not surprising that the company felt itself ill treated and turned to law and the courts for aid and protection from the arbitrariness and violence of the workers. Here a fundamental characteristic of *the law* may be noted. The company at once discovered that society had provided many laws having a possible ap-

[2] *Apex Hosiery Company* v. *Leader* 310 U.S. 469, 482 (1940). The quotations are from the statement of the case by Justice Stone.

plication to such a situation. In fact, it was not at all easy to choose which path to follow. To begin with, there were state laws that might be invoked. For example, it was clear that the law of Pennsylvania invited the company to seek damages for its destroyed property by bringing civil suit against the union in the state courts. Likewise, it suggested that the company might request proper state officials to bring criminal prosecution against the strikers for the commission of a variety of possible offenses resulting from their use of mob violence, and their wanton seizure and destruction of private property. But the company chose instead to turn to the federal courts and to invoke certain remedies available in federal law, charging specifically that the action of the strikers violated the Sherman Antitrust Act.

First of all, the Apex Hosiery Company sought governmental assistance in clearing the plant of its tenacious trespassers. This it received in the form of a writ of injunction restraining the strikers from further occupancy of the property.[3] Thereupon, the proper law-enforcement officials, acting pursuant to the writ, forcibly ejected the strikers. The company was now able to resume its normal operations.

But the company was not yet satisfied. During the seven weeks the strike had lasted much valuable business had been lost and wanton destruction of property had occurred. Accordingly, the company returned to the federal courts and asked for an award of damages against the union. This action, too, was brought on the basis of the Sherman Act. The processes of the law at once began to operate, and judges were soon involved in an attempt to render justice in the case. But first they found it necessary to ascertain what *the law* in the matter was. For presumably they were not to act as mere arbiters in the dispute, but were to refer to fixed rules which had been provided to meet just such a

[3] *Apex Hosiery Company* v. *Leader* 90 F. (2d) 155 (1937).

situation. At this point we may note a second important characteristic of *law*. Not only may there be a variety of laws with possible application to a specific situation. In addition the one actually invoked will probably need considerable interpretation before it can be applied to the case. In its possible relevancy to the *Apex* case the Sherman Act provided that "every contract, combination in the form of trust or otherwise, or conspiracy, in restraint of trade or commerce among the several States, or with foreign nations, is hereby declared to be illegal." And by way of a *civil* penalty for violations of this provision, the act invited persons injured as the result of the operation of such wrongful contracts, combinations, or conspiracies in restraint of commerce to seek treble damages for the loss they had suffered.[4]

The statute certainly seemed to hold forth some promise of help to the company, for by their action the strikers had brought to a halt a business having a substantial interstate aspect, and had specifically refused to permit the shipment in interstate commerce of stockings to the value of many hundred thousand dollars. But it was only a promise, for obviously the statute did not in so many words provide for relief in just such a situation as the one at hand. In its use of the words, "contract, combination . . . or conspiracy in restraint of trade . . ." the act's application to the activities of a labor union was not entirely clear. As it turned out, when the case reached the Supreme Court of the United States, after having passed through the lower federal courts, the nine members of the Court divided six to three in preferring an interpretation of the Sherman Act by which the company was finally refused its claim for damages.

To what considerations did the Court give attention in making its interpretation? Speaking through Justice Stone, the majority suggested three possible indications of the

[4]26 Stat. L. 209 (1890).

specific meaning of the words of a statute: namely, congressional intent as suggested at the time of the passage of the statute; traditional rules of common law on the same subject; and previous court rulings interpreting the statute.

Pursuing these three approaches to a solution of the legal problem in the case, the majority concluded the evidence indicated that the Sherman Act did not apply to the ordinary restraint upon commerce that might result from a strike, but only to that specific restraint which is intended to have, and does have, a substantial effect upon *commercial competition in the market.*[5]

Three dissenting justices, speaking through Chief Justice Hughes, suggested that the majority was mistaken in the official interpretation it was giving to the statute. They were of the opinion that the evidence from the same sources investigated by the majority indicated that a mere obstruction or prevention of the shipment of goods in interstate commerce, whatever the character of such restraint, so long as it is direct and intentional, amounts to a violation of the Sherman Act. So interpreting the statute, they felt that it had been violated by the strikers in the case at hand and that the wronged corporation was entitled to treble damages.[6]

Perhaps enough has now been said to show the need for some sort of governmental agency to interpret and apply general laws to specific situations. However, certain matters referred to in the discussion of the *Apex* case may be reconsidered at greater length in seeking a better understanding of the concept of a *government of laws* and also of the way in which the work of our courts is related to the total governmental process.

[5] *Apex Hosiery Company* v. *Leader* 310 U.S. 469, 493.
[6] *Ibid.,* p. 514.

The American System of Courts

In the first place, the story of the *Apex* case suggests that the business of providing a government of laws in this country is carried on by a variety of courts. To begin with, the distinction must be noted between state and federal courts. Because of the dual system of American government, involving as it does separate national and state governments more or less independent of each other, we may and do have two systems of courts: state courts to administer state law, and federal courts to administer federal law.[7] Such a division of the judicial function between two kinds of courts along federal and state lines may seem at first thought to be a relatively simple matter. Actually, it is an exceedingly complex arrangement. Recall that the Apex Hosiery Company, having decided to seek the aid of the law and the courts in its controversy with the hosiery workers, found that it could apparently turn in either direction. It might have turned to the courts of Pennsylvania and invoked the provisions of state law designed to provide assistance to one in the situation in which the company found itself. Indeed, as the affair finally turned out, it is clear that this is the direction which the company should have chosen, or, for that matter, might still choose after its failure in the federal courts. Justice Stone pointed out in his decision: "It is not denied, and we assume for present purposes, that . . . [the union members] by substituting the primitive method of trial by combat, for the ordinary processes of justice **and**

---

[7]It should be noted that a system of inferior federal courts with original jurisdiction to try cases involving federal statutes is by no means necessary. Such cases could be handled by state courts. But at least one federal appellate court would be needed to review the diverse decisions of state courts and establish uniformity in the interpretation and application of national statutes.

more civilized means of deciding an industrial dispute, violated the civil and penal laws of Pennsylvania which authorize the recovery of full compensation and impose criminal penalties for the wrongs done."[8] But instead the company chose to turn to the federal courts in an unsuccessful effort to invoke certain remedies under seemingly pertinent federal statutory provisions.

A brief explanation of the respective jurisdictions of federal and state courts is in order at this point. We may begin by examining the jurisdiction of the federal courts, noting that according to the theory of our American constitutional system the authority of federal courts to hear different kinds of cases is supposedly limited to certain specific situations, all other possible types of jurisdiction being reserved to state courts.[9] The specific types of jurisdiction granted to the federal courts under this principle may be grouped under two broad headings. In the first place, certain kinds of cases may be heard by the federal courts because of the nature of the subject matter of the litigation. Thus, if the facts of a case are such as to involve the federal Constitution, a federal treaty, or a federal statute, the case may be heard by a federal court. Likewise, any case arising within the fields of so-called admiralty or maritime law falls within the jurisdiction of the federal courts. In the second place, certain types of cases may be heard by the federal courts because of the nature of the parties to the litigation, irrespective of the subject matter. Within this category may

[8]*Apex Hosiery Company* v. *Leader* 310 U.S. 469, 483. Subsequent to this decision of the United States Supreme Court the Apex Company did bring suit for damages against the union in the Pennsylvania courts. However, the case was finally settled out of court when the union agreed to pay the sum of $110,000 to the company. *The New York Times,* June 21, 1941.

[9]*Constitution of the United States.* Tenth Amendment, "The powers not delegated to the United States by the Constitution, nor prohibited by it to the States, are reserved to the States respectively, or to the people."

be placed cases affecting ambassadors and other foreign diplomatic and consular agents, controversies to which the federal government is a party, cases between two or more state governments, and cases between a state government and a citizen of another state, or between citizens of different states.[10] With the exception of one or two minor types of case, all other possible types fall within the jurisdiction of the state courts.

Unfortunately, the respective jurisdictions of the federal and the state courts cannot, in practice, be kept as separate as this analysis might seem to indicate. Actually, there is a large but vague field in which the two jurisdictions overlap. The subject matter of a case may be such that both federal and state statutes are involved, and consequently the matter of federal or state jurisdiction may not be easy to determine. We have already seen how the Apex litigation seemingly involved both federal and state law and might have been considered by either type of court. Moreover, the jurisdiction of the federal courts within the constitutionally defined areas is not necessarily exclusive or, in some instances, even available. With the exception of the original jurisdiction of the Supreme Court, Congress is free to determine how much of this jurisdiction any given federal court shall possess. Congress may also provide for the exercise of jurisdiction within these federal areas by state courts.

The distinction between federal and state courts having been noted, we may go on to examine the distinction between different kinds of federal courts, since it is with certain aspects of the federal judicial process that we are to be primarily concerned. There are three main types of federal courts. At the bottom are the *district courts* of which there are eighty-six in the United States proper. These are the federal courts of original jurisdiction. That is, the average

[10]*Constitution of the United States*, Art. III, sec. 2.

case which may be heard at all in the federal courts is heard in the first instance by a district court. The Apex Hosiery Company began in a district court both of its actions against the hosiery union: the one for an injunction by which its plant might be cleared of sit-down strikers, and the other for treble damages under the Sherman Act.

Second, the United States has been divided into ten "circuits," and for each of these there is a *circuit court of appeals.* As the name indicates, these are courts which are almost exclusively concerned with appellate jurisdiction. That is, they review cases on appeal which have already been decided by the district courts. Naturally only a portion of the cases decided by the district courts will be reviewed by circuit courts. In the Apex litigation both district court rulings were appealed to and reviewed by a circuit court.

Third, at the top of our federal judicial structure stands the United States Supreme Court, the only federal court actually provided for in the Constitution, all the others having been organized by congressional statute under authority conferred upon Congress by the Constitution. The Supreme Court is almost exclusively a court of appellate jurisdiction. Only those cases to which a foreign diplomatic agent or a state government is a party may be heard originally by the Supreme Court.[11] These cases are relatively rare. The procedure by which the Supreme Court reviews cases decided originally by lower courts is technically rather complex and need be but briefly analyzed here. It is, of course, necessary to limit the number of cases reaching the highest federal court, since one such court can handle at best only a few hundred cases a year Between 1891 and 1925 Congress passed a series of statutes providing that many appeals to the Supreme Court should be by means of the writ of certiorari. The significance of this particular writ lies

[11]*Ibid.*

in the fact that it vests in the superior court a very great measure of discretionary power enabling it to select the cases that may come before it for review, and thus take jurisdiction only over those cases that present issues of major importance. Since 1925, in view of the widespread use of certiorari, appeal to the Supreme Court by individuals, *as a matter of right,* has been very largely curtailed.[12]

It should be pointed out that the United States Supreme Court reviews certain cases heard originally in the state courts. If the highest court in a state holds a federal statute or treaty invalid, or upholds a state law against the charge that it violates the federal Constitution or is repugnant to a federal law or treaty, an appeal to the Supreme Court may be made as of right by the aggrieved party. Moreover, the Supreme Court by certiorari exercises a discretionary right to review still other decisions of the state courts where a "federal question" is involved—such as the interpretation and application of a federal statute.[13]

Reference may also be made here to the fact that the judiciary in each state is organized in much the same hierarchal form as is the federal judiciary. There is, however, little uniformity in the forty-eight state systems. In general there are more different kinds of court at each of the three levels—original jurisdiction, intermediate appeal, and highest appeal—than is true of the federal system. Furthermore, there is no uniformity as to method of appointment and tenure. All judges associated with any of the federal courts herein described are appointed by the President of the United States by and with the advice and consent of the Senate, and hold office for life during good behavior. In a few states judges are similarly appointed, either by the gover-

[12]*Encyclopaedia of the Social Sciences* (New York: The Macmillan Company, 1932) III, 317.

[13]*Ibid.,* II, 131.

nor or the legislature, and hold office for life. But in the overwhelming majority of the states, judges are elected to office by the voters for limited terms, which vary greatly as to length.

The successive stages of the *Apex* litigation in the federal courts illustrate in rather striking fashion the vicissitudes that may be encountered by a case in its travels through the courts. In seeking to determine whether the Sherman Act did really govern the case, the different federal judges who passed upon the question were in wide disagreement. In the district court the company was successful in pressing its suit and received an award of treble damages against the union totaling $711,932.55. Thereupon the union appealed the decision to the circuit court of appeals and obtained a reversal. The decision of the circuit court denying the company damages was based on the grounds that the stoppage of interstate commerce resulting from the strike was not sufficiently substantial to support a decision that the Sherman Act had been violated, since only 3 per cent of the total flow of stockings in interstate commerce had been affected, and also that the evidence failed to show an *intent* on the part of the strikers to restrain interstate commerce. Finally, the company appealed the case to the Supreme Court, hoping for a reversal of the circuit court decision and a return to the original district court position. This reversal it failed to obtain. However, the Supreme Court did reject the reasons which the circuit court had offered in support of its decision. It concluded that the stoppage of interstate commerce was substantial and that the evidence did indicate an intent on the part of the strikers to bring about such a stoppage. However, the Supreme Court adhered to the decision reached by the circuit court, offering a new reason to the effect that the type of restraint present in the *Apex* case was not the kind of restraint of interstate commerce against which the words of the Sherman Act were directed.

Types of Law

An investigation of the *Apex* case also provides us with an opportunity to examine the different kinds of law which American courts are called upon to administer and which are, collectively, the basis, in theory at least, of our government of laws. Three types of law will be examined: statutory law, common law, and equity.

The most obvious form of law is a statute enacted by a legislative body. Where Congress or a state legislature has chosen to formulate a rule of society, such as one governing the relationship between an employer and his employees, it is superior to all forms of customary law which may previously have been utilized by courts in disposing of litigation arising within that particular field. As we have already seen in the *Apex* case, a statute such as the Sherman Act may need considerable interpretation by courts before it can be given specific application in a case involving particular individuals or circumstances. Nevertheless, a statute's existence is clear and definite. It is common knowledge that Congress has passed the statute known as the Sherman Act, which deals with the matter of monopoly control.

Common law, on the other hand, is judge-made law, often in the absence of any statute. This "common law" had its beginnings centuries ago in England when judges found it necessary, in deciding cases which litigants had brought before them, to make their own law in the absence of any other. According to a commonly accepted version of this historical process they manufactured law by drawing largely upon "those popular customs which were so long established and so generally followed that the courts resorted to them for the principles on which to decide the cases which were brought before them."[14] As a result of the gradual development of the common law there came to be recognized rules, for example, "that the eldest son alone is heir to his ancestor; —that property may be acquired and transferred by writing; —that a deed is of no validity unless sealed and delivered;— that wills should be construed more favorably, and deeds more strictly;—that money lent upon bond is recoverable by action of debt;—that breaking the public peace is an offense, and punishable by fine and imprisonment;—all these are doctrines that are not set down in any written statute or ordinance, but depend merely upon immemorial usage, that is, upon common law for their support."[15]

Equity is likewise a system of judge-made law, of English origin and development more or less simultaneous with that of the common law. In fact, to the layman equity seems hardly more than a mere supplement to the common law. Early in the development of common law it was discovered that in certain situations the inadequacy or total absence of traditional common-law remedies made it difficult for judges to render true justice. Accordingly, a special body of rules and a separate procedure were gradually worked out to handle these special cases. A good example of an equitable remedy is the writ of injunction which the Apex Hosiery Company sought from a federal court in an attempt to dislodge the sit-down strikers from its property. In the traditional common-law system a person whose property rights were being interfered with by another person or persons had no choice but to wait for the completion of the wrongful act and then to seek damages in the historic common-law

[14]L. B. Evans, *Leading Cases on American Constitutional Law* (2nd ed.; Chicago: Callaghan and Company, 1925) 142.

[15]Blackstone, *Commentaries on the Laws of England* (Chase, 3rd ed.; New York: Banks & Brothers, 1896) I, 68–69.

courts as provided by law. But in many such situations it seemed an injustice to the wronged individual not to provide him also with the necessary governmental assistance to prevent the continuation of the wrongful act, because in part or whole the resulting damage might be irreparable. Thus under available common-law remedies the Apex Hosiery Company might have found it difficult to collect damages, not so much for the physical destruction of its property as for the more intangible damage resulting from the loss of business. If the strike continued indefinitely the company might lose many of its customers permanently and never be able to regain the lost ground. For such loss the collection of adequate damages under law might be virtually impossible. It was for such reasons that the equitable remedy of the writ of injunction was developed to make it possible for a wronged person to seek the protection of the courts before the wrong against him was completed, or perhaps even begun. A court with equity jurisdiction gives this protection by issuing a writ forbidding the commission or continued commission of specific and allegedly illegal acts. Failure to observe such a writ renders the person who persists in the forbidden activity liable to punishment for contempt of court. In so far as an offense against the common law or statutory law may have been committed in an injunction case the common-law or statutory penalties for such an offense may also be applied. Thus after the Apex Hosiery Company had invoked an *equitable* remedy to prevent the workers from continuing their wrong against it, it attempted to invoke a *legal* remedy to obtain redress for the wrong already committed before the writ of injunction was granted.

The Role of the Judge in Lawmaking

Finally, an examination of the *Apex* case affords an opportunity to note the extreme difficulty which judges often encounter in their attempts to apply law to specific situations, whether the law be in the form of statute, common law, or equity. In good part the difficulty of the judge's task is the result of an extreme but necessary complexity in the law. Our legal system in the United States today does not consist of any single, straightforward catalogue of rules. Instead, we have a confusing intermingling of statutory law, common law, and equity. For one thing, in the frequent absence of a pertinent statute a court finds it necessary to base its decision in a given case upon the old rules of common law or equity, which are often less precise than the words of a modern statute. But even where there is a relevant statute, common law or judge-made law may still play a very important role. In the first place, when a legislature passes a statute it may simply be giving more definite form to a rule already well established in common law. The great English legal historian A. V. Dicey points out that "many Acts of Parliament . . . such as the Sale of Goods Act, 1893, or the Bills of Exchange Act, 1882, are little else than the reproduction in a statutory shape of rules originally established by the courts. Judge-made law has in such cases passed into statute law."[16] In the second place, even if a statute formulated by a legislative body does mark a break with common law and result in the legal expression of a public policy at least partially new, the influence of the common law may still be strong. The statute will be sub-

---

[16]A. V. Dicey, *Law and Public Opinion in England* (New York: The Macmillan Company, 1905) 360. Reprinted by permission of The Macmillan Company, publishers.

ject to interpretation and enforcement by the courts and, as Dean Pound suggests: "It is not what the legislature desires, but what the courts regard as juridically permissible that in the end becomes law. Statutes give way before the settled habits of legal thinking which we call the common law. Judges and jurists do not hesitate to assert that there are extraconstitutional limits to legislative power which put fundamental common law dogmas beyond the reach of statutes."[17]

In its decision in the *Apex* case the Supreme Court pointed out that the words of the Sherman Act were being interpreted in the light of the common law. "This Court has . . . repeatedly recognized that the restraints at which the Sherman law is aimed, and which are described by its terms, are only those which are comparable to restraints deemed illegal at common law. . . ."[18] True, the Court also insisted that this interpretation of the Sherman Act over a fifty-year period in the light of common-law tradition coincided exactly with what Congress had intended at the time it passed the statute, as was evidenced by the failure of Congress to repudiate this common-law influence in the judicial interpretation of the Sherman Act through subsequent amendments to the act. But the frequency of dissenting opinions in these Sherman Act cases and the extent to which even the majority interpretation of the act has shifted ground upon occasion prove that the original intent of Congress at the time it passed the act was somewhat nebulous, to say the least. The significant point is that the Supreme Court has been able to turn the enforcement of the Sherman Act in different directions and toward different goals, depending upon the interpretation of the act which a majority of the

[17]Roscoe Pound, "Law in Books and Law in Action." 44 *American Law Review* (Jan.–Feb. 1910) 27. Quoted by Haines, *op. cit.* (above, n. 1), p. 425.

[18]*Apex Hosiery Company* v. *Leader* 310 U.S. 469, 498.

justices happened to prefer at a given moment. And at certain moments common-law traditions seem to have carried much weight with the Court in its interpretation of the act.

And in the third place, even where, following the enactment of a statute, a court charged with its enforcement is motivated by no wish to reformulate the law in line with ancient doctrines of the common law, there is almost always a necessity for further development of judge-made law. What happens is perhaps something like this. The legislature passes a statute in a certain field. Years pass and the courts may render hundreds and even thousands of decisions under this statute. In the meantime conditions change. New problems arise. The courts do the best they can with the statute, interpreting it in the light of the new problems and inevitably adding to its meaning. As a result, the law—the law that actually operates and controls—is something more than the original statute. It is this statute plus many important court decisions clarifying and extending its meaning in the absence of any specific or further action by the legislature. These decisions which supplement the original statute become part of the common law.

In this process of statutory development and adaptation at the hands of judges, previous court decisions will presumably be followed in later cases where the factual background is of a similar character. This principle is referred to by lawyers with the Latin phrase *stare decisis*. In other words, we must note here the importance of *precedent* in our legal system, the idea that our law and our judicial decisions have a historical continuity—as opposed to a system by which courts might endeavor to render justice in each case anew, as though each case constituted a problem unto itself, in no way related to any previous problems which courts have disposed of. Unfortunately, this matter of precedents is by no means as simple or straightforward as has perhaps been indicated up to this point. For in actual practice, two cases are rarely, if ever, exactly alike. Consequently, when a lawyer agrees to handle a case for a client and goes to work preparing his arguments, or when a judge is asked to render a decision, both find that in seeking controlling legal principles it is necessary to read back through previous court opinions which will have been rendered in cases almost, but not quite, like the one at hand. Thus a judge may have a wide discretion in deciding in a given case to follow either precedent A, or precedent B, both of which seem to have considerable bearing on this case but which, unfortunately, are completely contradictory to one another. Let the judge follow A and he decides the case one way. Let him follow B and he must decide it in exactly opposite fashion. Which way will he decide?

Justice Cardozo has brilliantly illustrated the need for a choice between principles in some cases:

One principle or precedent, pushed to the limit of its logic, may point to one conclusion; another principle or precedent, followed with like logic, may point with equal certainty to another. In this conflict, we must choose between the two paths, selecting one or other, or perhaps striking out upon a third, which will be the resultant of the two forces in combination, or will represent the mean between extremes. Let me take as an illustration of such conflict the famous case of Riggs v. Palmer, 115 N.Y. 506. That case decided that a legatee who had murdered his testator would not be permitted by a court of equity to enjoy the benefits of the will. Conflicting principles were there in competition for the mastery. One of them prevailed, and vanquished all the others. There was the principle of the binding force of a will. . . . That principle, pushed to the limit of its logic, seemed to uphold the title of the murderer. There was the principle that civil courts may not add to the pains and penalties of crimes. That, pushed to the limit of its logic, seemed to uphold his title. But over against these was another principle, of greater generality, its roots deeply fastened in universal sentiments of justice, the principle that no man should profit from his own inequity or take advantage of his own wrong. The logic of this principle prevailed over the logic of the others. . . . One path was followed, another closed, because of the conviction in the judicial mind that the one selected led to justice. . . . In the end, the principle that was thought to be most fundamental, to represent the larger and deeper social interests, put its competitors to flight.[19]

We have noted the extent to which common law tends to dictate the content of statutory law or to influence its interpretation after its enactment. Perhaps an observation of even greater significance growing out of this discussion is that judges seem to participate in the legislative process. This truth has been so long recognized that it is no longer debatable. We can refer back two centuries and more to the famous remark of Bishop Hoadly: "Nay, whoever hath an *absolute authority* to *interpret* any written or spoken laws, it is *He* who is truly the *Law-Giver* to all intents and purposes, and not the person who first wrote or spoke them."[20] Or we can take the word of the recently retired Chief Justice of the United States: "The Court is the final interpreter of the Acts of Congress. Statutes come to the judicial test . . . with respect to their true import, and a *federal statute finally means what the Court says it means.* . . . Congress voluntarily leaves much to the Courts."[21] This

[19]Benjamin N. Cardozo, *The Nature of the Judicial Process* (New Haven: Yale University Press, 1921) 40–42. Reprinted by permission of the publisher.

[20]Bishop Hoadly's Sermon preached before the King, March 31, 1717, on "The Nature of the Kingdom or Church of Christ" (London: James Knapton, 1717). Justice Holmes is credited with calling a modern generation's attention to this phrase. 6 *Harvard Law Review* (April 1892) 33, n.

[21]Charles E. Hughes, *The Supreme Court of the United States* (New York: Columbia University Press, 1928) 229–32. (Italics added.) Reprinted by permission of the Columbia University Press.

was certainly true of the Sherman Antitrust Act. The Supreme Court itself points out in the *Apex* decision that "the prohibitions of the Sherman Act were not stated in terms of precision or of crystal clarity and the Act itself did not define them. In consequence of the vagueness of its language, perhaps not uncalculated, *the courts have been left to give content to the statute,* and in the performance of that function it is appropriate that courts should interpret its word in the light of its legislative history and of the particular evils at which the legislation was aimed."[22]

In short, it is not enough for a legislature to make law. Law must be implemented as well. This latter need can presumably be met in more than one way, and actually, as we will see later, we in the United States have tried more than one method of meeting the need. But usually, and for the most part, we have turned to the courts as a necessary agency standing somewhere between the legislative authority and the final executive power of government. It is important to note, then, obvious though the point may seem to be, that the courts are a part of the governmental process. They are not, as many people are inclined to believe, independent agencies in our society, set apart completely from the realm of politics.

Judicial Review

Up to now we have been examining the ordinary legislative and judicial processes—the process by which the rules of society, which we call laws, are formulated, interpreted, and applied to actual cases involving specific individuals. If we were seeking to describe the concept of a "government of laws" as it finds expression in England this would be essentially the complete story in rough outline. But for the United States it is only part of the story, for we have

[22] *Apex Hosiery Company* v. *Leader* 310 U.S. 469, 489. (Italics added.)

gone a step further than our English cousins in attempting
to establish a rule of law. In our efforts to achieve this goal
we have not been content to depend alone upon the ordinary forms—common law, equity, and statutory law. Instead, we have sought to perfect the concept by establishing
a "higher" or "superior" law over and above ordinary law.
More specifically, we have provided that public policies as
announced by our legislative bodies and enforced by administrative bodies must be formulated in accordance with
the principles of our Constitution. If they are not so formulated they fail to carry the weight of law and cannot prevail.
In short, an act of the legislative or administrative departments of government which is contrary to constitutional
principles is regarded as null and void. Furthermore, the
power to make such a declaration has come to be regarded
as resting in the courts. Thus the American judiciary not
only interprets and applies ordinary law as such law affects
the interests of private parties; it also interprets and applies
constitutional law as such law affects the powers and duties
of public officers to conduct the affairs of government. So
in the *Apex* case, in addition to the determination of what
the Sherman Act meant as applied to the situation at hand,
the question arose as to whether Congress even had the
authority under the higher law of the Constitution to pass
a law penalizing a labor union for restraining interstate commerce as the result of a local strike. As a matter of fact, this
question of constitutional law was not of serious importance
in the outcome of the *Apex* case and the Court quickly
concluded that Congress did possess such power and that
the real question was whether it had chosen to exercise it or
not. But the very fact that the issue of the constitutionality
of such a statute was raised at all illustrates the importance
of this additional level of law in the United States. If the
Court had considered it necessary to rule that a statute so

regulating a labor union was unconstitutional, that would
have been the decisive point in the case and it would not
even have been necessary to go on to determine whether
the union had in fact violated such a law.

It is this power of the courts over the other agencies of
American government that is commonly referred to by the
phrases "judicial review" or "judicial supremacy." The most
widely known, if not the most common, manifestation of
the process is to be seen in the invalidation of an act of
Congress by the Supreme Court of the United States. It
will readily be recognized that this somewhat unusual power
of the American courts is not necessarily related to or derived from the ordinary judicial function of law enforcement. That a court called upon to interpret and apply a
statute is under no compulsion of logic to ask first whether
the statute is valid in terms of some higher or constitutional
law must, of course, be admitted in view of the fact that
the courts in many countries possess no such additional
power. For example, in England there is a constitution,
but constitutional law tends to merge with common law
and statutory law, and the courts do not have the authority
to uphold this constitution, as a higher law, against the possibly conflicting provisions of statutory law enacted by
Parliament.

On the other hand, judicial power is not a great deal
more narrowly confined in England than in the United
States. As Professor C. G. Haines, one of the foremost
scholars in the field of American constitutional law, points
out:

Even if it be true . . . that there is no case on record in which
the clearly expressed will of the king or of Parliament was really
checked by the courts there were instances in which the courts
interpreting the common law changed the meaning of statutes,
refused to give them the effect intended, or to apply a rule of

his majesty in council until the King, Lords and Commons joined in an unmistakable mandate, which the courts reluctantly at times conceded it was their duty to obey. Short of such mandates clearly and unequivocally expressed there was a wide realm in which the courts applied the basic principles of reason of the common law and were seldom interfered with by either the king or Parliament.[23]

In other words, the common law in England has served in somewhat the same capacity as the American Constitution in providing certain fundamental legal principles which the courts utilize in checking the policies decided upon by the legislative department against a higher law.

As a matter of fact, it is extremely easy to exaggerate the importance of the special power of the American judiciary to declare statutes unconstitutional, and to overestimate the difference between the powers of the American and English courts in this respect. This is so because it has been customary for Americans to give relatively more attention to the power of the courts to invalidate statutes than to the power of the courts to interpret and apply statutes. It may be noted that Professor Haines in effect defines judicial review to include both of these aspects of the judicial process. He states: "The principles of law and political practice which place the guardianship of . . . constitutions primarily in courts . . . , *and the dominance of judge-made law in accordance with common-law standards and principles,* constitute the bases of what may appropriately be termed *the American doctrine of judicial supremacy."*[24]

It is clear, then, that according to the Anglo-American concept of government of laws, courts become a most im-

---

[23]Haines, *op. cit.* (above, n. 1), p. 36. Reprinted by permission of the University of California Press.

[24]*Ibid.,* p. 27. See also pp. 22–23. (First italics added.) Reprinted by permission of the University of California Press.

portant part of the political system, and that judges participate widely in the lawmaking process. This being so, it becomes of interest and importance to discover, if possible, the principles or controlling considerations, apart from whatever compelling force *stare decisis* may have, that influence judges in their exercise of political power. Presumably in a democracy such as ours this is a vital matter. In formulating public policy our lawmaking bodies in theory and usually in practice are controlled by and reflect public opinion. This relation between law and public opinion must now be examined.

Chapter II

The Struggle for Power

J OHN Chamberlain has recently referred to the role of government in a modern democracy, such as our own, by using the interesting phrase, "the Broker State."[1] Harking back to Rousseau and Jefferson, he argues that it is the function of the American government to serve as a broker—receiving, sifting, and evaluating the claims and assertions of the diverse economic and social groups that make up the body politic. Chamberlain is, of course, merely reworking the data and theories which a good many commentators on the American political scene have of late been advancing.[2] The picture provided by these observers, in so far as it is complete, is of a society made up of numerous so-called pressure groups, such as manufacturers, bankers, shop-

---

[1] John Chamberlain, *The American Stakes* (Philadelphia: J. B. Lippincott Company, 1940) Chap. I.

[2] A. L. Lowell, *Public Opinion and Popular Government* (new ed.; New York: Longmans, Green & Co., 1926) 60–67; E. P. Herring, *Group Representation before Congress* (Baltimore: Johns Hopkins Press, 1929); E. P. Herring, *The Politics of Democracy* (New York: W. W. Norton & Company, Inc., 1940); P. H. Odegard and E. A. Helms, *American Politics—A Study in Political Dynamics* (New York: Harper & Brothers, 1938); E. B. Logan (ed.), *The American Political Scene* (New York: Harper & Brothers, 1936) Chap. VI, "Pressure Groups and Propaganda," by H. L. Childs; E. E. Schattschneider, *Politics, Pressures and the Tariff* (New York: Prentice-Hall, Inc., 1935).

keepers, lawyers, farmers, laborers, consumers, and unemployed persons—to mention only a few of the more obvious and comprehensive classifications. Actually, most of these and other such groups have numerous subdivisions which are often more important as units than the broader factions of which they are parts. Thus wheat farmers and cotton farmers are apt to be in opposition to one another in their aims about as often as they are in agreement.

Pressure Politics in a Democracy

In any case, these pressure groups with their conflicting desires and interests are engaged in a more or less continuous rivalry and active struggle for position and power in society. Quite naturally a major portion of this combat takes place within the political arena, for government has economic policies to determine, important favors to bestow, and it naturally makes a difference which way the decisions go. For a long time it was customary to attack this theory of politics. Or if one accepted it as unfortunately correct, there was a tendency to deplore the situation and argue that unless the factions that make up American society could be persuaded to subordinate their own selfish interests to the interests of the entire people, and seek to advance the cause of "America," our nation could not progress further. But of late it has become more common to accept the inevitability of this conflict of social forces, and even to see in it a process that is perfectly consistent with the democratic idea, provided the bargaining power of the different groups can be more nearly balanced or equalized.[3]

Of course, it makes a difference how one fills in the rough

[3]See D. C. Blaisdell, *Economic Power and Political Pressures,* Monograph No. 26, Temporary National Economic Committee (Washington: Government Printing Office, 1941).

outlines of the theory. The Marxists, for instance, with their doctrine of the class struggle, are supporting one version of the theory. But theirs is a version which sees in the clash between the interests of certain groups in the body politic a gulf so wide that it can never be bridged. The fight is to the finish and the goal a final victory and complete seizure of power by the proletariat.

In contrast with the Marxists, Chamberlain and others have in mind a continuous contest between groups having important and substantial differences of opinion and aim, but which are never so far apart that they cannot live together in relative peace regardless of which group or combination of groups is for the moment nominally in power. As Chamberlain says, "democracy is what results when you have a state of tension in society that permits no one group to dare bid for the total power." And he adds: "The real test is: 'Has the way been left open for *my* group to fight for what it conceives to be its rights?' If the way is still open, then we have democracy."[4] But within the limits of this final necessity of a common meeting ground for the groups, Chamberlain talks bluntly of the attempts of the various groups to gain political favors as "limited rackets," and, moreover, sees nothing particularly to deplore in the situation. It is only when some one group harbors "strict racket" aspirations and begins to hanker for total power that democracy is threatened.

We are accustomed to seeing the main lines of the battle formed, and the struggle between groups waged, in what may be called the legislative arena. Legislators determine public policy. They decide whether the tariff on oil shall be raised or lowered, whether farmers shall be granted "parity payments," whether unemployed persons on govern-

[4]Chamberlain, *op. cit.* (above, n. 1), pp. 27, 31–32. Reprinted by permission of the J. B. Lippincott Company, publishers.

ment relief projects shall receive "prevailing wages," whether public utility holding companies beyond the second degree shall be abolished, and whether collective bargaining shall proceed along craft union or industrial union lines. Accordingly, it is not surprising that an American election should be contested in very vigorous fashion, with every pressure group seeking to sell its support as dearly as it can. Nor is it surprising that these same groups maintain elaborate lobbies in Washington and the state capitals and, regardless of whether they have won or lost in the election, continue their efforts to obtain favors from the government. The businessman has by no means discontinued his lobbying in Washington during the New Deal period on the ground that he can hope for nothing from an antibusiness, prolabor, profarmer administration. Instead, he has been more active in this respect than ever before and has won more than one important concession from the government, even though he may still prefer one of his own kind in the White House, and a businessman's Congress. Likewise, should the businessman one day gain this latter goal, another pressure group, labor, will hardly cease its struggle for power. It will undoubtedly lay plans to elect to public office in the next election men more sympathetic to it if it can, but meanwhile it will see its "main chance" in bargaining with whoever holds political office in the Broker State, and, like business in the New Deal years, it will win many concessions.

Pressure Politics and the Courts

An aspect of pressure politics which is frequently overlooked is that it may have an important influence upon the work of judges as well as upon elective officers of government. Pressure groups naturally concentrate their chief efforts in the legislative arena, for there it is that public policies are determined. But if a statute favoring collective bargaining is not final or definitive until courts have interpreted and applied it, can labor unions afford to ignore the use that is made of judicial power in this respect? Or if an N.R.A., which businessmen may or may not favor, does not become an established link in our national economic policy so long as the Supreme Court may possibly invalidate the whole affair, can businessmen overlook such exercise of judicial power?

It is inevitable that the struggle between pressure groups should often be transferred from the legislative to the judicial arena.[5] It does not follow that these groups will seek to employ the same technique in securing favorable court decisions that they would in persuading legislators to their point of view. But the influence is apt to be there, just the same, particularly in any case the outcome of which will have important implications affecting vital social or economic policies. Lawyers appearing before the Supreme Court have often departed from the exposition of strictly technical legal considerations in order to emphasize the broader clash between conflicting social forces which may be involved in a case. Joseph H. Choate's plea before the Supreme Court as an attorney in the Income Tax case in the 1890's that the court invalidate the tax and stop the "communist march" on private property remains an extreme example of the use of a nonlegal argument before that tribunal. Likewise, the following plea by George Wharton Pepper, former United States senator, in the A.A.A. case is perhaps too extreme to be typical: "But I do not want your Honors to think that my feelings are not involved, and that my emotions are not deeply stirred. Indeed, may it please your Honors, I believe I am standing here today to plead the cause of the America I have loved; and I pray Almighty God that not in my time

[5] Blaisdell, *op. cit.* (above, n. 3), pp. 73-79, 150-52.

may 'the land of the regimented' be accepted as a worthy substitute for 'the land of the free.' "[6]

Nonetheless, the nonlegal implications of virtually every case decided by the Supreme Court, and having an important social or economic background, are bound to be fairly apparent to the justices before the case is finally disposed of. Many justices have admitted that this is so Justice Holmes once said: "I think it most important to remember whenever a doubtful case arises, with certain analogies on one side and other analogies on the other, that *what really is before us is a conflict between two social desires,* each of which seeks to extend its dominion over the case, and which cannot both have their way. *The social question is which desire is stronger at the point of conflict.*"[7]

From the progress of English law during the nineteenth century Professor Dicey has given us an interesting example which reveals in admirable fashion the respective roles played by legislature and courts in the legislative process, and the extent to which the courts as well as the legislature may be subject to the influence of public opinion and the demands of pressure groups.[8]

From 1800 to 1870 the position of a married woman as to property rights depended almost entirely upon judge-made law, there being essentially no statutes on the subject. According to the old rule of the common law a woman upon marriage became merged legally with her husband and all of her property passed under his control. All of her income, likewise, went to her husband. As the century progressed, this state of affairs proved unsatisfactory even to the England of Queen Victoria, for it made it possible for a woman

[6]*United States* v. *Butler* 297 U.S.1, 44 (1936).

[7]Oliver Wendell Holmes, *Collected Legal Papers* (New York: Harcourt, Brace and Howe, 1920) 239. (Italics added.) Reprinted by permission of Harcourt, Brace and Company, publishers.

[8]Dicey, *op. cit.* (Chap. I, n. 16), pp. 369–96.

to fall hopelessly into the clutches of the type of villain or adventurer which many a nineteenth-century English novel depicted. Accordingly, pressure developed, particularly from the wealthier classes, for a change in the law which would give a woman some measure, at least, of financial independence from her husband. Indeed, this pressure had been felt even before the nineteenth century. As a result, through the response of the court of chancery to such pressure, there developed in equity certain new rules by which some relief was provided. At the time a woman's marriage settlement was made it became possible for her father to arrange her financial affairs so as to give her considerable independence from her husband.

This relief was welcome but it did not prove completely adequate. Equity, being a rival system to the common law, could not supersede the latter, and the two rules continued to exist side by side. The result was that the rule of equity protected only those women who had marriage settlements, namely the women of the wealthy classes. The average woman of the middle classes, having had no marriage settlement, found her situation controlled by the common law, and any property or income which came to her after marriage became merged with that of her husband. On the other hand, daughters of the poorer classes were not likely to be affected very much one way or the other by the absence or presence of remedial legislation.

It was not until 1870 that Parliament, in the first of a series of four acts, attacked this problem and endeavored to make its solution a matter of statutory law. Dicey suggests that up until that time the wealthier classes had been largely satisfied by the relief provided by equity, and that it was only following the Reform Act of 1867 that the middle classes were generally enfranchised and thus enabled to bring pressure upon Parliament. Moreover, Dicey observes that when Parliament did finally act, its legislation was to a considerable extent influenced by the rules of equity on the subject and in large part simply involved taking over the rules of equity in statutory form, thus making their application more universal. Finally, he points out that the failure of Parliament to write more satisfactory legislation than it did was in good part due to this very tendency simply to copy the rules of equity. That decision, in turn, was due to the pressure of the wealthier people who might have lost certain benefits still available under equity had Parliament attempted to formulate a scientific and progressive statute free from the influence of judge-made law.

Traditional Judicial Conservatism

If there is a sensitivity on the part of the judiciary to the main social forces of the community or nation, this question immediately suggests itself: How do judges react to these pressures? That they will not always react in the same way that members of the legislative and executive departments of government do is obvious. This is one reason why there is often a tendency for pressure groups to fight many of their battles over again before the judiciary, refusing to accept as final the decision of the so-called political divisions of the government. Often the judges are, on the average, older than these other public officials, often they are more conservative, and the hopes and fears of different social groups will be aroused accordingly.

There is nothing new about such a conclusion. Over forty years ago Professor Dicey, lecturing at the Harvard Law School, suggested in the following words the more conservative reaction of judges to certain social pressures:

The Courts or the judges, when acting as legislators, are of course influenced by the beliefs and feelings of their time, and are guided to a considerable extent by the dominant current of public opinion. . . . But whilst our . . . judges . . . are swayed by the prevailing beliefs of a particular time, they are also guided by professional opinions and ways of thinking which are, to a certain extent, independent of and possibly opposed to the general tone of public opinion. The judges . . . are men advanced in life. They are for the most part persons of a conservative disposition. They are in no way dependent . . . upon the favor of the electors. . . . They are more likely to be biassed by professional habits and feeling than by the popular sentiment of the hour. . . .

It is quite possible that judicial conceptions of utility or of the public interest may sometimes rise above the ideas prevalent at a particular era. . . . In the field of commercial law Lord Mansfield carried out ideas which, though in harmony with the best opinion of the time, could hardly have been, during the era of old toryism, embodied in Acts of Parliament. . . . However . . . we may, at any rate as regards the nineteenth century, lay it down as a rule that judge-made law has, owing to the training and age of our judges, tended at any given moment to represent the convictions of an earlier era than the ideas represented by parliamentary legislation. If a statute . . . is apt to reproduce the public opinion not so much of to-day as of yesterday, judge-made law occasionally represents the opinion of the day before yesterday. . . . The legislative action of the Courts represents in truth a peculiar cross-section of opinion, which may in more ways than one modify the effect of that predominent opinion of the day which naturally finds expression in a representative assembly. . . .[9]

An able student of American constitutional history, Professor Fairman, draws much the same conclusion as to the likelihood of judicial conservatism:

Looking back to times so remote that we may view them philosophically, we would agree that there was more of good

[9]*Ibid.*, pp. 361–68. Reprinted by permission of The Macmillan Company, publishers.

than bad in the Jeffersonian Revolution of 1800, in the rise of the common man as exemplified in Andrew Jackson, and in the triumph of nationalism over particularism under Lincoln. Yet in each case the justices put themselves in opposition to the popular instinct.[10]

Recently Robert Jackson, formerly Attorney General of the United States and now a Supreme Court justice, has re-iterated Dicey's conclusion in very similar words:

The Court, moreover, is almost never a really contemporary institution. The operation of life tenure in the judicial department, as against elections at short intervals of the Congress, usually keeps the average viewpoint of the two institutions a generation apart. The judiciary is thus the check of a preceding generation on the present one; a check of conservative legal philosophy upon a dynamic people, and nearly always the check of a rejected regime on the one in being.[11]

Likewise, Justice Holmes has pointed out that

When socialism first began to be talked about, the comfortable classes of the community were a good deal frightened. I suspect that this fear has influenced judicial action both here and in England . . . . I think that something similar has led people who no longer hope to control the legislatures to look to the courts . . . and that in some courts new principles have been discovered . . . which may be generalized into acceptance of the economic doctrines which prevailed about fifty years ago. . . .[12]

[10]Charles Fairman, "The Retirement of Federal Judges," 51 *Harvard Law Review* (1938) 397. Also available in *Selected Essays on Constitutional Law,* compiled and edited by a committee of the Association of American Law Schools (Chicago: The Foundation Press, 1938) I, 885, 886. Wherever law review articles have been reprinted in the *Selected Essays* series, both citations will be given.

[11]Robert Jackson, *The Struggle for Judicial Supremacy* (New York: Alfred A. Knopf, Inc., 1941) 315. Reprinted by permission of the publisher.

[12]Holmes, *op. cit.* (above, n. 7), p. 184. Reprinted by permission of Har-court, Brace and Company, publishers.

We may now recall the thesis of "a government of laws" which suggests that ours is a society governed according to fixed and known principles impartially and impersonally administered by judges. It is apparent that there is a contradiction between this mechanistic theory of government based upon the idea of certainty in the law, and the point of view which sees judges sharing in the lawmaking power and reacting to the varying demands of pressure groups. It would seem impossible that judges can render "equal justice under law" and at the same time reveal a sensitivity to the conflicting demands of opposing pressure groups We may, then, proceed to a more detailed examination of American judicial power, bearing in mind the dilemma which has been noted, and seeking further information which may enable us to make a more definite judgment in the matter. First, the story of the background and early beginnings of the power of judicial review will be briefly reviewed. Why was the American doctrine of judicial supremacy originally sanctioned? Was it because the Founding Fathers sought thereby to provide the necessary machinery to enable successive generations to live under a government of certain law? Or is there any evidence that it was, in part at least, the result of an earlier conflict between pressure groups which led one faction to seek aid and assistance from a powerful judiciary?

Second, certain significant decisions of the Supreme Court of the United States will be examined and their essential character noted. Are they primarily decisions proclaiming immutable legal principles or do they partake more of the character of awards in the struggle of social forces Let us now pursue the first of these paths.

Chapter III

The Genesis of Judicial Supremacy: The Federal and State Conventions

IN ALL of the bewildering mass of discussion and controversy which has centered about the work of the Supreme Court of the United States and its power under the American Constitution, one fact, at least, is quite clear: The Constitution does not *in so many words* authorize the Supreme Court, or any other court, federal or state, to declare acts of Congress unconstitutional.[1]

What is the answer to this historical puzzle? Have the courts merely usurped this great power? Or did the Founding Fathers, who in Philadelphia in 1787 formulated our Constitution, intend to provide definitely for the supremacy of the judiciary in our government? And if they did so intend, why were they so vague and indirect about their desire in the matter? Or, what is perhaps a more important

[1] *Constitution of the United States.* Art. III, sec. 1: "The judicial power of the United States, shall be vested in one Supreme Court, and in such inferior courts as the Congress may from time to time ordain and establish. . . ." Sec. 2: "The judicial power shall extend to all cases, in law and equity, arising under this Constitution, the laws of the United States, and treaties made, or which shall be made, under their authority; . . ." Art. VI, sec. 2: "This Constitution, and the laws of the United States which shall be made in pursuance thereof; and all treaties made, or which shall be made, under the authority of the United States, shall be the supreme law of the land; and the judges in every State shall be bound thereby, anything in the constitution or laws of any State to the contrary notwithstanding."

37

question, if it was their will that the courts should have the power to invalidate unconstitutional acts of the other agencies of government, for what reason, or reasons, did they choose to bestow this great power upon the courts? To seek answers to these questions requires first that we examine briefly the background of the Philadelphia Convention and the writing of the Constitution.

The General Point of View of the Framers

To begin with, many of the Founding Fathers were members of the wealthy property-holding and commercial class of the day which had supported revolution against Great Britain because it was convinced that the economic system which the mother country was endeavoring to force upon its colonies was not always operating in the best interests of the latter. But as the decade of the 1780's advanced, these wealthy and essentially conservative men had increasing cause to wonder whether they had done well to sponsor the break from England and its centralized, domineering government. For, as is usually true of great revolutionary movements, there was a growing tendency for men of more radical and possibly dangerous ideas to play an important part. Moreover, the break from the English commercial system had done some harm as well as good to the economic interests of the colonies. Stated bluntly, the times were bad, they seemed to be getting worse rather than better, and it almost looked as though the new country which had just won its freedom might not turn out so well after all. For example, George Washington wrote in 1786: "I feel, my dear General Knox, infinitely more than I can express to you, for the disorders which have arisen in these States. Good God! Who, besides a Tory, could have foreseen, or a Briton predicted them? . . . There are combustibles in every State, which a spark might set fire to."[2]

Charles A. Beard has described the grave concern with which men with substantial economic interests viewed the situation.[3] According to the Beard thesis these men were influenced by powerful personal economic motives in seeking important changes in the country's political system. While this Beard thesis has been generally accepted by scholars it has always remained the subject of academic controversy. Perhaps Beard did minimize unduly the extent to which the Founding Fathers were influenced by a belief in the desirability of certain fundamental political principles. Nonetheless, it seems quite clear that many of the most important people of the period had strong practical reasons for believing that the Articles of Confederation, which had gone into operation toward the close of the Revolutionary War, were a failure. "In short, the financial, creditor, commercial, and speculating classes in the new confederate republic were harassed during the critical period just as such classes had been harassed by rebellious patriots on the eve of the Revolution. From every point of view, as they saw the matter, they had valid reasons for wanting to establish under their own auspices on American soil a system of centralized political, judicial, and economic control similar in character to that formerly exercised by Great Britain."[4]

Washington stated the common view of these groups when he wrote: "I do not conceive we can exist long as a nation without having lodged somewhere a power, which

[2]George Washington, *Writings* (W. C. Ford, ed.; New York: G. P. Putman's Sons, 1891) XI, 103–4.

[3]See particularly his *An Economic Interpretation of the Constitution of the United States* (New York: The Macmillan Company, 1913).

[4]Charles A. and Mary Beard, *The Rise of American Civilization* (new ed.; New York: The Macmillan Company, 1937) I, 306. Reprinted by permission of The Macmillan Company, publishers.

will pervade the whole Union in as energetic a manner as the authority of the State governments extends over the several States."[5]

It is not surprising that the leaders of the country slowly evolved a plan of action. It was this plan which culminated in the Constitutional Convention held in Philadelphia in 1787, to which we may now give our attention. In all, some fifty-five men attended this meeting. Only twenty-nine were present when it was called to order and only forty-two were still present at the end, and of these, thirty-nine signed the finished document. That the majority of these men were relatively wealthy individuals possessed of varying property and commercial interests is a generally accepted estimate.[6] The radicals who had played important roles at various stages of the revolution, and with whom the conservatives had joined hands during that period, were absent. Sam Adams and John Hancock were missing. Patrick Henry could have been a member, but declined, as did six other men. His laconic explanation for this conduct was couched in these words, "I smelt a rat"! Thomas Jefferson and Thomas Paine were in Europe. In fact, only eight of the fifty-six men who had signed the Declaration of Independence were present. Furthermore, "not one member represented in his immediate personal economic interests the small farming or mechanic classes."[7] In other words, the type of man who was apt to be satisfied with the existing decentralized system and who would certainly have opposed any substantial move to strengthen the powers of the central government had little representation at Philadelphia.

[5]Washington, *op. cit.* (above, n. 2), XI, 53–54.

[6]Beard, *Economic Interpretation, op. cit.* (above, n. 3), pp. 149–51.

[7]*Ibid.*, p. 149.

The Background of Judicial Review

What was the attitude of the Framers of the Constitution on the subject of judicial review, and how was that attitude related, if at all, to the economic motivation which led so many of the delegates to favor a much more powerful government in this country? As already noted, such an investigation begins with the fact that the finished Constitution contained not a specific word on judicial review. But it does not follow that the Founding Fathers ignored the matter completely. It is clear that they were at least aware of the possibility of bestowing such power upon the courts. The power of courts to declare laws unconstitutional, it is true, was by no means a common phenomenon in the world of 1787. Indeed, it would have been difficult if not impossible to point to a single country in which such power clearly and fully existed. On the other hand, the power was not completely unknown, and much emphasis has been placed upon the fact that the Framers of the Constitution knew of the existence of certain courts that had actually exercised a similar authority.

What were the early precedents for judicial review with which the Founding Fathers were acquainted? The earliest date back to the colonial period before the Revolution. First of all, there was the curious *Dr. Bonham* case, an English decision which had been rendered nearly two centuries before in the year 1610. The actual nature of the litigation is no longer of importance to us. What is important, however, is that in the course of his decision the famous Chief Justice, Sir Edward Coke, in a somewhat incidental fashion, championed the principle of judicial supremacy, in the following words: "And it appears in our books that in many cases the common law will controul acts of parliament and sometimes adjudge them to be utterly void: for when an act of parliament is against common right or reason, or repugnant or impossible to be performed, the common law will controul it and adjudge such act to be void."[8]

Coke's thesis was never really accepted in England, and the subsequent English Revolution of 1688 involved a complete repudiation of the idea and led to the absolute *legislative supremacy* of Parliament in the English government.[9] But the *Dr. Bonham* case was known in the American colonies which, on the other hand, had not at once fully appreciated the significance of the change in the English political system brought about by the English revolutions of the seventeenth century. Accordingly, when in the second half of the eighteenth century the great controversy between the colonies and England began, and became centered in opposition to Parliament, Americans could not resist the temptation to use Coke's reasoning in the *Dr. Bonham* case. In 1761, in the *Writs of Assistance* case, James Otis asserted in his celebrated argument that any act of Parliament authorizing such writs was necessarily void as "against the constitution" and "against natural equity." Otis argued thus: "*If an act of Parliament should be made in the very words of this petition, it would be void. The executive courts must pass such acts into disuse.*" Later, Coke's thesis was utilized in urging resistance to the Stamp Act on the ground that such legislation was contrary to "higher law."[10] Thus, on the eve of the writing of the American Constitution, and long after England had repudiated the idea of a legislature's depend-

[8] 8 Co. 114a; 2 Brownl. 255 (1610). Quoted by T. F. T. Plucknett, "Bonham's Case and Judicial Review," 40 *Harvard Law Review* (1926) 30; also I *Selected Essays* 67, 71.

[9] However, common law has influenced the interpretation of statutes. See above, Chapter I.

[10] E. S. Corwin, "Marbury v. Madison and the Doctrine of Judicial Review," 12 *Michigan Law Review* (1914) 538; I *Selected Essays* 128, 144–45.

ence upon a higher law enforced by the courts, the idea was known and accepted in this country, in part at least, for a very practical reason, as opposed to a mere impersonal desire to support a commendable political principle.[11]

Second, the colonies had been familiar with the practice by which the legislative acts of the colonial assemblies had been subject to examination and review for compliance with English law by the Privy Council in London. According to one count, 8,563 acts of the colonies were examined by the Privy Council and 469, or 5.5 per cent, were disallowed. However, it is quite clear that a good many of these laws were annulled because they were regarded as inexpedient rather than because they were considered contrary to some higher law.[12] Nonetheless, the analogy to judical review is reasonably clear.

In the decade separating the beginning of the American Revolutionary War from the Philadelphia Convention, state governments had been set up and were operating in the thirteen states. When the Founding Fathers met in 1787 they were presumably aware of a small handful of cases in which the courts in these new state governments had apparently invalidated acts of state legislatures because they violated state constitutional provisions. There has been a great deal of controversy over the validity of these cases as bona fide precedents for judicial review, but it seems certain that they had some influence with the Philadelphia Convention. The most famous of these cases was that of *Trevett* v. *Weeden,* in which a Rhode Island court in 1786 pronounced null and void an act of the state Assembly purporting to require the acceptance of paper money as legal tender. The decision stirred up a bitter quarrel in Rhode Island, and the Assembly ordered the judges who had rendered the decision

[11] *Selected Essays* 67, 100.
[12] Haines, *op. cit.* (Chap. I, n. 1), pp. 44–59.

to appear before it for questioning. An attempt to remove them from office failed, but the Assembly did shortly drop several of the judges when their terms expired and appointed others to their places.[13]

The background of this case throws some interesting light upon the origin of judicial review in America. The invalidated law definitely involved the fundamental quarrel between rich and poor, creditor and debtor, which was rapidly taking shape during the 1780's. The enactment of the law was clearly a victory for the cheap-money advocates and indicated that the "radicals" of the day had gained much influence in the Rhode Island government. Conversely, the decision by which the statute was invalidated represented a distinct victory for conservatives and illustrated the potential value of judicial review as a possible instrument for use against legislative bodies too much inclined to favor the demands of dangerous factions within the body politic.[14]

Judicial Review in the Philadelphia Convention

While the flat issue of judicial review received little, if any, straightforward consideration by way of formal debate on the floor of the Constitutional Convention, a good deal of attention was given to a proposal, supported vigorously by Madison, that a council of revision be created, composed of a convenient number of members from the executive and judicial departments with authority to veto acts of Congress. But this proposal was defeated and the veto power was finally assigned to the president alone. It is interesting to

[13]*Ibid.*, pp. 105–12.

[14]*Ibid.* See also Homer C. Hockett, *The Constitutional History of the United States 1776–1826* (New York: The Macmillan Company, 1939) 172–77; E. S. Corwin, "Marbury v. Madison and the Doctrine of Judicial Review," 12 *Michigan Law Review* (1914) 538; I *Selected Essays* 128, 148–50.

note that some of the delegates offered in opposition to the council of revision proposal the argument that the judiciary would thereby gain a double check over legislation since they assumed the courts would also have the authority to declare laws unconstitutional. For example, Luther Martin argued that "as to the Constitutionality of laws, that point will come before the Judges in their proper official character. In this character they have a negative on the laws. Join them with the Executive in the Revision and they will have a double negative." James Wilson tried to answer this objection by pointing out that the check of judicial review would be exercised only for legal reasons, whereas "laws may be unjust, may be unwise, may be dangerous, may be destructive; and yet not be so unconstitutional as to justify the Judges in refusing to give them effect."[15] Accordingly, he favored giving judges the broader power to veto laws for reasons of wisdom and expediency, as well as constitutionality. But his argument was to no avail.

It is clear, then, that one of the reasons why the council of revision proposal was rejected was that some of the members assumed that the courts would exercise the power of judicial review, and they doubted the wisdom of conferring any further power of a similar character upon the judiciary. It was only in such indirect fashion that the power of judicial review received any attention—let alone approval—from the Convention.

In spite of the failure of the Convention ever to vote specifically on judicial review itself, most historians have been inclined to favor the conclusion that a great many of the delegates intended that the courts should exercise such power. Charles A. Beard has made a careful study of the views of the convention members. He concludes that of the

[15]Max Farrand, *The Records of the Federal Convention of 1787* (New Haven: Yale University Press, 1911) II, 73, 76.

twenty-five men "whose character, ability, diligence and regularity of attendance . . . made them the dominant element in the Convention, . . . seventeen . . . declared, directly or indirectly, for judicial control."[16] On the other hand, he argues that only five delegates, but one of whom was in the select group of twenty-five, seem to have gone on record as opposed to judicial review.[17]

This conclusion has been challenged by some historians. L. B. Boudin has perhaps been the outstanding advocate of the thesis that the Convention never indicated any intention that the courts were to exercise the power in question.[18] Professor Corwin, who reviewed Beard's book at the time of its appearance, challenged its data. He claimed that of the seventeen important, and eight unimportant delegates who Beard asserts favored judicial review, only eight "acknowledged the power on the floor of the Convention itself. . . . On the other hand the idea was challenged by four members of the Convention; and although . . . outnumbered . . . two to one . . . , popular discussion previous to the Convention had shown their point of view to have too formidable backing to admit of its being crassly overridden." He believes "that the Convention regarded . . . [the] question as still an open one when it adjourned."[19] On the other hand, Corwin did not feel that the power was "usurped" by the Supreme Court. Some twenty-five years later, after further contemplation of the matter, Corwin concluded: "Neither party, perhaps, has quite all the truth on its side.

[16]Charles A. Beard, *The Supreme Court and the Constitution* (New York: The Macmillan Company, 1912) 17–18. Reprinted by permission of The Macmillan Company, publishers.

[17]*Ibid.*, pp. 51 ff.

[18]L. B. Boudin, *Government by Judiciary* (New York: William Godwin, Inc., 1932) Vol. I, Chaps. III–X.

[19]7 *American Political Science Review* (May 1913) 330.

That the Framers anticipated some sort of judicial review of acts of Congress there can be little question. But it is equally without question that ideas generally current in 1787 were far from presaging the present vast rôle of the Court."[20]

Alternative Theories as to the Purpose of the Framers

If we accept as essentially correct the thesis that there was at least an inclination in the Convention in favor of judicial review, what reason can be offered in explanation of this attitude? Did the Founding Fathers support this judicial power as a matter of political principle, feeling perhaps that it was absolutely necessary if the commendable goal of a "government of laws" was ever to be reached in this country? Or did they perhaps have certain more practical or opportunistic reasons for their decision? The question has been answered both ways. Many historians have felt that in favoring judicial review the men of the Convention were influenced by a strong belief in certain fundamental principles rather than by personal or material considerations. It is asserted that out of the experiences of the colonial and revolutionary periods men had come to believe in the doctrine of a higher or natural law above legislative law; that they had come to have a profound distrust of legislative bodies and feared that the rights of individuals were constantly threatened by the abuse of legislative power; and that accordingly they established a written constitution as the fundamental law and authorized judges to act as guardians of this constitution by enforcing it against the improper laws which the legislature might enact. Professor A. C. McLaugh-

[20]E. S. Corwin, "The Constitution as Instrument and as Symbol," 30 *American Political Science Review* (December 1936) 1071, 1078. Reprinted by permission of the *American Political Science Review.*

lin, perhaps the most eminent of the historians who have taken this point of view, states:

> The doctrine of what is now called "judicial review" is the last word, logically and historically speaking, in the attempt of a free people to establish and maintain a non-autocratic government. It is the culmination of the essentials of Revolutionary thinking and, indeed, of the thinking of those who a hundred years or more before the Revolution called for a government of laws and not of men. . . .
>
> Over and over again in the Revolutionary argument we find assertion that Parliament was bound and limited by the constitution; the colonists attributed to Britain a principle which they were to make actual in their own constitutions; and the courts, when opportunity arose, assumed the right, in their independence, to act upon that principle and make the Revolutionary doctrine as real as their own position permitted.[21]

Charles A. Beard, on the other hand, denies that the Constitutional Fathers were "doctrinaires," fundamentally influenced by a belief in principles. Instead, "as practical men" they built "the new government upon the only foundations which could be stable: fundamental economic interests."[22] He asserts that men of property deliberately created the Constitution "as a bulwark against populism of every form," and that judicial review was but one of many provisions made for the protection of the interests of the wealthy against those of the masses. Supporters of the Constitution "must have rejoiced in the knowledge . . . that an independent judiciary was to guard the personal and property rights of minorities against all legislatures, state and national." And he suggests that those who disagree with the conclusion that

---

[21]Andrew C. McLaughlin, *A Constitutional History of the United States* (New York: D. Appleton-Century Company, 1935) 310, 317. Reprinted by permission of the publishers.

[22]Beard, *Economic Interpretation, op. cit.* (above, n. 3), p. 151.

the Founding Fathers intended to provide for judicial review must first of all "show that the American federal system was not designed primarily to commit the established rights of property to the guardianship of a judiciary removed from direct contact with popular electorates."[23]

Professor Haines is inclined to agree with the Beard thesis. He concludes:

The fact of the matter is that judicial review of legislation was adopted as a practical device to meet a particular situation by shrewd men of affairs who knew what they wanted and who seldom expressed clearly the reasons which prompted their conclusions. . . . The right of the judiciary to declare laws invalid, and thus to check the rapacity of legislative assemblies, was in the opinion of many to be the chief cornerstone of a governmental structure planned with particular reference to preserving property rights inviolate and to assuring special sanction for individual liberties.[24]

Needless to say, those historians, such as Beard and Haines, who have argued that the Founding Fathers were essentially practical men, primarily motivated in their work by realistic considerations rather than by principle, have been bitterly attacked on the ground that they are endeavoring to challenge and undermine the reputations of the greatest men in American history. Perhaps the best answer to these attacks has been made by another eminent American historian, Professor Schlesinger, who also stresses the economic motivation of the writing of the Constitution:

No discriminating reader need feel that such a presentation carries with it the imputation of ignoble or unworthy motives to the Fathers of the Constitution; rather, it forms an illuminat-

[23]Beard, *The Supreme Court and the Constitution, op. cit.* (above, n. 16), pp. 110–11, 126. Reprinted by permission of The Macmillan Company, publishers.

[24]Haines, *op. cit.* (Chap. I, n. 1), pp. 205, 217. Reprinted by permission of the University of California Press.

ing commentary on the fact that intelligent self-interest, whether conscious or instinctive, is one of the motive forces of human progress.[25]

Beard himself states unequivocally,

It is not merely patriotic pride that compels one to assert that never in the history of assemblies has there been a convention of men richer in political experience and in practical knowledge, or endowed with a profounder insight into the springs of human action and the intimate essence of government. . . . It is no less a cause for admiration that their instrument of government should have survived the trials and crises of a century that saw the wreck of more than a score of paper constitutions.[26]

The Silence of the Constitution on Judicial Review

The question still remains as to why the Fathers, if they possessed such a strong, practical reason for favoring judicial review, nonetheless remained silent in the Constitution on this important and controversial point, leaving its existence to be established by inference and interpretation. One possible answer is that the Convention may have regarded judicial review as having become, by 1787, a *normal function* of the courts. In other words, it was enough that the Convention established a system of courts—the existence of judicial review as a normal function of the courts was so firmly established that it followed without any question that the new federal courts were to possess such power. The difficulty with this explanation lies in its fundamental premise that judicial review was a common practice in 1787.

One other possible explanation is that the Fathers fully

[25]Arthur Schlesinger, *New Viewpoints in American History* (New York: The Macmillan Company, 1922) 189. Reprinted by permission of The Macmillan Company, publishers.

[26]Beard, *The Supreme Court and the Constitution, op. cit.* (above, n. 16), pp. 86–87. Reprinted by permission of The Macmillan Company, publishers.

intended the courts to exercise the power of judicial review, but were afraid that the idea would prove so unacceptable to the people at large that its inclusion in the Constitution in clear and unmistakable terms would make the ratification of the document impossible. But in all truth it must be admitted that this explanation has its difficulty, too. In the period between the adjournment of the Philadelphia Convention and the final action of the state conventions called to ratify the Constitution, the idea of judicial review was publicly discussed several times. If there was in fact a conspiracy on the part of the Framers to hoodwink the common people by slipping judicial review into the Constitution surreptitiously, there were' a number of the Fathers who failed to keep the secret and insisted upon letting the cat out of the bag. For instance, in the *Federalist Papers* written during the ratification struggle in an effort to win support for the Constitution, Alexander Hamilton made the following blunt statement:

The interpretation of the laws is the proper and peculiar province of the courts. A constitution is, in fact, and must be regarded by the judges, as a fundamental law. It therefore belongs to them to ascertain its meaning, as well as the meaning of any particular act proceeding from the legislative body. If there should happen to be an irreconcilable variance between the two, that which has the superior obligation and validity ought, of course, to be preferred; or, in other words, the Constitution ought to be preferred to the statute, the intention of the people to the intention of their agents.[27]

In the state ratification conventions the power of judicial review received little more attention than it had at Philadelphia but when referred to at all it was usually to assert its existence. John Marshall, future Chief Justice of the United

[27]*The Federalist* (Lodge edition; New York: G. P. Putman's Sons, 1888) 485–86 (No. 78).

States, was a delegate to the Virginia Convention and stated during the course of its deliberations:

If they [the legislature] were to make a law not warranted by any of the powers enumerated, it would be considered by the judges as an infringement of the Constitution which they are to guard. They would not consider such a law as coming under their jurisdiction. They would declare it void.[28]

Likewise, in the Connecticut ratifying convention Oliver Ellsworth made this explanation:

This Constitution defines the extent of the powers of the general government. If the general legislature should at any time overleap their limits, the judicial department is a constitutional check. If the United States go beyond their powers, if they make a law which the Constitution does not authorize, it is void; and the judicial power, the national judges, who, to secure their impartiality, are to be made independent, will declare it to be void.[29]

Similar statements were made in the conventions in several other states by men of various political positions. Even such radicals as Patrick Henry and Samuel Adams indicated their belief that the courts might invalidate legislation contrary to the Constitution. On the other hand, there were a few prominent leaders of the time who vigorously opposed the idea of giving such unlimited power to the judiciary.[30]

In any case during the period when the Constitution was before the states for ratification enough was said pro and con about the issue of judicial review that the conspiracy-of-secrecy explanation becomes rather unconvincing. At the

[28]Jonathan Elliot, *Debates in the Several State Conventions on the Adoption of the Federal Constitution*. . . . (Philadelphia: J. B. Lippincott Company, 1888) III, 553.

[29]*Ibid.*, II, 196.

[30]Haines, *op. cit.* (Chap. I, n. 1), pp. 135–43. It is also true that some of those who supported judicial review were thinking primarily of judicial invalidation of state laws rather than of federal laws.

same time, if one accepts the theory that the Framers did intend the courts to exercise this power, there is seemingly no other possible explanation of the silence of the Philadelphia Convention on judicial review than the secrecy or normal judicial function theses. Probably all points of view are in part correct. Some of the members of the Convention undoubtedly did feel that judicial review had become a normal function of the courts and that no specific provision was necessary. Some unquestionably favored judicial review but preferred to keep the Constitution silent on the point, uncertain what the public reaction would be. And finally some delegates were undoubtedly opposed to judicial review, or at least did not feel that any provision was being made for it in the Constitution. Certainly the matter was not one of the issues which occasioned great debate and controversy in the Convention.

The Paradox of the Constitution

One final question remains to be considered. Is there not a fundamental contradiction or inconsistency in the attitudes and work of the Constitutional Fathers as interpreted by the Beard school of historians? On one hand, according to Beard, the members of the conservative, wealthy class which played such an important role at Philadelphia preferred a new central government which would have vastly increased powers over those of the Confederation government and would be capable of pursuing vigorous policies favorable to the interests of this class. On the other hand, Beard asserts, these men undoubtedly supported judicial review so that the hand of the legislature might be restrained lest an uncontrolled government threaten property interests or minority rights.

Further contemplation of this situation makes it seem evident that what appears to be a serious inconsistency is at most a mild paradox. It seems as though the Founding

Fathers were both trying to eat their cake and have it too. Consequently, because of the operation of a dual, somewhat contradictory motivation, the Framers both strengthened the power of the national government and so arranged its organization as to minimize the danger of the use of this power in radical directions. In other words, Congress was granted strong powers through which to cope with the problems of the day, but, at the same time, conservative federal judges with a lifetime tenure might reasonably be counted on to enforce the Constitution against the extreme acts of the national legislature should that body one day fall under the sway of an ambitious and dangerous popular majority. Moreover, in so far as judicial review might operate to control state legislation, there is no difficulty in understanding the motivation of the Framers. That they distrusted the radical tendencies of the state legislatures and were anxious to curb such policies is entirely clear. Thus there is no inconsistency about the judicial review of state legislation by a *federal* judiciary.

We are indebted to Professor Edward S. Corwin for a further interesting analysis of this situation. In a paper read at the Harvard Tercentenary celebration he refers to the Constitution as both an *instrument* and a *symbol*. In its instrumental phase he views the Constitution as an agency for the exercise of positive political power, an agency for getting things done, an agency *"for the achievement of progress"*— all through the power of government.[31] This, he points out, was primarily the way the Framers saw their Constitution. "That the attitude of the members of the Federal Convention toward their task was predominantly instrumentalist and practical is clear at a glance. They had not gone to Philadelphia merely to ratify the past . . . but with *reform* in

[31]30 *American Political Science Review* 1072. This and the following excerpts are reprinted by permission of the *American Political Science Review*.

mind, and specifically the creation of *a strong, effective national government."*[32]

In speaking of its symbolic aspect, Corwin has in mind a Constitution of negative restraint, a document of limitations and prohibitions holding government within well-defined and narrow limits. This is the Constitution, for example, of the Bill of Rights which, as Corwin points out, was not the work of the Philadelphia Convention. This Constitution as a symbol is a

. . . consecration of an *already established order of things.* . . . [It] harks back to primitive man's terror of a chaotic universe, and his struggle toward security and significance behind a slowly erected barrier of custom, magic, fetish, tabu. While, therefore, the constitutional instrument exists to energize and canalize *public power,* it is the function of the constitutional symbol to protect and tranquilize *private interest or advantage as against public power.* . . .[33]

With which of these two phases of the Constitution is the institution of judicial review more closely associated? Seemingly it is an integral part of the symbolic Constitution. As Corwin points out:

. . . it may be remarked of constitutional negatism . . . that it must have remained impermanent and inefficient had it not found embodiment in an implementing institution. I refer, of course, to judicial review, and especially to the power of the Court to disallow acts of Congress on the ground of their being in conflict with the Constitution.[34]

This perhaps brings us back to the point of view that the Framers' Constitution was as much symbol as instrument if they intended to provide for judicial review. But we may recall that while Corwin agrees with Beard that the Framers

[32]*Ibid.,* p. 1073.
[33]*Ibid.,* p. 1072.
[34]*Ibid.,* p. 1078.

did make such provision he argues that "ideas generally current in 1787 were far from presaging the present vast rôle of the Court."[35] Moreover, as we shall shortly see, judicial review is not necessarily inharmonious with the Constitution as an instrument. Remember that judicial review refers not so much to the actual invalidation of legislation as it does merely to the right of the courts to pass upon such legislation In so far as judicial review commits the Constitution, as higher law, to the protection of the courts, there is no compulsion that judges must declare laws to be improper. What if the judges choose to be impressed by the strong instrumental qualities of the Constitution, by the degree to which it does provide "for the achievement of progress"? Under such circumstances may not judicial review become the means whereby the widening of governmental power is approved and glorified rather than curtailed and denounced?

As early as the career of John Marshall, the first great Chief Justice of the United States, the usefulness of judicial review for both instrumental and symbolic purposes became apparent. John Marshall was a member of the Federalist party and certainly a stanch and loyal successor to the line of men who dominated the scene at Philadelphia. Like them he was torn in two directions. And so it is that he is the author of two of the greatest decisions in Supreme Court history, one of which, *Marbury* v. *Madison,* is the rock upon which judicial review, the symbol of restraint, rests, and the other, *McCulloch* v. *Maryland,* a sanction for the idea of an expanding Constitution, sustaining down through the years an ever-changing program of vigorous governmental action. Let us now examine these two cases, turning first to the initial invalidation of congressional legislation through judicial review, and noting the character of the "official apology" offered for such conduct.

[35]*Ibid.*

★　　　★　　　★　　　★　　　★　　　★

Chapter IV

The Genesis of Judicial Supremacy: *Marbury* v. *Madison*

THE case of *Marbury* v. *Madison* stands out like a lone landmark in the early history of judicial review.[1] A decade and a half elapsed between the Philadelphia Convention in 1787 and this first decision of the Supreme Court invalidating congressional legislation. More than half a century then separates *Marbury* v. *Madison* from the second case in which the Court invalidated an act of Congress, and it was not until after the Civil War that the Supreme Court began to exercise this power with any frequency. It is perhaps too much to say that without the decision in *Marbury* v. *Madison* the judiciary might never have attempted to assert control over federal legislation, but certainly the importance of this early assertion of the power by John Marshall cannot be overestimated.

The Political Background of the Case

Marbury v. *Madison* is remembered today for the great opinion of Chief Justice Marshall establishing the famous

---

[1] I Cranch 137 (1803). There were earlier cases in which the Court exercised the power of judicial review to the extent of passing upon the constitutionality of federal and state laws, but in these cases the decisions upheld the legislation. See *Hylton* v. *United States* 3 Dallas 171 (1796), and *Calder* v. *Bull* 3 Dallas 386 (1798). The first case in which the Supreme Court held a state law void under the federal Constitution was *Fletcher* v. *Peck* 6 Cranch 87 (1810). But state laws had earlier been invalidated by lower federal courts.

constitutional principle of judicial review. What is not always remembered is that the case grew out of a background in which there were strong political overtones. In the national election of 1800 the Federalist party, which had inherited the traditions of the Founding Fathers and had completely dominated the national government during the first decade of its existence, had the misfortune to lose control of both Congress and the presidency. Wishing to save what it could, and aided by a lame-duck session of Congress which was to meet following the election, it had until March 4, 1801, to accomplish its purpose. Accordingly, it determined to make at least one arm of the government, the judiciary, safe for the Federalist cause. During the closing weeks of the Adams administration legislation was enacted creating numerous new judicial positions, and President Adams hastened to fill these new offices with deserving members of the party before his term expired, thereby creating the famous chapter in history of the "midnight judges." Professor McLaughlin relates:

Here was a golden opportunity for the office-seeker and for the extension of party influence. The indignation of the Republicans might have been tempered, had they been given the chance of filling the new offices with their own party adherents. But no such opportunity was granted them. With an eye for detail, Adams patiently proceeded to appoint to the new positions none but members of his own party before he hurried away in his carriage . . . . The Republicans . . . could not quietly accept the new act; they were irritated at the sight of a party, beaten in the election and deprived of control in the political branches of the government, now taking refuge in the judiciary where they would be free from popular pressure and might be able to perpetuate their obnoxious and unpopular doctrines. So bitter was the feeling, so extreme the partisanship, that the freedom and the independence of the judiciary were endangered.[2]

[2]McLaughlin, *op. cit.* (Chap. III, n. 21), pp. 288–89. Reprinted by permission of D. Appleton-Century Company, Inc., publishers.

Among Adams's last-minute appointments was one naming an obscure gentleman, William Marbury, to the relatively unimportant position of justice of the peace in the District of Columbia. The appointment was perfectly proper and legal. The president had acted under the authority of an admittedly constitutional statute, and the Senate had confirmed the appointment. Unfortunately for Marbury, there was a final slip in the plan. President Adams went out of office before Marbury's commission had been delivered to him. The next day, March 4, 1801, the new president, Thomas Jefferson, ordered his Secretary of State, James Madison, to refrain from delivering the commission to Marbury. Without this document Marbury could not take office.

The matter was now carried to the Supreme Court by Marbury under a provision of the Judiciary Act of 1789 authorizing the Court to issue writs of mandamus in certain situations. Specifically, Marbury asked the Court that it issue such a writ compelling Madison to deliver the commission. The decision in the case was written by Chief Justice Marshall, himself a Federalist only recently appointed to his office by one of President Adams's last official acts. In fact, he had been Secretary of State in the Adams administration and his was the responsibility for the failure to deliver the Marbury commission before Adams left office. It has even been suggested that this personal relation to the case should have, according to judicial ethics, disqualified Marshall from participating in the decision.[3]

Marshall's Opinion in Marbury *v.* Madison

A considerable portion of the chief justice's opinion in the case is devoted to an irrelevant consideration of the seeming merit of Marbury's contentions, and the soundness of the

[3]Haines, *op. cit.* (Chap. I, n. 1), p. 194.

writ of mandamus as the proper legal remedy for him to invoke. Marshall supported Marbury's claim to such a writ and seized the opportunity to criticize the Jefferson administration for its treatment of Marbury. The irrelevancy of these parts of the opinion is made apparent when Marshall goes on to conclude that the Court is powerless to help Marbury and that it will not issue a writ of mandamus. How was such a conclusion reached? In what might seem like unnecessary action in view of the relatively simple point upon which the Court was asked to rule, Marshall decided that before disposing of the case on its merits the Court should re-examine that portion of the Constitution dealing with the organization and authority of the judicial department of government, namely, Article III. Proceeding to do so, the Court presently discovered what seemed to be a contradiction between this third article of the Constitution and the pertinent clause of the Judiciary Act of 1789. The words of the Constitution appeared to limit absolutely the original jurisdiction of the Supreme Court to just two types of cases, those in which a state government, or a diplomat from a foreign country, was involved as a party to litigation. In all other cases the jurisdiction of the Supreme Court was to be appellate only.

To Marshall's way of thinking Congress was endeavoring by law to extend to the Supreme Court a third type of original jurisdiction, the right to decide cases in which requests were made for a writ of mandamus. We may at this point agree with Marshall that a contradiction did exist in fact between the Constitution and the provisions of the congressional statute, although, as will later be seen, there was a way whereby the Court might have interpreted the statute to have avoided this contradiction. Did it necessarily follow that the Court should proceed to invalidate the law? Marshall begins rather glibly:

The question, whether an act, repugnant to the constitution, can become the law of the land, is a question deeply interesting to the United States; but, happily, not of an intricacy proportioned to its interest. It seems only necessary to recognize certain principles, supposed to have been long and well established, to decide it.[4]

Continuing, he points out that ours is a constitutional system:

The powers of the legislature are defined and limited; and that those limits may not be mistaken, or forgotten, the constitution is written. To what purpose are powers limited . . . if these limits may, at any time, be passed by those intended to be restrained? . . . It is a proposition too plain to be contested, that the constitution controls any legislative act repugnant to it; or, that the legislature may alter the constitution by an ordinary act.

Between these alternatives there is no middle ground. The constitution is either a superior paramount law, unchangeable by ordinary means, or it is on a level with ordinary legislative acts, and, like other acts, is alterable when the legislature shall please to alter it.

Which should it be? Obviously, the law must give way to the Constitution. But was it up to the courts so to rule?

If an act of the legislature, repugnant to the constitution, is void, does it, notwithstanding its invalidity, bind the courts, and oblige them to give it effect? . . . This . . . would seem . . . an absurdity too gross to be insisted on. . . .

It is emphatically the province and duty of the judicial department to say what the law is. . . . If two laws conflict with each other, the courts must decide on the operation of each.

So if a law be in opposition to the constitution; if both the law and the constitution apply to a particular case, so that the

[4]*Marbury v. Madison,* 1 Cranch 137, 175.

court must either decide that case conformably to the law, disregarding the constitution; or conformably to the constitution,
disregarding the law; the court must determine which of these
conflicting rules governs the case. This is of the very essence
of judicial duty.

If, then, the courts are to regard the constitution, and the constitution is superior to any ordinary act of the legislature, the
constitution, and not such ordinary act, must govern the case to
which they both apply.

Those, then, who controvert the principle that the constitution
is to be considered, in court, as a paramount law, are reduced to
the necessity of maintaining that courts must close their eyes on
the constitution, and see only the law.

That, of course, would never do. Such a "doctrine would
subvert the very foundation of all written constitutions."

But Marshall was not yet through. Completing his remarks
on the general character of constitutional government, the
position of ordinary law and the role of the courts thereunder,
he examined the American Constitution in detail and discovered two provisions of great importance to his thesis. The
first of these was:

The judicial power shall extend to all cases . . . arising under
this constitution.

Could it be the intention of those who gave this power, to say
that in using it the constitution should not be looked into? That
a case arising under the constitution should be decided without
examining the instrument under which it arises?

This is too extravagant to be maintained.

And if this were not enough, what about the requirement
that a judge take an oath to support the Constitution? How
could he possibly fulfill that oath if he might not examine the
content of the Constitution in order to determine whether a
law was consistent with it? If he might not, Marshall concludes, "If such be the real state of things, this is worse than

solemn mockery. To prescribe, or to take this oath, becomes equally a crime."[5]

Rejoinder to Marshall

It is interesting to note that Marshall's opinion is devoid of any historical evidence to support his conclusion. It is based solely upon logical reasoning concerning the nature and content of our Constitution. As such, it is a most impressive document. Nevertheless, the fundamental point in his logic—that a judge confronted with a conflict between a law and the Constitution is compelled to choose one or the other and must necessarily uphold the Constitution and render null and void the law—is not unassailable.

The use of similar logic to reach conclusions exactly opposite to those arrived at by Chief Justice Marshall's logic has perhaps never been better employed than by Justice Gibson of the Pennsylvania Supreme Court in a dissenting opinion in 1825 in the case *Eakin* v. *Raub*. Following closely the sequence of points in Marshall's famous opinion, he reasons, in part, as follows:

The Constitution and the right of the legislature to pass the act, may be in collision. But is that a legitimate subject for judicial determination? If it be, the judiciary must be a peculiar organ, to revise the proceedings of the legislature, and to correct its mistakes; and in what part of the Constitution are we to look for this proud preëminence? . . . *It is the business of the judiciary to interpret the laws, not scan the authority of the lawgiver;* and without the latter, it cannot take cognizance of a collision between a law and the Constitution. . . . The oath to support the Constitution . . . must be understood in reference to supporting the Constitution, only as far as that may be involved in . . . [the judge's] official duty; and, consequently, *if his official duty does not comprehend an inquiry into the authority*

[5]*Ibid.*, pp. 176–79.

of the legislature, neither does his oath. . . . The official oath
. . . relates only to the official conduct of the officer, and does
not prove that he ought to stray from the path of his ordinary
business to search for violations of duty in the business of
others . . . .

But do not the judges do a positive act in violation of the
Constitution, when they give effect to an unconstitutional law?
. . . The fallacy of the question is, in supposing that the judiciary adopts the acts of the legislature as its own; whereas the
enactment of a law and the interpretation of it are not concurrent acts. . . . The fault is imputable to the legislature, and on
it the responsibility exclusively rests. In this respect, the judges
are in the predicament of jurors who are bound to serve in capital
cases, although unable, under any circumstances, to reconcile it
to their duty to deprive a human being of life. To one of these,
who applied to be discharged from the panel, I once heard it
remarked, by an eminent and humane judge: "You do not deprive a prisoner of life by finding him guilty of a capital crime;
you but pronounce his case to be within the law, and it is therefore those who declare the law, and not you, who deprive him
of life."[6]

It should further be noted that Marshall's reasoning is
capable of being turned against the very Court that used it.
For, as Charles A. Beard has pointed out, the President of
the United States also acts under the Constitution and has
taken an oath to support it.[7] Let us take a specific case. When
the Supreme Court rendered its decision in 1935 in the
Schechter case by which it invalidated the National Industrial
Recovery Act, President Roosevelt was obviously irritated

[6]12 Sergeant and Rawle (Pennsylvania Supreme Court) 330 (1825). Quotation from the report of the case in Robert E. Cushman, *Leading Constitutional Decisions* (7th ed.; New York: F. S. Crofts & Co., 1940) 183. (Italics
added.)

[7]Charles A. Beard, *American Government and Politics* (8th ed.; New
York: The Macmillan Company, 1939) 44–46. Justice Gibson also makes
this point.

and thought that the Court had acted incorrectly. As it was, he did not permit his irritation to go beyond a sharp comment to the effect that the Court apparently wished to return the country to "horse and buggy days." But suppose he had reasoned as follows: This is a bad decision. The Supreme Court is misinterpreting the Constitution. It has rendered a decision which conflicts with the Constitution (and certain eminent constitutional experts would have supported him at this point). I have taken an oath to support the Constitution. Therefore, I cannot as chief executive observe and enforce this decision and at the same time follow the Constitution. My oath requires that I do the latter rather than the former. Accordingly, I will ignore this decision of the Supreme Court and assume that it is null and void.

Such a line of reasoning would not have differed materially from the logic Marshall actually employed in rendering his decision in *Marbury* v. *Madison*. Furthermore, Congress, too, could employ this same type of logic should it in turn wish to ignore or invalidate action either by the president or by the courts. Obviously, we could hardly afford to have the three departments of government employing such reasoning against one another, for the affairs of the government would soon be in a state of chaos. But granted that it would be impossible for all three agencies so to conduct themselves, it is at least permissible to ask why it should fall within the peculiar province of the courts to act as watchdogs of the Constitution and invalidate the improper acts of the other two agencies, any more than it should fall within the peculiar province of the president, or of Congress, to act in such a capacity. It may be argued that courts are no more important in their way than are executives or legislatures. According to the theory of separation of powers, each supposedly has a function to perfom: Congress legislates, the Court adjudicates, the president administers. There is nothing magic or divine about the second of these three processes any more than there is about the other two. So it is entirely proper to point out that, if he had chosen to do so, Chief Justice Marshall might have reasoned: We are aware of the maximum limits of judicial power and we do not intend to exceed them. Here is a congressional statute that gives us the right to issue writs of mandamus. Here is Marbury with a seemingly good claim that such a writ be issued against Madison. Accordingly, we have no choice but to issue the writ asked for, and anyone who suggests to us that the statute is unconstitutional is in the wrong place. Let him go over to the body that passed the law and argue with them. They took an oath to uphold the Constitution and it is their business to keep that oath.

In a sense, of course, these attempts to quibble about the logic or scope of the actual opinion and decision in *Marbury v. Madison* are just as academic as arguing that the Convention of 1787 did not intend the courts to exercise such a power. Nearly a century and a half has passed since *Marbury v. Madison,* and, right or wrong, the Supreme Court is not now likely to rebuke Marshall by reversing or altering the ruling in the *Marbury* case. On the other hand, it is barely possible that a realization of the thin logical ice upon which Marshall skated, and the historical fact that presidents and Congresses have shown a great modesty and self-restraint in observing judicial decisions, may persuade present and future judges to show a little similar modesty. Such a result would be particularly fortunate in those cases in which the courts invalidate acts of the other departments of government even though not all of the participating judges are agreed that there is in fact a contradiction between a statute and the Constitution. Justice Stone has made a statement in a dissenting opinion that may well be placed alongside Justice Gibson's warning concerning the limitations and fallibility of judicial power: ". . . while unconstitutional exercise of power by the executive and legislative branches of the government is subject to judicial restraint, the only check upon our own exercise of power is our own sense of self-restraint."[8]

Alternative Paths Open to Marshall

Two further alternatives were open to Chief Justice Marshall in disposing of the case. In the first place a way was open whereby the relevant portion of the Judiciary Act of 1789 might have been interpreted to avoid any conflict between the statute and Article III of the Constitution. It has been pointed out that the wording of the act was sufficiently general that it might have been held to provide that the power given to the Court to grant writs of mandamus was to be exercised only in cases reaching the Court on appeal or in the two types of cases which the Constitution permitted it to hear by exercise of original jurisdiction. Had the Court so interpreted the law it would have had to refuse jurisdiction in the case as it actually did, but without the necessity of invalidating a law in order to reach such a result.[9]

Second, Chief Justice Marshall might have taken the point of view that Article III of the Constitution, involving as it does the organization and jurisdiction of the judiciary, belonged to the peculiar province of the courts to protect. Accordingly, any law which sought to impose upon the Court a task in connection with its judicial function which seemed to be forbidden by the Constitution might be resisted. The relevant portion of the Judiciary Act of 1789 could then have been invalidated on the basis of such reasoning, and a limited version of judicial review established. This power would have

[8]*United States* v. *Butler*, 297 U.S. 1, 78–79 (1936).

[9]Edward S. Corwin, "Marbury v. Madison and the Doctrine of Judicial Review," 12 *Michigan Law Review* (1914) 538; I *Selected Essays* 128, 132–33.

enabled the Court to invalidate, as it later did, certain laws dealing with the judicial process, such as those which the Court felt attempted to impose nonjudicial duties upon it.[10] As a matter of fact, with the single exception of the invalidation of the Missouri Compromise in the *Dred Scott* case, all acts of Congress invalidated by the Supreme Court up to 1868 did concern matters of court organization and jurisdiction.[11] But in *Marbury* v. *Madison,* Marshall chose to base his decision upon the much broader ground that the Court must refuse to enforce any act of Congress which it considers contrary to the Constitution, regardless of whether the act is one pertaining to the work of the judiciary or dealing with some other matter altogether.

Marshall's Purpose in Marbury v. Madison

Enough has now been said about the situation in which the Court found itself in deciding the case of *Marbury* v. *Madison* to indicate that it had several alternative paths available, almost any one of which might have been followed with logical and legal justification. Why did Chief Justice Marshall choose the path that he did? It may be conceded that the decision in the case was in part the result of the justices' conclusions on the high level of constitutional principles, but there were certainly other factors of a more realistic character which influenced a Federalist Court in its decision.

It may be noted that the Court did not render the most obvious "political" decision available. It refrained from exercising a power which Congress had granted to it and which in the case at hand it might have used in partisan fashion to accomplish an act of judicial interference with the conduct

[10]See, for example, *Gordon* v. *United States* 2 Wallace 561 (1865); *United States* v. *Evans* 213 U.S. 297 (1909); *Muskrat* v. *United States* 219 U.S. 346 (1911).

[11]Haines, *op. cit.* (Chap. I, n. 1), p. 401, n.

of administrative affairs of the government by the President of the United States and his first assistant, the Secretary of State. In other words, the Court might have tried to force Jefferson and Madison to give Marbury his commission, and Federalists the country over would have applauded. But instead, in an act of seeming self-abnegation, the Court said "No" and dismissed the case for want of jurisdiction. There are two possible reasons, apart from the compulsion of the Constitution, for this action.

In the first place, Marshall and his colleagues were undoubtedly deterred from a decision ordering Madison to deliver Marbury's commission because of a fear that Jefferson and his Secretary of State might flatly refuse to obey such a court order and, succeeding in such refusal, thereby weaken respect for the power of the judiciary. Or worse still, the Republican administration might even have attempted to take drastic steps of reprisal against the Court. As it was, even though the Court refrained from granting Marbury the writ he was seeking, Marshall's obiter dictum in his opinion —that Marbury seemed to have a very good case against Madison—stirred up a hornet's nest of criticism by Republicans against the Court. Indeed, as Professor Corwin has said, "The case in fact smells strongly of powder, for the battle between the chief justice and President Jefferson was already on."[12] The Federalist Court, then, went as far as it dared in its opposition to the Jefferson administration. Further it dared not go, for fear of goading Republicans beyond the endurance point. After all, the Federalists held only the judiciary and in the face of a determined onslaught against them by president and Congress, their position would surely have proved untenable.

But, it may be asked, if Marshall thought it wise for the

[12]E. S. Corwin, "Judicial Review," *Encyclopaedia of the Social Sciences,* VIII, 457, 601.

Court to avoid deciding the case on its merits, why did he not seize upon the argument already discussed: that the Act of 1789 did not authorize the Court to issue a writ of mandamus in a case like the one at hand? In that way, as has been pointed out, the Court could have dismissed the case for want of jurisdiction without declaring a statute invalid.

It looks very much as though Marshall and his Court wanted to exercise the power of judicial review and declare congressional legislation void. Does it not seem, then, in the second place, that Marshall was playing for much higher stakes than a mere decision supporting the Federalist position in the petty squabble involving Marbury and his claim to the office of justice of the peace? In the pages of American history William Marbury was an insignificant figure at best, and what matter if he be sacrificed for a worthy cause? Having read his lecture condemning Jefferson and Madison for their highhanded action, the chief justice went on to accomplish his greater purpose of establishing once and for all in very positive fashion a strong precedent for the power of judicial review. Professor Haines has thus indicated the importance of the chief justice's action: ". . . Marshall, who was an ardent Federalist, was aware of a rising opposition to the theory of judicial control over legislation, and he no doubt concluded that the wavering opinions on federal judicial supremacy needed to be replaced by a positive and unmistakable assertion of authority."[13] Another eminent constitutional historian, Andrew C. McLaughlin, agrees that "the learned Justice really manufactured an opportunity to declare an act void."[14]

Marbury v. *Madison* plainly reveals John Marshall in a

---

[13]Haines, *op. cit.* (Chap. I, n. 1), p. 202. Reprinted by permission of the University of California Press.

[14]A. C. McLaughlin, "Marbury v. Madison Again," 14 *American Bar Association Journal* (March 1928) 155, 157.

moment in which he is profoundly impressed by the restrictive or symbolic aspects of the Constitution. In such a
moment the John Marshall of greatest fame perhaps seems
somewhat out of character. This is not John Marshall, the
Federalist, the great nationalist, who did so much during his
three decades as chief justice to build up the power and
prestige of the central government by constantly emphasizing
the strong instrumental value of the Constitution. But, at the
same time in *Marbury* v. *Madison* Marshall is by no means
completely out of character. It may be argued that he was
remaining perfectly loyal to the wishes of the Founding
Fathers who had sought to strengthen the powers of the
national government but who had also apparently sought to
make provision for judicial review. In other words, Marshall
was invoking that power for the first time at just such a
moment when the Fathers probably intended it should be
exercised. Jefferson had become president and his party had
won control of Congress. The opposition had obtained complete control of the political branches of the government. Is
it not obvious that from the point of view of the Founding
Fathers and the Federalist party the time had come to point
out that the Constitution as a higher law did place restraints
upon Congress and that the Supreme Court as guardian of
the Constitution had power to enforce those restraints?

In *Marbury* v. *Madison* we see Chief Justice Marshall suggesting that the Supreme Court was duty-bound as a matter
of unescapable principle to enforce the Constitution as a
symbol of restraint upon congressional authority through the
exercise of its power of judicial review. We may now go on
and observe how Marshall and the Court, still claiming to be
acting solely according to the requirements of fixed constitutional principles, used its power of judicial review to
place its stamp of approval upon the idea of the Constitution
as an instrument of expanding national power.

Chapter V

The Meaning of the Constitution:
Instrument and Symbol

"W<small>E</small> <small>MUST</small> never forget that it is a *constitution* we are expounding." Thus spoke Chief Justice Marshall of the United States Supreme Court more than a century ago in his famous opinion in *McCulloch* v. *Maryland*.[1] The Constitution as an instrument of positive power; the Constitution as a symbol of negative restraint: to which of these concepts was Chief Justice Marshall referring? To one familiar only with the Marshall of the *Marbury* decision it might well seem that he had in mind the symbolic concept of the Constitution and that he was thinking primarily of the authority of the Court to enforce the Constitution by calling a halt when governmental agencies attempt to exceed fixed constitutional limits in the exercise of political power. On the other hand, his choice of words was such that it is not impossible that he was referring to the strong instrumental qualities of the Constitution conducive to the exercise of broad, far-reaching powers. Obviously, the wisest way to bring to an end any uncertainty concerning the meaning of the chief justice's words is to examine *McCulloch* v. *Maryland*.

The Background of McCulloch v. Maryland

Just two years after the Constitution went into operation Congress created the First Bank of the United States. From

[1] 4 Wheaton 316, 407 (1819).

the beginning this bank was the center of political controversy and in 1811 its charter was allowed to lapse. However, in 1816 because of the financial disturbances which followed the War of 1812, Congress authorized the incorporation of a Second Bank of the United States. At once the controversy was renewed. In general, both banks were supported by the Federalists and opposed by the anti-Federalists who were followers of Jefferson. Specifically, the Second Bank had made many enemies by first pursuing unwise fiscal policies which encouraged an overexpansion of credit, and then by about-facing and pursuing conservative policies which contributed to the ruin of many state banks which had imprudently encouraged undue speculation during the first period. In the ensuing financial depression the Bank of the United States was widely attacked as the tool of the "money trust." Much of the opposition to the bank came from the South and West, where many of the farmers and people of the small towns were suffering bitterly because of the scarcity of money and the generally deflationary conditions which they attributed to the bank's policies. As had been true in the 1780's, this dissatisfaction among the poorer and more radical classes led to vigorous political demands which were heeded by many state legislatures. One state after another passed laws directed against the bank and designed to curtail its activities. Among these state laws, and quite typical of them, was one enacted by the Maryland legislature which in effect required the Baltimore branch of the Bank of the United States either to pay an annual sum of $15,000 to the state or to pay a heavy tax on the paper used for its bank notes. So serious was the threat inherent in these state laws that the bank was forced to take up the challenge. In Maryland, James W. McCulloch, the cashier of the Baltimore branch, issued bank notes without complying with the law, an action that soon resulted in litigation which eventually came before the Supreme Court of the United States in 1819.[2]

One of the arguments advanced by Maryland before the Supreme Court was a claim that the whole bank program was unconstitutional owing to the absence of any express or enumerated power in the Constitution giving Congress the right to take the action it had. In short, Maryland invited the Court to declare the Bank Act of 1816 invalid. McCulloch and the bank, in turn, asked the Court to invalidate the Maryland tax law on the ground that it was an improper interference by a state with the valid program of an agency of the federal government. Accordingly, the Court found it necessary to answer two questions: first, did Congress have the power to incorporate a bank; and second, if it did, could a state tax such a bank? A unanimous Court answered the first question in the affirmative and the second in the negative.

Marshall's Opinion in the McCulloch Case

In his opinion Chief Justice Marshall at once admitted that the federal government is a government of "enumerated powers" and "can exercise only the powers granted to it."[3] Moreover, he conceded that among the powers of the federal government actually enumerated in the Constitution there is not a word about establishing a bank or creating a corporation. But he was by no means ready to go on from such observations to a conclusion that Congress had once more passed an unconstitutional statute. On the contrary, utilizing all of those powers of logic and persuasion which he had employed so effectively to reach a contrary result in *Marbury* v. *Madison*, he proceeded to argue magnificently that Congress had acted

[2]See Cushman, *op. cit.* (Chap. IV, n. 6), and Charles Warren, *The Supreme Court in United States History* (Boston: Little, Brown and Company, 1922) I, 499–540.

[3]*McCulloch* v. *Maryland* 4 Wheaton 316, 405.

within the permissive limits of the Constitution. Reasoning first of all from the general nature of the Constitution, as he had done in his *Marbury* opinion, he asserted that Congress's express powers carry after them certain implied powers: ". . . it may with great reason be contended, that a government intrusted with such ample powers, on the due execution of which the happiness and prosperity of the nation so vitally depends, must also be entrusted with ample means for their execution. The power being given, it is the interest of the nation to facilitate its execution."[4]

Among the "ample" powers expressly granted to the federal government Marshall found those "to lay and collect taxes; to borrow money; to regulate commerce; to declare and conduct a war; and to raise and support armies and navies" to be significant in the light of the case at hand. The creation of a bank as a means of executing such powers the chief justice was inclined to feel proper from the very nature of the Constitution and the powers granted by it. But moving on from such general reasoning to more specific argument, he pointed out that among the powers expressly granted to Congress was that of making "all laws which shall be necessary and proper, for carrying into execution the foregoing powers."

What did these words mean? It was obvious that they were capable of being variously interpreted. Depending upon the particular emphasis given to the clause "necessary and proper," the words might be considered as granting Congress power to pass all laws which in a *convenient* manner would tend to *facilitate* the exercise of its other express powers. Or they might mean that Congress could pass only those laws *absolutely indispensable* to the exercise of the other powers. If the first interpretation were to be followed, then the law creating the bank might well be upheld in view of the function the bank could perform as the fiscal agent of Congress

[4] *Ibid.*, p. 408.

in facilitating the exercise of such express congressional powers as those listed by Marshall. But if the second interpretation were to be preferred, the law was probably unconstitutional, for the bank was hardly indispensable to the exercise of these powers of Congress.

The chief justice preferred the more generous and lenient interpretation, and in his decision he sought to prove that the evidence indicated the necessary and proper clause should be so defined, although actually a Supreme Court, contrary-minded, could have produced substantial evidence and reasoning to the opposite effect. But the great chief justice proceeded to develop his thesis of the broad and extensive powers of Congress, and arrived at the following sweeping conclusion:

We admit, as all must admit, that the powers of the government are limited, and that its limits are not to be transcended. [See *Marbury* v. *Madison!*] But we think the sound construction of the constitution must allow to the national legislature that discretion, with respect to the means by which the powers it confers are to be carried into execution, which will enable that body to perform the high duties assigned to it, in the manner most beneficial to the people. Let the end be legitimate, let it be within the scope of the constitution, and all means which are appropriate, which are plainly adapted to that end, which are not prohibited, but consist with the letter and spirit of the constitution, are constitutional.[5]

Thus it was that Congress ventured to suggest, and the Supreme Court agreed, that the powers of the national government were not to be regarded as limited solely to the ones expressly enumerated in the Constitution but were to be considered as including all those that might be reasonably implied from those expressly stated.

Having in this fashion sanctioned the concept of broad

[5]*Ibid.*, p. 421.

federal power, Marshall and his Court went on to an answer to the second question in the case which makes the Court's nationalist inclination doubly apparent. Federal law is supreme within its own field. "The power to tax involves the power to destroy." Therefore, "the states have no power, by taxation or otherwise, to retard, impede, burden, or in any manner control, the operations of the constitutional laws enacted by Congress to carry into execution the powers vested in the general government. This is, we think, the unavoidable consequence of that supremacy which the constitution has declared."[6] Accordingly, the Maryland statute taxing the bank was declared void.

The McCulloch Decision and Constitutional Principles

In view of the storm center of controversy which the Bank of the United States had become by 1819 it is not surprising to learn that Chief Justice Marshall's opinion in the *McCulloch* case was about as bitterly and widely attacked as had been the earlier *Marbury* opinion. Moreover, the criticism came in many instances from the same sources. In both cases, it was primarily the Jeffersonian Republicans, the back-country farming people, who were antagonized by the decisions. It should be noted, however, that in both situations there was little criticism of judicial review as such. Indeed, most of the irritation caused by the *McCulloch* decision resulted from the failure of the Court to declare an act of Congress void. The opposition had little enthusiasm for Marshall's view of the Constitution as an instrument rather than a symbol and was inclined to view with grave concern the resulting extension of national legislative power over that of the states.

There is no suggestion in the words of the Court's opinion

[6]*Ibid.*, pp. 431, 436.

that the case had any political implications whatsoever. The chief justice seems completely oblivious of the controversy that was raging around the bank. His opinion in the case, as had likewise been true of his *Marbury* opinion, contains almost no reference to the realistic side of the litigation involved. Instead, both opinions are exercises in pure constitutional interpretation. There are not even references to earlier decisions that might constitute precedents for the cases at hand. Marshall gives the impression of a judge who is completely immersed in an analysis of the Constitution, seeking only to discover certain fundamental principles which will dictate decisions which can and must be rendered without any reference to the personal or political realities of the situations. The following passage in the *Marbury* opinion might equally well have occurred in the *McCulloch* opinion: "It seems only necessary to recognize certain principles, supposed to have been long and well established, to decide . . . [the case]."[7]

In the light of this judicial attitude toward the Constitution it will not be inappropriate for us to make a brief examination at this point of a number of these principles which the courts have repeatedly purported to discover in the Constitution and which they have constantly emphasized as the basis of their decisions. What is the character of these principles? Are they clear and unmistakable as to meaning? Do they lay down fixed rules by which the propriety of the activities of public officers may be easily determined? Obviously, the true nature of the power exercised by the courts in judicial review cases will be profoundly affected by the answers to these questions. It is one thing if the Constitution clearly establishes a system of limited government operating within the restricted realm of specifically granted powers. It may at least be argued that ours is then in truth *a government of*

[7]*Marbury v. Madison* 1 Cranch 137, 175 (1803).

laws and that the Supreme Court but performs an automatic duty when it enforces the higher law of the Constitution against the acts of a misguided Congress. Justice Frankfurter has pointed out that this view is widely held:

. . . multitudes of Americans seriously believe that the nine Justices embody pure reason, that they are set apart from the concerns of the community, regardless of time, place, and circumstances, to become the interpreter of sacred words with meaning fixed forever and ascertainable by a process of ineluctable reasoning.[8]

In fact, a present member of the Supreme Court has recently insisted upon the correctness of this point of view in the following words:

There should be no misunderstanding as to the function of this court. . . . It is sometimes said that the court assumes a power to overrule or control the action of the people's representatives. This is a misconception. The Constitution is the supreme law of the land ordained and established by the people. All legislation must conform to the principles it lays down. When an act of Congress is appropriately challenged in the courts as not conforming to the constitutional mandate the judicial branch of the Government has only one duty,—to lay the article of the Constitution which is invoked beside the statute which is challenged and to decide whether the latter squares with the former. All the court does, or can do, is to announce its considered judgment upon the question.[9]

On the other hand, it is quite a different matter if the principles of the Constitution are something less than crystal

[8]Felix Frankfurter, *Law and Politics*, edited by Archibald MacLeish and E. F. Prichard, Jr. (New York: Harcourt, Brace and Company, 1939) 108. Reprinted by permission of the publishers.

[9]Justice Roberts's opinion in *United States* v. *Butler* 297 U.S. 1, 62–63 (1936).

clear. The concept of limited government operating under a higher law then becomes somewhat blurred; the Constitution fails to achieve the "prolixity of a legal code" and becomes instead a broad essay on government, an instrument to be used by Congress and Court alike in political as well as legal fashion to sustain or reject ever-changing governmental programs.

The Principles of Federalism and Implied Power

We may briefly examine three points at which the Constitution is said to establish fundamental principles of government. In the first place our Constitution establishes two levels of government, national and state, and the relationship between these two types of government is said to depend upon the principle of *federalism*. According to this principle these two kinds of government are more or less independent of each other. They divide the powers of government in such a way that each has an area of activity which it can call its own. Each is then supposed to maintain a "hands-off" policy as to the power of the other. All of this is quite different from the English political system, where there are, to be sure, divisional units of government in addition to the national unit, but subdivisions which are created by and constantly subject to this national government. According to the principle of federalism, our states depend for their continued political power upon no whim or favor of men in Washington, but upon the word of the Constitution itself.

The successful operation of any such scheme involving an integrated system of two essentially independent governments must necessarily depend upon a careful and fairly clear-cut division of power between the two. This division the Constitution purports to achieve. Faced with the necessity of making a division of political powers between two levels of government, the Founding Fathers in 1787 pursued the plan of enumerating one by one the powers of the national government, leaving it to be assumed that the remainder belonged to the states. However, this inference was not sufficiently strong to suit some people, and almost at once, as a part of the Bill of Rights, the Tenth Amendment was added to the Constitution, providing specifically that all powers not granted to the government of the United States nor actually forbidden to the states are reserved to the state governments or to the people.

According to the word of the Constitution the bare outline of national and state powers is quite clear. In the first place, certain powers are granted to the national government. Congress is expressly authorized to declare war, to raise and support an army, and to provide and maintain a navy. Second, certain other powers are quite clearly reserved to the state governments. Congress is granted no authority to establish public schools or to control ordinary human relationships in such fields as marriage, divorce, and crime. So it may well be supposed·that these are powers reserved to the states. Third, there are a few powers which rest with neither government, being specifically prohibited to both. For example, both Congress and the state legislatures are expressly forbidden to pass ex post facto laws and bills of attainder.

It would be a happy thing if we could stop at this point with the principle of federalism providing such a clear-cut and workable formula for determining in actual practice the line between the powers of the government in Washington and the powers of the states. Unfortunately, we cannot. For one thing, powers granted to one or the other of the two governments are not necessarily exercised exclusively by either. They may in some instances be shared in concurrent fashion. It is clear, for example, that the grant of the taxing power to Congress does not amount to a denial of this power to the states. It was certainly intended that both governments should be able to use such a power. It should be noted that a few powers are both expressly granted to Congress and expressly denied to the states. This is true of the power to coin money, and of the treaty power. On the other hand, such a power commonly associated by the average person with the national government as the authority to regulate interstate commerce is not necessarily an exclusive possession of the government in Washington. The states may, and upon occasion sometimes do, regulate interstate commerce.[10]

As a result of this exercise of concurrent powers the line between central and state power becomes somewhat blurred. However, the resulting uncertainty, so far as our description has gone, is not too serious a matter. It is true that many of the powers granted to Congress are not exclusive and may be considered in the technical sense as belonging to the state governments as well. But there is at this point a subsidiary constitutional principle providing for the *supremacy of federal law*. The Constitution clearly states that the laws of the United States which are made in pursuance of the Constitution shall be the supreme law of the land, anything in the laws of the states to the contrary notwithstanding.[11] In other words, a state may perhaps in certain ways regulate interstate commerce but only in so far as such regulations are consistent with, or permissible under, the policy Congress may have chosen to establish. In those fields, then, where both federal and state government may sometimes be active, federal law is supreme.

But there is a much more serious blurring of the principle of federalism. It might be supposed, and indeed it was at first argued by many people, that it follows from the princi-

[10]See *Cooley* v. *Board of Wardens of Port of Philadelphia* 12 Howard 299 (1851).

[11]Constitution of the United States, Art. VI.

ple of federalism and the idea of the enumeration of the powers of the national government that this government is limited first and last to the exercise solely of those powers *expressly* enumerated in the Constitution. But we have seen that the Supreme Court in its decision in *McCulloch* v. *Maryland* rejected this supposition and concluded that Congress might exercise in addition to its express powers such further powers as could reasonably be *implied* from its enumerated powers. The far-reaching effects of this decision have long since become evident. For example, did the Constitution expressly provide that Congress might establish a postal system? Then it was determined, by implication, that Congress might make certain offenses, such as embezzlement, or the distribution of obscene literature, federal crimes if any use of the mails was made in the commission of these offenses.

Or did the Constitution expressly state that Congress might raise and support an army? Then it was held, again by implication, that Congress could enact sedition laws preventing newspapers from printing anything which might obstruct the sale of government bonds—notwithstanding the express prohibition in the Constitution directing Congress to pass "no" law abridging the freedom of the press. Did the Constitution expressly authorize Congress to raise money for the promotion of the general welfare? Then a comprehensive system of national old-age insurance became permissible.

Or again did the Constitution provide that Congress might regulate interstate commerce? Then by implication Congress found it within its power to enact legislation controlling any number of things that might well have seemed to lie outside the scope of national power—radio broadcasting, transactions on the New York Stock Exchange, dissension between Henry Ford and his workers, railroad rates between two cities in the state of Texas, the statement on the label of a can of tomatoes or the contents of a box of ladies' face powder

—all of these fell within the scope of implied congressional power to be derived from the commerce power. What is more, Congress found that it might endeavor to make the control of such matters more effective through the creation of manifold regulatory agencies such as the Interstate Commerce Commission, the Federal Trade Commission, the Federal Communications Commission, the Securities and Exchange Commission, and the National Labor Relations Board, none of which was even remotely provided for by the express terms of the Constitution and all of which have been created on the basis of implied power.

We may now reconsider the constitutional principle of federalism. It is clear at once that the idea of federal implied power has itself become something in the nature of a subsidiary constitutional principle which is not in all ways consistent with the concept of federalism. On the basis of the original principle alone it might have been possible to evolve in time a working formula by which the line between the powers of the national government and those of the state governments could have been drawn in reasonably clear and satisfactory fashion. But once the admission was made that Congress possessed implied as well as express power, the limits of national authority became extremely difficult to determine. For how far did one propose to go with this business of implied power? What laws could Congress pass upon its basis without invading the realm of state power and where must Congress finally stop? The difficulty was—and is—that such questions can have no fixed or certain answers, for the process of implication is never fixed or certain. It may be said that the well of implication is bottomless. Yet we must stop somewhere or there would be no end to the power of Congress. But does not any stopping point have to be selected more or less arbitrarily? Congress may do this, but it may not do that. Why?

It may be said that the ideas of federalism and implied power constitute a pair of rival constitutional principles which are in more or less opposition to each other. Moreover, it has become clear that the principle of federalism has a strong *symbolic* significance, for it has often been used by the courts to curb the expansive tendencies of Congress and the state legislatures. For example, this symbolic value of the principle may be seen in the decision of the Supreme Court invalidating the original Agricultural Adjustment Act.[12] Congress, in attempting to regulate agriculture along national lines, was declared to be improperly invading the realm of state power and therefore exceeding the scope of national power under our federalism.

On the other hand, the rival principle of implied power has strong *instrumental* potentialities and has often proved a more than adequate basis upon which to sanction increased national governmental activity. The instrumental value of this principle may be seen in the decision of the Supreme Court sustaining the second Agricultural Adjustment Act.[13] Here it was declared that while the regulation of agriculture might have seemed to be a power reserved to the state governments, actually congressional authority to accomplish such a purpose could be implied from the express power to regulate interstate commerce.

So it is that for a century and a half we have had under our Constitution only a vague, general dividing line between central and local government. Great extremes of centralization and decentralization have been and continue to be possible within the limits of the Constitution. During the regime of Chief Justice Marshall the tide was a strongly nationalist one, and the Court rendered many decisions sanctioning the broadening scope of federal power. Then under Chief Justice

[12]*United States* v. *Butler* 297 U.S. 1.
[13]*Mulford* v. *Smith* 307 U.S. 38 (1939).

Taney the nationalist tide ebbed somewhat, and the Court became more concerned with safeguarding "states' rights."[14] This Taney period ended in a violent explosion, and for a time judicial authority was at a minimum while the political and military arms of the government were winning a great new nationalist victory. Since the Civil War the states' rights and nationalist forces have been engaged in an almost continuous struggle for dominance, and each has had its moments of success. Of late we have been witnessing a strong and almost unprecedented tendency toward centralization which, it seems finally, is entirely proper under the Constitution. It almost appears as though the Constitution has at last become an unlimited instrument of nationalism, and that the symbolic and restraining value of the federalism principle is about to disappear from sight. But probably it is much too early to conclude that the pendulum is at last through swinging, and it is entirely possible that we may yet witness a recrudescence of federalism.

In any case it is clear that we have available an extensive freedom of action in both directions under our Constitution. This freedom may be an entirely desirable thing. But let us not delude ourselves with too much talk about principle, or too much talk about the higher law of the Constitution which establishes a nice and exact balance between the government in Washington and the government in the states. Moreover,

[14] Recent authors have pointed out that the contrast between the nationalism of the Marshall Court and the interest in state power of the Taney Court has been exaggerated. See Warren, *op. cit.* (above, n. 2), Vol. II, Chap. XXI, Carl Swisher, *Roger B. Taney* (New York: The Macmillan Company, 1935), and B. F. Wright, *The Contract Clause of the Constitution* (Cambridge: Harvard University Press, 1938) Chap. III. Neither Marshall nor Taney was interested in nationalism or states' rights solely as matters of principle. Both men were largely influenced by their social and economic views, and in this respect there is little doubt that Taney's philosophy was such that he was often led to the placing of emphasis upon state power.

it is well to remember that in the final analysis it is an agency of the national government, the Supreme Court of the United States, that resolves whatever conflict may exist between the concepts of federalism and national implied power. The loyalty of this Court to its own government can become of tremendous importance, a fact which was made very clear by the record of the Marshall Court in its wholehearted support of the nationalist movement during the first three or four decades of our present system.

The Principle of Limited Government

A second fundamental principle which the courts declare finds expression in our Constitution is that of *limited government*. According to this principle the Constitution makes a delegation of political power to governmental agencies, in the name of the people. But this delegation of power is not complete. There are certain potential political powers which no government in our country has any authority to exercise and which the people have chosen to withhold from their political rulers. This limitation is accomplished in two ways. In the first place, it is asserted that undelegated powers cannot be exercised. This is particularly true of the national government since it is presumably drastically *limited* in that it may exercise only those powers actually granted to it, others being reserved to the states or to the people. At this point the principle of limited government is obviously closely identified with the principle of federalism. Second, the operation of the principle is to be seen in the numerous express limitations which the Constitution places upon one or both governments. For example, the national government is forbidden to levy export taxes, the state governments are forbidden to pass laws impairing the obligation of contracts, and both governments are ordered not to deprive persons of their lives, liberty, or property, without due process of law. In a strong sense the long list of civil liberties enumerated in the Bill of Rights amounts to a prohibition upon federal power, and in so far as the Supreme Court has ruled that the Fourteenth Amendment re-enacts these prohibitions and applies them to state government, the limitation of both governments is effected. Moreover, the Supreme Court has declared that in addition to the express prohibitions contained in the Constitution there are certain other prohibitions which may be implied from the Constitution but which are no less effective for being merely implied. For example, the Court has ruled that Congress may not use its taxing power for a regulatory purpose, such as discouraging child labor.[15] Or, it may be pointed out, that at the same time the Supreme Court was formulating the *implied power* doctrine in *McCulloch* v. *Maryland* as a basis for upholding the bank it was denying a state government the right to tax this bank on the theory that there is an *implied prohibition* against the taxation of agencies of the federal government by the states.

Enough has now been said to indicate the strong suggestion of the limited character of political power which pervades the Constitution. But, as was true of the principle of federalism, this principle is strongly offset at many points by certain countertendencies which are present in the Constitution. It is clear that the possession by the national government of implied, in addition to express, power tends to offset the concept that national government is limited in that it may exercise only those powers actually granted to it. Moreover, numerous Supreme Court decisions make it clear that virtually all of the express prohibitions which operate upon the national and state governments are to be regarded as relative rather than absolute. For example, the power of the national government to declare and conduct a war has several times been

[15]*Bailey* v. *Drexel Furniture Co.* 259 U.S. 20 (1922).

used to justify the placing of relatively drastic restrictions upon freedom of speech and freedom of the press, even though the First Amendment specifically forbids Congress to restrict these rights. In such cases the Supreme Court is called upon to weigh the positive exercise of an undeniable power of government against the restrictive force and scope of just as undeniable a prohibition. Power and prohibition may be evenly matched contenders in such a battle, and the decision may well go in either direction. This is, of course, merely another illustration of Corwin's thesis that the Constitution is both an instrument and a symbol. The principle of limited government is perhaps the strongest aspect of the symbolic Constitution. But at the same time the Constitution bestows such strong instrumental power upon our governmental agencies that it has often seemed that the Constitution is not much of a limiting force upon these agencies and that the only effective restrictive force is public opinion. In other words, if the people want something done, whatever that something may be, ways and means of securing action have often been found within the Constitution. The record of the national government during the Civil War and the World War may be cited as evidence of this truth.

In the case of the state governments the relative rather than absolute quality of the limited-government principle is easily illustrated. The failure of the Constitution to enumerate state powers, and its suggestion, instead, that the great residue of political power is reserved to them, considerably upsets the concept that they are governments of limited powers only. For example, one of these reserved powers is the so-called *police power,* which in a general way authorizes a state to take whatever steps are necessary to foster and protect the general welfare of its people. This situation will be examined in considerable detail in a later chapter, but it may be noted here that there is a definite lack of harmony between the idea that a state possesses a broad power to promote the health, safety, morals, and general welfare of its people, and the express prohibition forbidding that state to deprive persons of life, liberty, or property, without due process of law. If the Constitution is viewed in its instrumental capacity, a state statute providing for compulsory vaccination may well be approved as a necessary measure in the interests of public health. But if emphasis is to be placed upon the symbolic character of the Constitution it is at least possible to claim that this statute deprives persons of their liberty without due process of law and is thus unconstitutional. As a matter of fact, the Supreme Court was once asked to decide just such a case, and the justices who sat in the case could not agree whether it was a matter of the proper exercise of a valid constitutional power, or a definite violation of an express constitutional prohibition.[16]

The Principle of Separation of Powers

Finally, the principle of *separation of powers* may be noted. According to this idea, government is a threefold process and is organized into three divisions, one for each process, all three being kept separate and distinct from one another. Chronologically speaking, the first thing a government does is to determine upon certain policies which are presumably in the public interest. This is known as the legislative or law-making process, and under our Constitution such power in the national government is granted to Congress. Second, it becomes necessary to interpret such general policies in the light of their specific application to certain individuals or situations. This is known as the judicial process, and national power here is granted to the Supreme Court and other fed-

[16]*Jacobson* v. *Massachusetts* 197 U.S. 11 (1905).

eral judicial bodies. Finally, the completion of the process of government requires that policies as adopted by the legislature and as interpreted and applied by the courts be uniformly enforced or carried out. This is known as the administrative process, and its performance is assigned to the executive division, headed in our national government by the president, with countless department heads, subordinates, and members of administrative commissions to assist him. Lawmaking, law interpretation, law enforcement—these are the three aspects of government.

Why did the Constitutional Fathers place such emphasis upon this idea of separation of powers? Is it not an inevitable characteristic of any system or type of government? The answer is "yes" and "no." It may be said that the three processes themselves are inevitably present in any form of government. But the Fathers supposedly had something more than the mere threefold character of the governmental process in mind. In addition they proposed that the actual exercise of each of these powers should be by a separate agency of government more or less independent of the other two. Thus it is said that the legislative power rests in an *independent* Congress, the executive power in an *independent* president, and the judicial power in an *independent* Supreme Court. The reason for this arrangement was that it would make possible the creation of a strong government with great powers, yet at the same time presumably prevent our government from ever becoming arbitrary or tyrannical or perhaps falling into the hands of one dangerous faction or party, particularly a mob-majority, since no single agency of government would possess more than one third of the sum total of political power, and each was to be selected in different fashion.

But again in separation of powers we have a principle that has its counterpart in a supplementary principle. In this case, the latter is known as the principle of *checks and*

balances. Having divided government into a threefold process and having assigned each of the three parts to a supposedly independent agency, the Constitutional Convention
proceeded to authorize or pave the way for an almost endless
amount of interference with, or "checking" of, the affairs of
each department, in turn, by the other two.

They provided that the president, although chief executive
of the government, should exercise numerous legislative
powers, including the right to call Congress in special session,
the right to recommend the enactment of specific laws, and
the right to veto laws that he disapproves.

To the Congress, the Fathers gave several powers enabling
it to interfere with or check the president's conduct of the
affairs of the executive department. Executive appointments
are subject to a vote of confirmation by the Senate, and members of the executive department, from the president on
down, are subject to impeachment and removal from office by
Congress. Perhaps the most striking illustration of the manner and extent to which Congress has control over the executive division of government is to be seen in the amazing fact
that, apart from the office of the presidency and that of the
vice-presidency, all of the ten executive departments, the
several score administrative commissions, and the hundreds
of bureaus, divisions, and subdivisions associated with the
executive departments have been created by act of Congress.[17]
What is more, they are subject at any moment to revision,
alteration, or even outright abolition by Congress. The
National Labor Relations Board is an administrative agency,
the peculiar function of which is to administer that part of
our national labor policy set forth in the Wagner Act. The
board is thus a part of the executive process of government.
But it was created by Congress, and should Congress decide

[17]It is true that a few of these agencies have been created by executive
order of the president, but only under authority granted to him by Congress.

to abolish it, only a presidential veto could prevent such action; and even that may be overridden by Congress.

The Convention of 1787 also provided for several checks over the federal judiciary. It gave the president control over the courts by permitting him to name all federal judges. Then it provided a legislative check of both executive and judiciary by requiring that judicial appointments by the president be confirmed by the Senate. Or again, the very existence of all federal courts, save one, the Supreme Court, depends upon acts of Congress. Which means again that as Congress creates, so it may alter and abolish. Similarly, the very power of the federal courts to hear cases is subject in many ways to the control of Congress. Finally, Congress may impeach and remove federal judges from office and more than once has done so.

But lest one conclude that our federal judges are hardly more than helpless pawns in the game of government, we need only recall that the checks at this point are not all one-sided by any means, and that the judiciary has claimed for itself an important check over both Congress and the administrative officers of government through the operation of its power of judicial review.

The dichotomy which exists within the Constitution on this matter of the separate spheres of the three agencies of government can be illustrated by reference to two contrasting Supreme Court decisions. In 1920 President Wilson removed from office the postmaster of Portland, Oregon, without complying with the terms of a congressional statute which provided that the president could not remove such an officer without obtaining the consent of the Senate. Litigation resulted and the Supreme Court finally upheld the president's action by holding that the statute which he had seemingly violated was unconstitutional. It based this decision upon the principle of separation of powers, pointing out that in passing a statute restricting the president's removal power Congress was endeavoring to cross the line and interfere with the president's control of the executive affairs of government.[18]

In 1933 President Roosevelt removed a member of the Federal Trade Commission from office, again in a manner contrary to the procedure set forth by congressional statute. Again litigation resulted, and this time the Court ruled against the president, although it might have seemed that its earlier decision had paved the way for subsequent presidential removal of any and every officer within the executive department of government without any regard for the attitude of Congress. But the Court was impressed by the claim that the Federal Trade Commission, while essentially a part of the executive sphere of government, acted at times in quasi-legislative and quasi-judicial capacities. Because of this, the Court concluded that it was the president and not Congress in this case who was violating the separation-of-powers principle and that Congress had a valid right to check the president in the removal of such an officer whose duties may be said to cut across the lines of the three spheres of government.[19] In other words, the Court was in effect stressing the idea of checks and balances as opposed to the idea of a pure separation of powers, the result being that it ended up with exactly the opposite decision from what might have been expected in the light of the postmaster case. Moreover, what may seem like a logical distinction between these two decisions, in the light of the varying character of the offices concerned, becomes somewhat less impressive when it is noted that it may be said of almost any executive officer that he sometimes acts in a quasi-legislative or quasi-judicial capacity. A postmaster, for example (or certainly the postmaster general), is sometimes compelled to make rules or to render

[18]*Myers* v. *United States* 272 U.S. 52 (1926).

[19]*Rathbun* v. *United States* 295 U.S. 602 (1935).

findings as to the permissible use of the mails by certain individuals or concerns under questionable circumstances. In so acting does he not become a quasi-legislative or quasi-judicial agent?

The Constitution as Instrument and Symbol

It need not be concluded that these pairs of rival principles just described so completely offset one another that they add up to zero. We Americans do have a Constitution. It does contain certain ideas about government. There is something to the idea of federalism. It is far from being meaningless. After all, in addition to our national government we do have forty-eight more or less vigorous state governments carrying on very substantial and reasonably independent programs. Moreover, the dividing line between the powers of these two types of government has been relatively clear in some respects. Such things as public education or the control of local governments and their activities have been pretty largely functions of the state governments. Military activity and foreign affairs have been almost completely functions of the national government. Likewise, there is something to the idea of separation of powers. It cannot be denied, for example, that our chief executive, the president, has greater independence of the legislature than is true of the chief executive under parliamentary government. On the other hand, it must be admitted that there seem to be a great many possible exceptions to these principles. At least they do not always provide as certain an answer in a given situation as one would expect when that situation is supposedly governed by "principle." Justice Holmes once put somewhat the same idea in these words: "General propositions do not decide concrete cases. The decision will depend on a judgment or intuition more subtle than any articulate major premise." [20] So it seems

[20]Dissenting opinion, *Lochner* v. *New York* 198 U.S. 45, 76 (1905).

impossible to draw any other conclusion than that constitutional principles are merely general ideas or guideposts, and that the Constitution as a whole is hardly more than a collection of such ideas and guideposts.

By way of summarizing the discussion of principles just completed, and at the same time introducing the examination of judicial review in operation, the dual character of the Constitution may once more be stressed. As a symbol of restraint the Constitution contains certain principles capable of being utilized by the courts to hold nonjudicial agencies of government within more or less narrow bounds. Thus federalism may be used to restrict national government activities on the score that this is necessary to prevent an encroachment upon powers reserved to the states. Vice versa, state activity may be prevented lest federal territory be entered. Second, the principle of limited government has obvious symbolic import for purposes of judicial limitation of the governmental program. It need only be declared as to either a federal or state law that it deprives a person of his life, liberty, or property, without due process of law, to obtain a ruling that government is exceeding the limitations imposed upon it. Finally, the principle of separation of powers can be utilized to restrict governmental activity wherever it appears that the strict threefold character of the governmental process is being threatened. Here, too, it is the Constitution as symbol which is being emphasized.

But when circumstances and the occasion seem to call for increased governmental activity, the Court need only point the way down the ample instrumental thoroughfares of the Constitution. Thus the doctrine of implied powers has a strong instrumental value sufficient upon occasion to offset any seeming barrier in the form of federalism. Likewise, the same doctrine—or in the case of the states, the reserved-power principle of the Tenth Amendment—and the police power particularly, have instrumental values that may easily be used to overcome the negative purpose of the limited government principle. Finally, the checks-and-balances principle, providing, as it does, undoubted right to each of the departments of government to participate in many ways in the work of the other two, has an instrumental value entirely sufficient to silence any command to halt in the name of separation of powers.

Returning to Chief Justice Marshall's warning phrase that "we must never forget that it is a *constitution* we are expounding," it now seems clear that while he was adamant about the presence in the Constitution of the implied-power principle, he was using that principle to strengthen the instrumental values of the document. He was certain that his decision in *McCulloch* v. *Maryland* was the inexorable result of an immutable principle. But the principle he was insisting upon was the tolerant one of flexibility. In effect, he was arguing that the Constitution may be regarded as a broad essay on the essential character of our government, deliberately written in words general in meaning and capable of interpretation and expansion to meet changing needs. This is a "constitution intended to endure for ages to come, and, consequently, to be adapted to the various *crises* of human affairs. To have prescribed the means by which government should, in all future time, execute its powers, would have been to change, entirely, the character of the *instrument,* and give it the properties of a legal code." [21] Again he points out that a constitution, complete down to the last detail and intended to be all-inclusive, "would partake of the prolixity of a legal code, and could scarcely be embraced by the human mind. It would probably never be understood by the public." Instead, he goes on to say, it is far better that the Constitution indicate only the general direction of our political life, "that

[21] *McCulloch* v. *Maryland* 4 Wheaton 316, 415. (Second italics added.)

only its great outlines should be marked, its important objects designated, and the minor ingredients which compose those objects be deduced from the nature of the objects themselves."[22] That this was the idea the Constitutional Fathers had of their work, he concludes, is not to be doubted.

But there had been an earlier occasion, as we have seen, when Marshall was inclined to apply the exact words of the Constitution pretty rigidly so as to give a restrictive rather than an expansive result. Moreover, it is clear that some of Marshall's successors on the Supreme Court have had little enthusiasm for the great doctrine announced in *McCulloch* v. *Maryland*. Accordingly, it will now be wise to examine in some detail the actual operation of judicial review in one or two fields of constitutional interpretation. First of all let us take the power of Congress to regulate interstate commerce, which reveals the Constitution in one of its strongest instrumental aspects, and note the extent to which the Supreme Court has been consistent in championing this clause as an instrument of power. Second, we may turn to the due-process-of-law clauses and investigate the consistency which the Court has shown in utilizing these restrictive phrases to emphasize the symbolic quality of the Constitution.

[22]*Ibid.*, p. 407.

Chapter VI

The Supreme Court in Action: Interstate Commerce

Our Constitutional Fathers went to Philadelphia by stage-coach. There were no trains. There were no automobiles. Moreover, in 1787 there were no telephones and there was no radio. A person burned wood from his own wood lot, and not coal from West Virginia. The chicken for his Sunday dinner came from his own barnyard, and not from a neighboring state. Small wonder, then, that the Constitution contained no specific references to matters like these. Instead, the Convention dealt in general terms. Congress was granted power to regulate commerce *among* the several states. By the terms of the Tenth Amendment power to regulate commerce *within* the states was presumably reserved to the state governments. But where was the line to be drawn between these two aspects of the nation's economic activity? Or to rephrase the question in the light of the present—how far can Congress go on the basis of powers granted to it in 1787 in attempting to cope with and control the economic and social problems of a highly industrialized, modern society?

The Supreme Court and the Commerce Clause

Let us take an example. Not so many years ago people began to grow concerned about the increasing number of automobiles that were being stolen and demanded that the government do something about this serious problem. The first responses came from local and state governments, and for a while they were reasonably successful in curbing the thefts. But two factors—the steady mechanical improvement in the automobile and the simultaneous construction of a nation-wide network of high-speed highways—made it an increasingly simple matter for a thief to drive a stolen automobile across state lines. The individual state governments soon found that their constitutional power to cope with this problem was inadequate, since the authority of each state came to an end at its borders. Consequently, Congress was soon asked to attack this problem along national lines. At once doubts were expressed as to whether the national government had any power to deal with such a matter. However, congressmen could not afford to be deaf to the clamor that they "do something" about stolen automobiles. It occurred to them that they might be able to call the driving of a stolen automobile across the lines between two states "commerce among the states," and the punishment of the thief a "regulation" of such interstate commerce. Here, then, is an actual illustration of the essential problem involved in the exercise of the national commerce power.

The attitude of the Supreme Court toward the development of the commerce power as an instrument of national authority will now be examined. It may, however, first be noted in passing that several other congressional powers have been of significance in this constitutional development. From time to time Congress has used its taxing and spending powers, its postal power, its monetary powers, and its so-called war powers, in attacking social and economic problems. But, by and large, the extension of national authority has been dependent upon the commerce power. Either a federal law making it a federal crime to drive a stolen automobile across state lines rests upon the commerce power or it is probably beyond the power of Congress to enact.

No attempt will be made to trace the development of the commerce power over the last century and a half. One or two high lights in the earlier years will be noted, but our main purpose will be to examine the varying views of the commerce power which have prevailed in recent years. Particular attention will be given to the work of the Supreme Court in this process of interpreting the commerce clause of the Constitution. What role has the Court been playing? As Congress has endeavored to use the commerce power to meet an ever-increasing number of national problems, and as the Court has passed upon the validity of specific exercises of the power, what has been the true character of the latter process? Has the Court merely been enforcing the Constitution by automatically sanctioning what that document clearly permits, and by invalidating whatever lies beyond its terms? Or has the Court been acting more in the capacity of a legislative body, a political arm of the government, which is susceptible to social and economic pressures of both a progressive and a reactionary character, and which passes finally upon the wisdom or feasibility of each new policy? Changing the emphasis from the Court back to the Constitution, we should keep such questions as these in mind as we examine commerce cases. What do the words "commerce among the several states" include? Do they refer only to the actual movement of goods and persons across state lines, or do they extend to various types of economic activity, such as manufacturing, or buying and selling, if these are carried on along national lines?

Needless to say, the Supreme Court has decided commerce power cases in two ways. In some it has upheld the exercise of power by Congress; in others it has condemned action which Congress has taken. That there should be two such types of decisions is not in itself surprising or significant.

After all, in some instances Congress may simply have been going too far, while in others it has stayed within proper limits. What is significant to note is the degree of consistency which the Court has been able to show in marking out constitutional guideposts by which certain types of laws can be sanctioned and others condemned.

The Initial Interpretation of the Clause

The first case involving the commerce clause of the Constitution did not reach the Supreme Court until 1824. This was *Gibbons* v. *Ogden,* in which Chief Justice Marshall wrote another of his famous opinions.[1] The facts of the case are interesting. To Robert R. Livingston and Robert Fulton, the famous inventor, the state of New York had granted an exclusive right to control the navigation of its waters by steamboat. From these men Ogden in turn received a license to engage in such navigation. Gibbons, on the other hand, was endeavoring to operate steamboats between New York and New Jersey under a license granted to him by the national government. Litigation resulted and the case eventually reached the Supreme Court. That Court found it necessary to decide whether the granting of a license to Gibbons by the national government was a proper action under the congressional power to regulate interstate commerce, and if it was, whether the attempt of the state of New York to grant an exclusive license to Livingston and Fulton was valid. For our purposes the important part of the decision is that dealing with the question—what is commerce? From our present-day point of view it is surprising to find that the Court was somewhat in doubt as to whether transportation and navigation were included in the term. Strangely enough, all concerned with the case seemed agreed that commerce included the

[1] 9 Wheaton 1 (1824).

concept of "traffic" in the sense of business, or "buying and selling," but Ogden contended that the commerce clause gave Congress no authority to control navigation or transportation. In his opinion, Chief Justice Marshall rejected this contention, ruled that Congress possessed authority to regulate interstate transportation, and concluded that, accordingly, the attempt of New York to grant an exclusive right to engage in such transportation was invalid.

It seems clear that in including the regulation of transportation within the commerce power the chief justice thought he was sanctioning one of the less obvious rights of Congress under that power. A careful reading of Marshall's opinion makes it obvious that he was anxious to broaden national power in the commerce field. Marshall points out that the commerce "power, like all others vested in Congress, is complete in itself, may be exercised to its utmost extent, and acknowledges no limitations, other than are prescribed in the constitution."[2] It has been said of the opinion in *Gibbons* v. *Ogden* that "it was perhaps the only genuinely popular decision which Marshall ever handed down. It was received with widespread expressions of approval, for it was, as one writer has put it, 'the first great anti-trust decision.' "[3] The Supreme Court was undoubtedly influenced, in arriving at its decision, by the obvious desirability of frustrating the attempt of New York to hamper commercial progress through the fostering of a monopoly. But for Marshall there was perhaps an even more important motivation in the case. He was probably concerned less with the antitrust tendencies of his decision than he was with the impetus which it gave to the national government's control of the country's economic activities. Marshall's great biographer has said that his opinion did "more to knit the American people into an indivisible

[2]*Ibid.,* p. 196.

[3]Cushman, *op. cit.* (Chap. IV, n. 6), p. 275.

Nation than any other one force in our history, excepting
only war."[4] It is important to note that the chief justice's
ruling was perfectly consistent with his own intense loyalty
to Federalist traditions and was equally harmonious with the
strongly nationalist sentiments, which had prevailed at Philadelphia in 1787. Marshall, then, started the commerce clause
upon its constitutional course in a way calculated to enhance
its importance and prestige and in a manner that would have
seemed eminently suitable to the Founding Fathers.

Reaction in the 1890's

We may now turn to a decision rendered nearly three quar-
ters of a century later. During this long interval the Supreme
Court, with few exceptions, such as the exclusion of insurance
companies from congressional control, continued to sanction
a broad exercise of the commerce power by the national
government. In the year 1890 Congress enacted the famous
Sherman Antitrust Act, declaring illegal every combination
in restraint of interstate commerce. Shortly thereafter the
national government took steps to prosecute five sugar refining companies located in the state of Pennsylvania for
violation of the law. The companies offered as their defense
the argument that, whether they were guilty of an attempt
to create a monopoly or not, the alleged monopoly was in
manufacturing and not in commerce. In its decision in *United
States* v. *E. C. Knight Company* the Court accepted this argument, and stating that "commerce succeeds to manufacture,
and is not a part of it," concluded that Congress had no right
to control the process of manufacturing on the basis of its
commerce power.[5] However, the Court avoided invalidating

[4]A. J. Beveridge, *The Life of John Marshall* (Boston: Houghton Mifflin
Company, 1919) IV, 429-30.

[5]156 U.S. 1 (1895).

the Sherman Act by holding that Congress had intended it to apply only to monopolies in trade and transportation, and not manufacturing, and that the Department of Justice had erred in its interpretation of the law in invoking it against the sugar refining companies. Justice Harlan alone dissented. Because of the close relationship between the attempt at monopoly control which was here being made within the state of Pennsylvania, and the subsequent trading in sugar across state lines, he felt that Congress's commerce power must necessarily extend to the control of the former if the latter were to be protected. But in 1895 Harlan's was a voice crying in the wilderness.

There is a subtle but very important contrast between the decisions in *Gibbons* v. *Ogden* and *United States* v. *E. C. Knight Company* which illustrates the significant change in emphasis which had occurred in the Court's view of the extent of the commerce power. Where Marshall had sought to broaden the scope of the power by extending it to include interstate movement of goods, and transportation generally, the Court of the *Knight* case had swung around to a position where it was virtually limiting the commerce power to the regulation of transportation and was excluding almost everything else. It may be noted that the Sugar case was decided by one of the most conservative groups of justices who have ever sat on the Court. It is hard to avoid the conclusion that this decision, which virtually nullified "the Sherman Act, and kept it nullified during the most critical period in our industrial history, when most of the great trusts were formed,"[6] was a rather deliberate product of the laissez-faire philosophy which was then dominant among the justices. In the same year that it decided the Sugar case, the Court handed down two other extremely conservative opinions, one invalidating the income tax, in *Pollock* v. *Farmers' Loan and*

[6] E. S. Corwin in 12 *American Bar Association Journal* (March 1926) 171.

Trust Co.,[7] and the other upholding a sweeping antilabor injunction in *In re Debs.*[8] These three decisions combined to bring down upon the Court one of the greatest storms of criticism in its entire history.[9]

It would be incorrect to infer that the decision in the Sugar case marked an end to the liberal interpretation of the commerce power for which Marshall had set the precedent. It did, however, constitute fair warning by the Court that no longer could Congress count on the judiciary to ratify any use it might choose to make of the power, and that henceforth the Court might, upon occasion, call a halt to its extension of the commerce power. That such a warning should have been given by a conservatively minded Court at that particular moment is not surprising, for in a very important sense Congress had only just begun to explore the possibilities of utilizing the commerce power for important regulatory purposes. In the words of the conservative historian of the Supreme Court, Charles Warren, the Interstate Commerce Act of 1887 was "the *first* important exercise by Congress of its power under the Commerce Clause" and the Sherman Act of 1890 was but "the third important example of the exercise by Congress of . . . [this] power."[10] In fact, Warren asserts that "until the year 1903, Congress had confined the exercise of its powers under the Commerce Clause almost entirely to the subject of intoxicating liquor, common carriers and trusts."[11]

[7]158 U.S. 601 (1895).

[8]158 U.S. 564 (1895).

[9]Warren, *op. cit.* (Chap. V, n. 2), III, 421–26.

[10]*Ibid.*, III, 451, 455. (Italics added.) This and the following excerpt are reprinted by permission of Little, Brown and Company, publishers.

[11]*Ibid.*, III, 457.

The Commerce Clause as a Basis for a Federal Police Power

In 1903 the Supreme Court upheld a statute based upon the commerce power which, while relatively unimportant in itself, illustrated a new use, far-reaching in significance, which Congress might make of this power in a new century destined to present for governmental consideration an infinite number of complicated social and economic problems. In 1895 Congress had passed a statute making it a crime to send lottery tickets across state lines. The act was based upon the commerce power, and in *Champion* v. *Ames,* Justice Harlan, speaking for the majority of the Court, upheld the law. He stated that "if the carrying of lottery tickets from one State to another be interstate commerce [and the majority thought it was], and if Congress is of the opinion that an effective regulation for the suppression of lotteries, carried on through such commerce, is to make it a criminal offense to cause lottery tickets to be carried from one State to another, we know of no authority in the courts to hold that the means thus devised are not appropriate and necessary. . . ."[12] Interestingly enough, Justice Harlan had been the lone dissenter in the Sugar case. And prophetically, four justices dissented from his opinion in the Lottery case.

It is important to note that on its face the lottery ticket statute actually was a regulation of interstate commerce. Congress did not seek to prohibit the lottery evil outright. Instead, it simply denied the use of interstate channels to such an enterprise. It was upon this basis that the Court found it possible to uphold the legislation. The significance of this decision is quite obvious. It meant, in effect, that Congress might exercise, what amounted to a federal police power over such

[12] 188 U.S. 321, 358 (1903).

matters as public morals, public safety, and public health wherever a use of the channels of interstate commerce was involved. Where the commerce power had previously been used primarily to regulate, foster, or promote commerce for its own sake, railroad regulation being a good example, it now seemed that Congress might seek to regulate social and economic practices within the states, provided only that at some point they involved a crossing of state lines.

Congress was not slow in making a wide use of this new interpretation of the commerce power. In rapid succession, statutes were passed providing for the federal control of many matters which had usually been considered as subject only to the operation of the police power of the states. The Pure Food Act, the Meat Inspection Act, the Narcotics Acts, the White Slave Act, and other similar laws were passed by Congress upon the basis of the commerce power. Finally, in 1916, Congress passed the first Child Labor Act, which was designed to curtail child labor by prohibiting the transportation in interstate commerce of goods manufactured by concerns employing children contrary to certain standards laid down in the statute. In general, the employment of children under fourteen years of age or of children between fourteen and sixteen for more than eight hours a day or six days a week by a manufacturer was to result in a blocking of the channels of interstate commerce to his products. Naturally enough such a statute was enacted only after a bitter legislative struggle, and its passage antagonized conservative business interests which were opposed to control of economic enterprise by government, particularly the national government. Accordingly, the law was soon challenged in the courts, for while the decision in *Champion* v. *Ames* might have seemed to constitute a favorable precedent for upholding the law, the decision in the Sugar case—to the effect that commerce succeeds to manufacture and is not a part of it—had never been repudiated by the courts and certainly encouraged an attack upon the child labor law.

When the issue reached the Supreme Court in 1918, in *Hammer* v. *Dagenhart,* it held that the statute was unconstitutional in that it represented an attempt by Congress to control not commerce, but manufacturing, and thus involved an illegal encroachment upon the powers reserved to the state governments by the Tenth Amendment. The Court said: "To sustain this statute would not be in our judgment a recognition of the lawful exertion of congressional authority over interstate commerce, but would sanction an invasion by the federal power of the control of a matter purely local in its character, and over which no authority has been delegated to Congress in conferring the power to regulate commerce among the States."[13] Justice Holmes, who wrote the dissenting opinion in this five-to-four case, argued that the statute was valid because on its face it was clearly a regulation of interstate commerce since it prohibited the shipment of certain goods across state lines. He argued that the Court had no right to invalidate the law because of its indirect or secondary purpose: that of attempting to control certain conditions in the manufacturing stage by reaching a situation that existed before transportation began. After all, on its face the act did deal only with the movement of goods in interstate commerce. It did "not meddle with anything belonging to the States. They may regulate their internal affairs and their domestic commerce as they like. But when they seek to send their products across the state line they are no longer within their rights. . . . Under the Constitution such commerce belongs not to the States but to Congress to regulate."[14]

Whether one agrees with Holmes's dissenting opinion or not, it may be admitted that the majority opinion itself pos-

[13]247 U.S. 251, 276 (1918).
[14]*Ibid.,* p. 281.

sesses a certain logic and reason. For it *was* obvious that Congress was trying to reach behind the interstate movement in question to control something that occurred before such movement even began. In short, it was using its power to prohibit certain types of commerce as a sort of threat to bully manufacturers into discontinuing the use of child labor. Viewed in the light of this information, the majority decision is not unconvincing, although, of course, it is based on the premise of the *Knight* case that "commerce" is restricted virtually to transportation, a premise that may be challenged. But when one attempts to reconcile this majority opinion with decisions concerning other similar regulatory statutes under the commerce power, logic and consistency are absent. For example, it is difficult to reconcile the decisions in the child labor and lottery ticket cases. The facts of the two cases were very similar, yet the statute in the one case was held to be a valid exercise of the commerce power, while the statute in the other case was invalidated.

Did the majority in the Child Labor case admit its departure from the *Champion* v. *Ames* precedent and specifically reverse it? By no means. Instead, it made a rather labored effort to harmonize the majority decisions in the two cases. It argued that in the *Champion* case "the use of interstate transportation was necessary to the accomplishment of harmful results," while in the *Hammer* case "the goods shipped are of themselves harmless."[15] All of which would seem to prove nothing. For a lottery ticket is also in itself a perfectly harmless object—it is just a piece of paper. Or on the other hand, in the Child Labor case it could have been said, just as easily as in the Lottery case, that "the use of interstate transportation was necessary to the accomplishment of harmful results." If employers of child labor could not ship their products across state lines they would soon enough have

[15]*Ibid.*, pp. 271–72.

desisted from the evil of employing child labor. Of course, it may be argued that in the Lottery case Congress was trying to reach an evil that occurred after interstate commerce had taken place, whereas in the Child Labor case the evil took place before the interstate movement began. But should that factor have made any difference to the Supreme Court, since it is evident that the continuation of either of these social evils necessitated the continued use of the channels of interstate commerce? Or if it did make a difference, one wonders how the Court would have ruled in the Child Labor case had the statute in question prohibited the shipment of raw materials across state lines to factories employing child labor. That would have put the evil on the postinterstate side. But would such a difference in facts have altered the ruling of the Court in the case?

There were other decisions in earlier cases which the Court endeavored in the Child Labor case to distinguish from the decision of the moment. For instance, the Court had previously upheld federal statutes which made it a crime to take a woman across state lines for immoral purposes or to send impure foods or drugs across state lines. Again it may be argued that a woman herself, or a can of spoiled tomatoes, is a perfectly harmless object as it moves across state lines. It does not clog or disrupt the channels of interstate commerce any more than does a pure woman or a pure can of tomatoes. In both instances the regulation of a certain type of commerce by Congress is just an excuse to reach a general social evil which is related to interstate commerce only incidentally. Yet the Court upheld both statutes.[16] But when it came to the later Child Labor case the Court refused to admit that its ruling was in any way inconsistent with these earlier decisions.

There is another example in the later question of the con-

[16]*Hoke* v. *United States* 227 U.S. 308 (1913); *Hipolite Egg Co.* v. *United States* 220 U.S. 45 (1911).

stitutionality of the National Motor Vehicle Theft Act, which has already been referred to. When this law, making it a federal crime to drive a stolen automobile across state lines, reached the Supreme Court, it was upheld unanimously. The Court said: "Congress can certainly regulate interstate commerce to the extent of forbidding and punishing the use of such commerce as an agency to promote immorality, dishonesty or the spread of any evil or harm to the people of other States from the State of origin." Having said this, Chief Justice Taft tried to reconcile the ruling with the earlier contrary decision in the Child Labor case by suggesting that "articles made by child labor and transported into other States were harmless, and could be properly transported without injuring any person who either bought or used them."[17] Yet it is obvious that the very words Taft employed to defend the National Motor Vehicle Theft Act could have been used to sustain the Child Labor Act. It was true, perhaps, that the transportation in interstate commerce of child labor products did no harm to the buyer or seller, but certainly it did harm. For example, it could almost certainly have been shown that the carrying of such products into a state that itself had rigid child labor restrictions created pressure upon that state to relax its control because of the ruinous competition of the lower-priced child labor products with its own products, higher priced because of higher labor costs. In such a situation interstate commerce clearly became "an agency to promote . . . the spread of . . . evil or harm to the people of other States from the State of origin."

Finally, it is enlightening to examine the still later question of the constitutionality of the federal kidnaping legislation passed after the kidnaping of the Lindbergh baby. This statute made it a federal crime to take a kidnaped person across state lines. So ready were the federal courts to sustain it that the

[17]*Brooks* v. *United States* 267 U.S. 432, 436, 438 (1925).

issue never went beyond a federal circuit court of appeals, which ruled: "To prohibit the use of the channels of interstate commerce to facilitate the crime of kidnaping is clearly within the power of Congress."[18] One can thoroughly approve this decision and yet find in it some cause for wonder and concern. After all, the child labor law did have something to do with such concepts as *economic enterprise, business, trade,* and *commerce,* which the Framers of the Constitution had in mind when they wrote the commerce clause.[19] Yet it was held to be beyond the scope of Congress's commerce power, whereas committing the crime of kidnaping does seem just a bit remote from things *economic,* unless the idea of ransom serves that purpose. Yet the courts did not hesitate about including this act within the scope of Congress's power to regulate *commerce.* It may also be noted that the federal kidnaping legislation even goes so far as to provide that if a kidnaping is not cleared up within seven days a presumption shall arise that the kidnaper has taken his victim across state lines and that this presumption shall be sufficient to authorize investigation of the crime by federal agents.

In this same respect it is somewhat amusing to note that in some of the White Slave cases the courts ruled that it was perfectly proper for Congress, upon the basis of the commerce power, to make it a crime to take a woman across a state line for an immoral purpose, even though there was no financial aspect to the transaction.[20] Thus far had the Court come in excluding economic considerations from the word "commerce," and in emphasizing its seeming identification with the mere act of transportation across state lines.

[18]*Bailey v. United States* 74 F. (2d) 451, 453 (1934).

[19]See W. H. Hamilton and D. Adair, *The Power to Govern* (New York: W. W. Norton & Company, Inc., 1937) Chap. III, for an interesting discussion of the probable meaning the people of 1787 attached to the words in the commerce clause.

[20]*Caminetti v. United States* 242 U.S. 470 (1917).

Most of the commerce power cases thus far examined have this much in common: each involves a statute which on its face obviously provides for the regulation of interstate commerce. But in several of these cases the Court concerned itself with the question whether this was not just a subterfuge on the part of Congress in an effort to reach and control some problem lying beyond interstate activity and perhaps having no very close or necessary relation to it. In most of such cases the Court has been inclined to uphold the legislation under attack by permitting itself to be impressed by the obvious argument that interstate commerce is in fact being regulated. But in the Child Labor case the Court declared the legislation void because it was more impressed by the fact that Congress was really trying to regulate some social evil which was only incidentally related to interstate commerce. It is hard to avoid the conclusion that the varying outcome of these cases was affected by a personal as well as a legal motivation on the part of the justices. Where legislation directed against such admitted social evils as the theft of automobiles or kidnaping has been in question, judges have not been at all inclined to erect any constitutional barriers in the way of federal action. After all, public opinion has been almost unanimous in demanding action against these evils and even an ultraconservative has little inclination to oppose such a tide. Where a social practice was not quite so recognizably evil, and some opinion has opposed governmental "meddling," as was perhaps true of the lottery traffic, judges have begun to entertain constitutional doubts about the validity of federal legislation. Finally, when Congress endeavored to employ its commerce power against a highly controversial evil touching the field of business enterprise, and encountered the opposition of a vociferous, although perhaps minority, faction of the American people, a Supreme Court dominated by a conservative majority interposed a legal objection.

It may be argued that there is little reason to be disturbed about the ruling in the Child Labor case since it is the only decision in which the Court refused to sanction the use by Congress of the commerce clause for federal police power purposes. The weakness in this argument is that this one adverse decision struck down the most important congressional attempt to make use of a national police power in the field of business enterprise. Moreover, the decision in *Hammer* v. *Dagenhart* undoubtedly laid a strong restraining hand upon Congress for the following decade and a half, and discouraged further attempts to develop the commerce power in that direction.

The Commerce Clause and the Control of Local Enterprise

We may now turn to another and somewhat different development of the commerce power which has been taking place in the present century and which has resulted in a second and highly interesting type of Supreme Court decision. Some time after the inauguration, in 1887 and 1890, of a policy of federal regulation of such economic enterprises as railroads and trusts, it slowly became apparent that it was not always sufficient merely to control the interstate aspects of these problems. As the nation made further economic progress and its industrial system became more and more highly centralized and closely integrated, it became increasingly difficult to separate the strictly interstate aspects of such enterprises from the purely local or intrastate. Accordingly, Congress became more and more inclined to provide, here and there, for federal regulation of admittedly local economic activity on the theory that this activity often has such a close and substantial relation to interstate enterprise that federal regulation becomes legitimate, both in the sense of economic necessity and in that of constitutional validity. Naturally enough, neither of these contentions was admitted by everyone. The business interests affected by such a program of increasing federal control offered particularly strong opposition. They began by challenging in Congress itself the claim of the economic necessity of such regulation, and when Congress rejected their arguments and legislated anyway, they shifted their campaign of resistance to the courts, where they argued that the new policy was unconstitutional.

The famous decision in *Schechter Poultry Corporation* v. *United States* by which the Court in 1935 invalidated the National Industrial Recovery Act makes a good, although not strictly chronological, starting point for an examination of this second type of commerce case.[21] It will be recalled that the N.I.R.A. provided for the formulation of so-called "codes of fair competition" for the separate trades and industries covered by the act. Each code was to contain rules and regulations governing the business, trade, and labor practices of each industry or occupation, and by restoring order in each unit of our national economy, was presumably designed to help bring about a return of prosperity to the nation generally. Congress based the statute upon the commerce power, arguing that there existed, because of the depression, certain obstructions to the free flow of interstate commerce, and that this legislation was designed to remove these obstructions.[22]

Inevitably, the statute resulted in much litigation, and the case which finally brought the law before the Supreme Court

[21] 295 U.S. 495 (1935).

[22] The relevant portion of the statute reads as follows: "Section 1. A national emergency productive of widespread unemployment and disorganization of industry, which burdens interstate and foreign commerce, affects the public welfare, and undermines the standards of living of the American people, is hereby declared to exist. It is hereby declared to be the policy of Congress to remove obstructions to the free flow of interstate and foreign commerce which tend to diminish the amount thereof; . . ."—48 Stat. L. 195 (1933).

concerned the Schechters, who ran a wholesale poultry business in Brooklyn, New York. They had been accused of violating certain of the provisions of the code which had been adopted by the poultry business. Accordingly, they had been prosecuted by the federal government under the terms of the N.I.R.A., which provided certain penalties for noncompliance with the law or codes. Specifically, the Schechters had violated such provisions in their code as the one forbidding the sale of unfit or diseased chickens and another prohibiting a dealer from giving a favored customer any choice of chickens when the latter bought less than a full crate. (Instead, the customer was supposed to take the run of the coop.) The Schechters offered as their primary defense the argument that the statute was unconstitutional in its application to them.

There were three fundamental grounds upon which the Schechters challenged the constitutionality of the N.I.R.A., but the Supreme Court considered only two. It first considered and accepted the argument that the act was unconstitutional because, in authorizing the formulation of codes, Congress had improperly delegated legislative power to the president and the code authorities. Our interest here, however, centers in the second argument advanced against the law to the effect that since the Schechters' business was a local one in Brooklyn, Congress had exceeded its commerce power in passing a law providing for the regulation of such a business. It was admitted by all parties to the case that the Schechters' business was in the ordinary sense of the word local or intrastate in character. However, the government attempted to justify the statute as a valid exercise of the commerce power by arguing that the business of the Schechters was closely related to and affected interstate commerce. For instance, about 95 per cent of the chickens handled by the company had come originally from other states. Moreover, other concerns of an admittedly interstate character having business relations with the Schechters or doing business in competition with them would certainly be affected by the generally healthy or unhealthy state of the Schechter business. For example, if the Schechter Corporation cut either the wages of its employees or the price of its chickens, such action might well set in motion a cycle of wage cutting or price cutting which would soon move beyond the confines of Brooklyn, New York, and affect the practices of chicken dealers in other states.

This argument failed to impress the Supreme Court, and in a unanimous decision Chief Justice Hughes ruled that the statute was invalid, that Congress had exceeded the scope of its commerce power, and that in violation of the Tenth Amendment it was attempting to encroach upon the powers reserved to the state governments. The argument advanced in support of the law proved too much, said the Court, and if it were accepted there would be no type of local business which could not be brought under federal control because of some slight relation to, or effect upon, interstate commerce.

Again, when this decision is considered by itself it seems entirely reasonable and logical. After all, it was the result of a unanimous agreement among the justices. But as was true of the group of commerce cases already examined, there are other decisions in cases somewhat comparable to the *Schechter* one which seem definitely to raise doubts about the consistency of the Court's approach to this aspect of the commerce problem. For instance, in 1922 the Court in the case *Stafford* v. *Wallace,* with only one dissenting vote, had upheld the Federal Packers and Stockyards Act of 1921, by which the activities of certain commission men or livestock dealers had been subjected to federal control. The activities of these men were largely confined to the great stockyard and slaughterhouse cities of the Middle West. It was thought that they were engaging in certain monopoly practices which were contrary to the best interests of the meat business, and also of the buying public. As the result of considerable pressure Congress had finally provided for their regulation. Admittedly, the activities of these agents, so far as their immediate scope was concerned, were confined to the packing house centers and were not interstate in character. However, the Court upheld the act on the theory that these men, while engaged in purely local activity themselves, were but a part of a broader current or stream "of commerce from one part of the country to another which . . . [was] ever flowing . . . [and was in its] very essence the commerce among the States . . . which historically it was one of the chief purposes of the Constitution to bring under national protection and control." In its decision the Court declined "to defeat this purpose in respect of such a stream and take it out of complete national regulation by a nice and technical inquiry into the non-interstate character of some of its necessary incidents and facilities when considered alone and without reference to their association with the movement of which they were an essential but subordinate part."[23]

Naturally the government attorneys in the *Schechter* case called the Court's attention to the *Stafford* decision and suggested that it constituted a favorable precedent for upholding the National Industrial Recovery Act. But the Court thought the facts of the two cases were quite different. It said there was "no warrant for the argument that the poultry handled by the defendants at their slaughterhouse markets was in a *'current'* or *'flow'* of interstate commerce and was thus subject to congressional regulation. . . . So far as the poultry herein questioned is concerned, the flow in interstate commerce had ceased. The poultry had come to a

[23]258 U.S. 495, 519 (1922). See also, *Swift and Co.* v. *United States* 196 U.S. 375 (1905).

permanent rest within the State."[24] Of course, the Court was right in suggesting that the facts of the two cases were not identical. In the *Stafford* case the packers received the cattle from the Western states, and subsequently dressed meat was shipped all over the country for sale to the consumer. In the *Schechter* case, while the chickens had been brought into New York from other states, they were sold and consumed in the same state in which the challenged business practices had occurred. Consequently, the facts in the *Schechter* case were such that it became more extreme to apply the "current of commerce" principle to them. It would have represented an additional step forward, even a considerable step. But the point is, it was a possible step. Had the Court wished to sustain the National Industrial Recovery Act it could have done so upon the "current of commerce" theory, and have written a favorable decision based upon the *Stafford* precedent. Or to state such a conclusion somewhat differently, it is difficult to see wherein the same vague words of the Constitution, which made it possible for the Court to uphold federal regulation of livestock dealers in Chicago under the commerce power, absolutely compelled the Court to rule that federal regulation of chicken dealers in Brooklyn was not permissible.

Another earlier case was of great importance as a precedent had the Court wished to sustain the N.I.R.A. This was the *Shreveport Case*. Briefly stated, it involved the power of Congress and its agent, the Interstate Commerce Commission, to control railroad rates between points within the same state. The facts of the case are curious and interesting. The commission had fixed rates between the city of Shreveport, Louisiana, and certain points in eastern Texas for which Shreveport is the natural trade center. Motivated by a natural desire to keep Texas trade safe for the Texans, the govern-

[24]*Schechter Poultry Corp.* v. *United States* 295 U.S. 495, 543.

ment of that state had endeavored to fix the rates between the eastern Texas points and such cities as Dallas and Houston so low that these eastern points would trade with the Texas cities even though they were further away than was Shreveport. At this point the I.C.C. threw a monkey wrench into these plans and ordered the intra-Texas rates raised to the same level as the interstate Texas-Louisiana rates. Litigation resulted and in a seven-to-two decision delivered by Justice Hughes (who also wrote the opinion in the *Schechter* case) the Supreme Court upheld the right of the federal government to regulate the local or intrastate commerce in this situation on the theory that it had "such a close and substantial relation" to interstate commerce that the satisfactory control of one required the simultaneous and identical control of the other.[25]

Of course, this decision, too, was suggested to the Court in the *Schechter* case as a favorable precedent upon which the N.I.R.A. might be sustained. But again the Court decided that there was a difference of degree between the facts of the two cases. And to give that difference of degree the strong support of a definite legal principal, the Court, in defining its rule about federal control of local commerce "related" to interstate commerce, went a bit further than it had in any previous case. It said: "In determining how far the federal government may go in controlling intrastate transactions upon the ground that they 'affect' interstate commerce, *there is a necessary and well-established distinction between direct and indirect effects.* The precise line can be drawn only as individual cases arise, but the distinction is clear in principle."[26] And,

[25]*Houston, E. & W. Texas Ry. Co.* v. *United States* (The *Shreveport Case*) 234 U.S. 342, 351 (1914).

[26]*Schechter Poultry Corp.* v. *United States* 295 U.S. 495, 546. (Italics added.) On the establishment of a "new" principle see Thomas Reed Powell, "Would the Supreme Court Block a Planned Economy?" 12 *Fortune* (August 1935) 48, 49, 128.

in the case at hand, to invalidate the National Industrial Recovery Act, the Court had only to say that the relationship between the Schechter brothers' business and interstate commerce was indirect. But where was the line to be drawn between direct and indirect effects? Why should not the Court have accepted the extensive and weighty evidence presented by the government purporting to show the close interrelation between such a business as that of the Schechters and other aspects of national commerce, and have concluded that the existence of a "direct effect" had been proved? Again, it could have done so and have written an entirely convincing and acceptable opinion growing out of the *Shreveport* ruling.[27] Or, for that matter, it is entirely proper to ask where in the Constitution the Court found any "clear principle" (to use Hughes's own words) compelling it to draw a line between local businesses having direct or indirect effects upon interstate commerce, and making possible federal control of one, and impossible federal control of the other.

The "direct-and-indirect-effects" rule formulated by the Court in the *Schechter* case is a somewhat curious one and clearly illustrates the essential weakness of many such rules. It is virtually worthless so far as providing any workable rule enabling future congressmen, justices, businessmen, or anyone else, to determine how far national legislation may go on the basis of the commerce power in controlling local commerce. Everything depends on where the line is to be drawn between those local situations that directly affect interstate commerce and those that only indirectly affect it.

---

[27] See the decision in the lower federal court upholding the N.I.R.A. in part, *United States* v. *Schechter Poultry Corp.* 76 F. (2d) 617 (1935). See also C. G. Haines, "Judicial Review of Acts of Congress and the Need for Constitutional Reform," 45 *Yale Law Journal* (1936) 816; I *Selected Essays* 844, 865–68, for an argument that the Supreme Court might legitimately have upheld the N.I.R.A. On this point likewise, see the Powell article cited in the preceding footnote.

And the Court says it will draw that line "only as individual cases arise."

Two subsequent decisions in which the Court applied this formula will now be examined. The first of these followed very shortly after the *Schechter* ruling and concerned the question of the constitutionality of the first Guffey Coal Act, a statute by which Congress in effect attempted to re-enact the N.I.R.A. in regard to one industry—the business of mining bituminous coal. Congress had considerable reason to hope that the Court might uphold such a law, by placing it on the "direct" rather than the "indirect" side of the formula, in view of the undeniable fact that a very great part of the coal affected by the act moved across state lines after it was mined and was widely distributed and sold throughout the country. The case, *Carter* v. *Carter Coal Company*, found the nine justices in almost hopeless disagreement. It proved difficult to secure a majority for any decision. Finally, however, six justices agreed that coal mining only indirectly affected interstate commerce and that in so far as the act provided for federal control of the wages and hours of coal miners it was unconstitutional. These justices ignored persuasive evidence showing a close and substantial relation between the status and welfare of coal mining and the general business life of the nation. Certainly coal mining has a much more "direct" effect upon interstate commerce than the business of the Schechter brothers. Nonetheless, the majority justices held that "the only perceptible difference between that case and this is that in the *Schechter* case the federal power was asserted with respect to commodities which had come to rest after their interstate transportation; while here, the case deals with commodities at rest before interstate commerce has begun. That difference is without significance."[28]

This statement perhaps begged the question, for the Court

[28]298 U.S. 238, 309 (1936).

was by no means ruling that for a local situation directly to affect interstate commerce it must be related to that commerce at both ends—both before and after. Presumably a relationship at either end is sufficient, provided only that that relation is "direct."[29] But instead of examining the evidence as to whether coal mining has such a direct effect the Court went off on a tangent about there being no difference between coal that is shipped across state lines *after* it is mined, and chickens shipped across state lines *before* they are killed and eaten! Then in a statement which denies all meaning to the decisions in the *Shreveport* and *Stafford* cases and even to Chief Justice Hughes's formula in the *Schechter* case, Justice Sutherland, speaking for the majority, said: "The federal regulatory power ceases when interstate commercial intercourse ends; and correlatively, the power does not attach until interstate commercial intercourse begins."[30] Had such reasoning prevailed in the *Shreveport* and *Stafford* cases it is hard to see how they could have been decided in the way they were.

The decisions of 1935 and 1936 found the Supreme Court standing firmly against the expansion of the commerce clause. But 1937 was to tell a different story.

When the fifty-eight lawyers hired by the American Liberty League advised their clients that the National Labor Relations Act was without a doubt unconstitutional and that it was safe to refrain from complying with its terms, they had good reason to feel that the advice they were offering was

[29]In 1938 the Supreme Court did, in fact, hold in *Santa Cruz Fruit Packing Company* v. *N.L.R.B.* 303 U.S. 453 that the commerce power extended to the local production of goods where no raw materials were brought in from outside a state and where only 37 per cent of the finished goods were shipped out of a state, provided the local conditions being regulated had a "direct" or "close and substantial" effect upon interstate commerce.

[30]298 U.S. 238, 309.

not simply fathered by the wish of their clients but was actually based upon sound legal considerations. For the Wagner Act, like the Guffey Coal Act, was passed by Congress in 1935 shortly after the Supreme Court decision invalidating the N.I.R.A.

In effect, the Wagner Act revived the labor provisions of the National Industrial Recovery Act. It created an administrative commission to be known as the National Labor Relations Board and authorized it to do two things. One was to enforce that portion of the Wagner Act which listed certain "unfair labor practices" on the part of the employer by ordering employers to cease and desist from such practices as fostering a "company union," or discharging workers solely because they are active in the labor union movement. The other was to enforce the statute's collective bargaining guarantee by conducting elections among workers to enable them to decide what labor union, if any, was to represent them for purposes of collective bargaining when it came time to meet with the "boss." The act was based upon the commerce power. Congress had endeavored to support the constitutionality of such legislation by pointing out that strikes, lockouts, unfair labor practices, refusals to bargain collectively, and similar employer-employee conflicts have the unfortunate effect of diminishing the flow of raw materials and finished goods in interstate commerce. The act, said Congress, was thus designed to restore interstate commerce to a condition of stability and prosperity by preventing such conflicts.

But this was essentially the same argument that had failed to convince the Court of the constitutionality of the N.I.R.A. In other words, Congress was attempting to control a local situation, namely, the relationship between an employer and his workers, on the theory that this local situation "affects" interstate commerce. But as we have seen, the Court seemed interested in whether this effect was "direct" or "indirect." Presumably there was no more reason to suppose that the Court would sustain the Wagner Act when applied to a business like that of the Schechter brothers or the Carter Coal Company than there had been that it would sustain the National Industrial Recovery Act or the Guffey Coal Act when they were applied to the very same businesses.

The question of the validity of the Wagner Act finally reached the Supreme Court early in 1937. Two important facts in the background of the case may be noted. One was that the bitter controversy in Congress over President Roosevelt's proposal to enlarge the Supreme Court had been raging for some weeks when the decision was announced, and the outcome of this issue in Congress was still uncertain. The other was that the personnel of the Court was as yet unchanged. It still consisted of the same nine justices who had participated in the N.I.R.A. and Guffey Coal Act cases. Mr. Roosevelt had not yet appointed a single new justice to the Court.

In accepting jurisdiction in the litigation over the Wagner Act the Supreme Court agreed to review simultaneously the decisions of the lower courts in five separate cases, all of which raised the question of the constitutionality of the Wagner Act. It will be remembered that in the Recovery Act litigation, while dozens of cases involving all sorts of different businesses had arisen in the lower courts, only one of these cases was reviewed by the Supreme Court. The issue of the statute's validity depended in the final analysis entirely upon the outcome of a case involving its application to the wholesale poultry business. At the time government attorneys had been somewhat criticized for their selection of the *Schechter* case as the one to appeal to the Supreme Court for a test of the validity of the Act. It was argued that the facts of that case were not too fortunate from the government's point of view and that there had been available for appeal other and better cases where the businesses involved had a much closer relation to interstate commerce than did a chicken business in Brooklyn. The suggestion was that the facts of one of these other cases might have made it easier for the Court to sustain the N.I.R.A. on the basis of its direct-effect doctrine had it been at all inclined to render such a decision. In determining the constitutionality of the Wagner Act, the Court was asked to and did review the findings of five separate opinions of the lower courts in cases involving the great Jones and Laughlin Steel Corporation, the Associated Press, a bus company, a manufacturer of automobile and truck trailers, and a small clothing manufacturer.[31] Conceivably the Court might thereby have upheld the Wagner Act in its application to the facts of one or more of these cases while invalidating it as to the others. In brief, a "mixed" decision might have been rendered.

Nonetheless, in all five cases the issue was essentially the same, although the facts varied, and as it turned out all were decided the same way. Each company had presumably violated the Wagner Act by discharging workers because of union activity. The National Labor Relations Board had entered each case, examined the facts, and issued orders directing that discharged workers be re-employed and given back pay for the period they were out. The companies resisted these orders and litigation resulted. When the cases reached the Supreme Court the facts of the cases were not in dispute, and it was agreed by all parties concerned that the Labor Board had merely been performing its duties as required by the statute. Indeed, the companies agreed that they

[31]*The Wagner Act Cases*, 301 U.S. 1 (1937). The titles and citations of the five cases are as follows: *N.L.R.B.* v. *Jones & Laughlin Steel Corp.* 301 U.S. 1; *N.L.R.B.* v. *Fruehauf Trailer Co.* 301 U.S. 49; *N.L.R.B.* v. *Friedman-Harry Marks Clothing Co.* 301 U.S. 58; dissenting opinion to the above three decisions, 301 U.S. 76; *Associated Press* v. *N.L.R.B.* 301 U.S. 103; *Washington Coach Co.* v. *N.L.R.B.* 301 U.S. 142.

had violated the law. The sole question before the Court was the constitutionality of the act, and for our purposes here we may limit ourselves to the consideration of the question whether Congress was acting within the Constitution in using its commerce power to control relations between employers and workers in the manufacturing process.

The Court chose the *Jones and Laughlin* case as the one in which to render its definitive decision.[32] In the opinion written by Chief Justice Hughes, the Court by a five-to-four vote upheld the constitutionality of the Wagner Act. In this and the other cases the Court took cognizance of the fact that each of these businesses affected by the Wagner Act had imported a majority of its raw materials from outside the state in which it did its manufacturing, and had also shipped more than half of its finished products to other states for sale.[33] For this reason the Court concluded that each of the businesses had a "close and substantial" relation to interstate commerce and were thus subject to congressional control.

What about the N.I.R.A. and Guffey Coal Act decisions? Was it necessary to reverse them? By no means, for the Court simply asserted that in each of the cases at hand there existed a "direct" effect upon interstate commerce, and thus they fell upon the opposite side of the fence and were to be "distinguished" from the *Schechter* and *Carter* decisions. At first thought this "distinction" seems perfectly logical and reasonable. After all, every one of the businesses involved in the Wagner Act cases was definitely more closely related to interstate commerce than that of the Schechters. But on further

[32]This was somewhat surprising. Since the Court was sustaining the Wagner Act in its application to all of the cases one might have expected that the Court would write its definitive opinion in the case where interstate commerce was least involved, namely the clothing manufacturer case (*N.L.R.B.* v. *Friedman-Harry Marks Clothing Co.*)

[33]With the exception of the bus company and Associated Press cases, where there was direct activity in interstate commerce.

thought it would seem that the most important issue confronting the Court in these cases was not the difference in the character of the various businesses affected by the Recovery and Wagner acts, but rather the difference in the laws themselves, since presumably about the same businesses were controlled in either instance. Justice McReynolds, speaking for the minority of four, points out that "every consideration brought forward to uphold the [Wagner] Act . . . was applicable to support the [Recovery and Guffey Coal] Acts."[34] One cannot help wondering how the Court would have ruled had it been compelled to determine the constitutionality of the N.I.R.A. in a case involving the Jones and Laughlin Steel Corporation.

And what about the coal business in the *Carter* case? Was it, after all, so very different from the businesses involved in the Wagner Act cases so far as its effect upon interstate commerce was concerned? True, it was not tied to interstate commerce both coming and going, but only on the going side. But on that one side it would be difficult to find a local economic activity more closely related to interstate enterprise. The overwhelming proportion of the coal mined in the relatively few coal-producing states is shipped into the many noncoal-producing states for sale. Moreover, while in the original Wagner Act cases the Court was able to point to a relationship in each instance to the occurrence of interstate commerce both before and after the local activity being regulated, it by no means insisted that such a condition must exist if it is to rule that a local situation directly affects interstate commerce and is thus within congressional control.[35]

In spite of the technical consistency which the Court un-

[34]301 U.S. 77.
[35]The Wagner Act has since been applied to local activity which is related to interstate commerce in only one direction. See *Santa Cruz Fruit Packing Company* v. *N.L.R.B.* 303 U.S. 453 (1938).

doubtedly maintained through all of these decisions, the fact remains that in the practical sense the outcome of these cases was very different. The constitutionality of three great federal statutes had been questioned before the Supreme Court. All three had been enacted on the basis of the commerce power, and all provided for substantial federal control over the manufacturing (or mining) process as carried on by essentially the same individuals or corporations. But two of the laws were invalidated on the ground that Congress had exceeded the limits of its commerce power, while the third was given the Court's sanction on the theory that it fell within those limits.[36]

It is impossible to leave the Wagner Act cases without making at least some reference to the possibility that political as well as legal considerations may have had some influence upon the Court. As has already been mentioned, these decisions were handed down during the heat of the battle over the Roosevelt plan to reform the Supreme Court. There is little doubt that these decisions had a profound effect upon the outcome of that struggle. If the Wagner Act was, surprisingly enough, constitutional, then much of the force was gone from the president's argument that a reactionary Court was misinterpreting the Constitution and thwarting the wishes of a great majority of the American people as unmistakably indicated in the 1936 election. So it was to be. The president lost his fight. But the Court has not since invalidated any federal law on the ground that the commerce power is being exceeded. Professor Powell's comment on the 1937 rulings of the Court, "A switch in time saves nine," may be facetious but it is not without an element of truth.[37]

[36]This discussion is confined to the interstate commerce aspect of these cases and ignores the other constitutional issues, such as the question of delegation of legislative power, that may have been present in any of them.

[37]Thomas Reed Powell, "From Philadelphia to Philadelphia," 32 *American Political Science Review* (February 1938) 1, 24.

The Commerce Power Bursts Its Bonds

One final case remains to be examined, a case which provides a fitting and decisive conclusion to each of the two
types of commerce cases which have been considered. On
February 3, 1941, a unanimous Court, speaking through Justice Stone, upheld the constitutionality of the federal Fair
Labor Standards Act, more commonly known as the "Wages
and Hours Act." The passage of this law by Congress in
1938 was the culmination of a long and often bitterly fought
struggle to establish legislation prescribing maximum hour
and minimum wage levels for workers. Efforts to provide a
"floor for wages, and a ceiling for hours" had had their origin
about half a century before when a few pioneering state legislatures took the first steps toward the limitation of the working week and working day. Until the period of the New Deal,
attempts to enact such legislation had been largely confined
to the states, and, as will be pointed out in the next chapter,
were constantly hampered by constitutional barriers erected
by the courts under the due process clause of the Fourteenth
Amendment.[38] The effectiveness of state wages and hours legislation had also been considerably limited for a second reason
—the unwillingness of all state legislatures to pass such laws.
The effect of these differing standards was to make some in-
dustrialists leave the more progressive states to locate their
plants in states with lower standards. Because of this it was
inevitable that labor and reform pressure-groups should turn
to Congress and demand the enactment of legislation creating
a uniform national policy.

The federal Fair Labor Standards Act of 1938 provided for
ultimate national standards of a forty-hour maximum work
week and a minimum wage scale of forty cents an hour, with

[38]See below, pages 150–161.

time and a half for overtime work. The law was based upon the commerce power, and two devices were utilized to give it teeth. In the first place, it forbade the shipment in interstate commerce of products manufactured under labor conditions which failed to conform to the wage and hour standards specified in the act. This will immediately be recognized as the same device which Congress had endeavored to employ in implementing the first federal child labor law. In the second place, the law prohibited the very act of producing goods destined for interstate shipment, except in conformity with the prescribed wage and hour standards. This device, in turn, closely resembles the implementing provisions of the National Industrial Recovery and Wagner Acts.

The validity of the act was determined in *United States* v. *Darby Lumber Company*.[39] The Darby Lumber Company produced lumber and shipped "a large part" of it out of the state of production.[40] It was prosecuted by the federal government under the act for failure to comply with certain of the prescribed labor standards. The company conceded the validity of the factual case against it and based its defense on the contention that the statute was unconstitutional since it exceeded the limits of Congress's commerce power. The Supreme Court rejected this claim and upheld Congress in its use of both of the implementing devices found in the act.

In upholding the provision denying the use of the facilities of interstate commerce to producers who fail to abide by the prescribed labor standards the Court championed the right of Congress to prevent the use of interstate commerce as a means of spreading evils from one state to another, recognized that the shipment of goods produced under sublabor

---

[39] 85 Law. ed. Advance Opinions 395 (1941). See also *Opp Cotton Mills* v. *Administrator of Wage and Hour Division* 85 Law. ed. Advance Opinions 407 (1941).

[40] Note the similarity between these facts and those of the *Carter* case.

standards constituted such an evil, and specifically repudiated the doctrine of *Hammer* v. *Dagenhart*. Justice Stone pointed out:

> While manufacture is not of itself interstate commerce the shipment of manufactured goods interstate is such commerce and the prohibition of such shipment by Congress is indubitably a regulation of the commerce. . . .
>
> The motive and purpose of the present regulation is plainly to make effective the Congressional conception of public policy that interstate commerce should not be made the instrument of competition in the distribution of goods produced under substandard labor conditions, which competition is injurious to the commerce and to the states from and to which the commerce flows. . . .
>
> Hammer v. Dagenhart has not been followed. . . .
>
> The conclusion is inescapable that Hammer v. Dagenhart, was a departure from the principals [*sic*] which have prevailed in the interpretation of the commerce clause both before and since the decision and that such vitality, as a precedent, as it then had has long since been exhausted. It should be and now is overruled.[41]

In upholding the provision forbidding the production of goods destined for interstate commerce except under the prescribed labor standards, the Court frankly admitted that this was a regulation of intrastate commerce but insisted that the right of Congress to regulate such commerce under certain circumstances had long since been recognized. Justice Stone stated:

> The power of Congress over interstate commerce is not confined to the regulation of commerce among the states. It extends to those activities intrastate which so affect interstate commerce or the exercise of the power of Congress over it as to make regulation of them appropriate means to the attainment of a legiti-

[41] 85 Law. ed. Advance Opinions 395, 399, 400–1, 402.

mate end, the exercise of the granted power of Congress to regulate interstate commerce. . . .

Our conclusion is unaffected by the Tenth Amendment which provides: "The powers not delegated to the United States by the Constitution nor prohibited by it to the states are reserved to the states respectively or to the people." The amendment states but a truism that all is retained which has not been surrendered. . . .

From the beginning and for many years the amendment has been construed as not depriving the national government of authority to resort to all means for the exercise of a granted power which are appropriate and plainly adapted to the permitted end.[42]

The decision in *United States* v. *Darby Lumber Company* seems to make it plain that the Court is finally willing to permit Congress to exercise an extensive federal police power wherever the element of interstate commerce is present. The Court, in effect, sanctions the doctrine of Justice Holmes's dissenting opinion in *Hammer* v. *Dagenhart* that these federal quasi police-power measures are, after all, on their face regulations of interstate commerce, and that the Court has no business speculating as to the secondary and possibly improper motives that may have induced Congress to make such uses of the commerce power. In the second place, the decision reaffirms the principle of the *Shreveport Case* that Congress may regulate local commerce which "affects" interstate commerce. It is significant that there is no word in the decision about "direct and indirect effects," no attempt to prove that the production of lumber locally for later shipment in interstate commerce has a "direct" effect upon such commerce. Instead, the Court is content to return to the simpler phraseology of some of its earlier decisions, pointing out merely that the effect in question is "substantial."

[42]*Ibid.,* pp. 402–3, 405, 406.

Whether this means that the more rigid formula of the *Schechter* case is to be discarded permanently, it is perhaps too early to say. But the *Darby* decision does at least indicate a great willingness on the part of the Court to be realistic about the connection between local production and interstate trade:

Congress, to attain its objective in the suppression of nation-wide competition in interstate commerce by goods produced under substandard labor conditions, has made no distinction as to the volume or amount of shipments in the commerce or of production for commerce by any particular shipper or producer. *It recognized that in present day industry, competition by a small part may affect the whole and that the total effect of the competition of many small producers may be great. The legislation aimed at a whole embraces all its parts.*[43]

The decision in the *Darby* case certainly marks a whole-hearted return by the Court to Marshall's nationalisitic interpretation of the commerce power. Indeed, about the only further step the Court might take in its general reasoning concerning the commerce power would be to cease denying that manufacture is not of itself commerce and conclude that where goods are produced for, or affect, interstate trade, the act of production is a phase of the total process of commerce. But as long as the Court is willing to sanction federal regulation of manufacturing because of its "substantial effect" upon commerce, to demand this further and final step is perhaps unnecessary.

The Commerce Clause and Judicial Review: Summary

The fact seems to be pretty well established that the United States Supreme Court has not succeeded through the

[43]*Ibid.*, p. 405. (Italics added.)

years in interpreting the commerce clause in such a consistent fashion as to give it any certainty or finality. It may be admitted that a selection of cases involving the commerce power can be made that will show the Court to have been reasonably consistent in its development of constitutional law in this area. It may also be granted that the cases we have examined have been selected to show the Court at its inconsistent worst. But they by no means exhaust the list of inconsistent decisions on important social and economic questions which affect the people of the country in a vital way. It certainly has made a difference that from time to time the commerce power has been held to extend to such practical problems as white slavery, kidnaping, purity of foods and drugs, stolen automobiles, the traffic in lottery tickets, abuses in stockyard practices, and the fixing of railroad rates; but not to extend to such other practical problems as child labor, coal mining, sugar refining, and the wages and hours of workers in the poultry business.

At times it has surely been difficult to say with any degree of certainty on the basis of legal precedents just what the commerce power permitted and what it did not. The failure of the fifty-eight Liberty League lawyers to predict correctly the Court's ruling on the constitutionality of the Wagner Act is sufficient proof of the existence of this difficulty. Of course, at the moment even a poor lawyer can guess that the Supreme Court of 1941 is likely to be quite consistent about following only those precedents, from the time of Marshall to the present, which sanction the broadest interpretation of the commerce power. But it must be remembered that this was and is merely one possible interpretation. There was and is no inevitability about it.

A careful examination of the background and decisions in the commerce power cases makes it very difficult to believe that the primary motivation of the justices in such situations is a mere judicial search for correct legal principles and a desire to avoid incorrect ones. The truth of the matter seems to be that in such a vague, general provision as the commerce clause of the Constitution, the Supreme Court has a perfect instrument with which to exercise its power to govern. It cannot be denied that the precedents on the commerce power are so numerous, conflicting, and flexible that the Court is in a position to rule either way it wishes in doubtful cases on controversial issues. Accordingly, the justices may, like congressmen, endeavor to solve social and economic problems, and at the same time support the claims of certain pressure groups and oppose those of others. Can anyone doubt that Chief Justice Marshall was aware of the importance of the economic background of the *Gibbons* case, and that in rendering the opinion he did he was trying to clear away what to him appeared to be a very serious barrier to the sound economic development of the country along national lines? On the other hand, can it be doubted that the majority justices in the *Knight Company* case were aware of the economic significance of the antitrust drive gathering momentum under the Sherman Act, and that from their point of view the decision they rendered, curtailing that program, represented a wise and desirable *governmental* policy in the light of the facts of the problem? Or again is it not obvious that the unanimous *Darby* decision was substantially conditioned by the attitudes of five new justices recently appointed by a progressive, nationalist president, who were joined by one liberally inclined justice who carried over from an earlier period and two other less liberal carry-over justices who had certainly not failed to be impressed by the signs of the times? As late as 1935 it was still possible to hold back the clock. But after 1936, 1937, and 1940 that could no longer be done. This is not to suggest that the Supreme Court no longer has any choice in its interpretation of the commerce power, but only that its area of possible choice has shifted, moving so far in a nationalist direction as to lop off a considerable area of possibility at the other end.

It would be a bold man who would conclude that the pendulum is at last through swinging. At the same time it is reasonable to suppose that the judicial view of the commerce power so firmly announced by Chief Justice Marshall in *Gibbons* v. *Ogden* and so belatedly championed by the Supreme Court in the Wagner Act and Wage and Hour Act cases will not readily be set aside again. For the present and the near future, at least, the Court's interpretation of the commerce clause is evidence of an instrumental Constitution, incarnate and triumphant. But it should be remembered that it was not enough for the forces within our democratic society which were contending for development of the *instrument* to win their point with Congress and the president. The Court, too, had to be convinced.

★　　★　　★　　★　　★　　★

Chapter VII

The Supreme Court in Action: Due Process of Law

O_{NE} of the strongest of all the *instrument-symbol* conflicts in our constitutional system is the clash between due process of law and the police power. The former is a constitutional limitation expressly prohibiting any governmental activity which is considered to deprive any person of his life, liberty, or property, without due process of law. The police power, on the other hand, has come to be considered as bestowing a vast authority upon the states to foster and protect the health, safety, and morals of the people, and in a general way to promote the public welfare. It is one of those powers which the Constitution fails to grant expressly to the national government and which accordingly is presumably reserved to the state governments by the Tenth Amendment.[1] However, as we have already seen, the national government has succeeded in recent times in utilizing certain of its powers, particularly the commerce power, to accomplish purposes identical with those which the state police power is designed to serve. For example, the federal pure food and drug acts have an obvious relation to public health, but since Congress possessed no straightforward police power through which it might estab-

[1] "The powers not delegated to the United States by the Constitution, nor prohibited by it to the States, are reserved to the States respectively, or to the people."

lish such a policy, it enacted this legislation upon the basis of its commerce power.

The Police Power and Due Process of Law

Between these two constitutional points—the power, and the limitation—there is considerable room for conflict. A state passes a law prohibiting the operation of poolrooms for profit. In justification of such a statute it may clearly be argued that it is necessary to protect public morals and is thus a proper measure under the police power. But it may just as clearly be argued that it deprives persons of their liberty and property without due process of law and is thus an improper measure contrary to the principle of limited government. Which is to prevail—power or limitation?

Before proceeding further it may be noted that the police power is by no means the only one that comes in conflict with the limitation of due process of law. The exercise of certain other positive governmental powers, such as the taxing power, or the power of eminent domain, may well result in such conflict. Likewise, this limitation is by no means the only specific manifestation of the concept of limited government. There are others, such as the prohibitions against the passage of ex post facto laws, laws impairing the obligation of contracts, or the denial of the equal protection of the laws. But the clash between the police power and due process of law is perhaps the most important single illustration of the broad conflict between rival constitutional principles, and will certainly be an adequate means of throwing light upon this conflict for our purposes.

It may be noted further that there are two due process of law clauses in the Constitution, one in the Fifth Amendment, one in the Fourteenth Amendment.[2] The wording is almost

[2]Fifth Amendment: ". . . nor shall any person . . . be deprived of life, liberty, or property, without due process of law; . . ." Fourteenth Amend-

identical, the only difference being that the Fifth Amendment places a limitation upon the national government, and the Fourteenth upon the state governments. The effect of the limitation is presumably the same in either instance. In so far as the national government uses its commerce and other powers for the same purposes for which the states use their police power it might expect to find the Fifth Amendment restraining it to the same degree that the Fourteenth restrains the states. Actually, this exercise of federal power has involved nothing like the clash with the due process clause of the Fifth Amendment that the exercise of state power has with the similar limitation of the Fourteenth Amendment. There are, of course, instances of federal statutes invalidated because they were considered as falling short of due process of law requirements, but they are not numerous. It does not follow from this that the courts have necessarily been stricter in their application of the principle of limited government to state power than to federal power. It is true that the Fifth Amendment has assumed nothing like the importance of the Fourteenth as a barrier against government activity. But the point to be remembered is that in the case of federal legislation the courts have chosen to emphasize the importance of another barrier, the principle of federalism, as the means for judicial review and possible annulment of such legislation. For example, we have already seen how the Supreme Court invalidated the National Industrial Recovery Act on the ground that Congress was using its commerce power to encroach upon powers reserved to the states. The act might well have been attacked as a violation of the due process of law clause of the Fifth Amendment, and indeed it was, but the Supreme Court found it unnecessary to examine such an

ment: ". . . nor shall any State deprive any person of life, liberty, or property, without due process of law; . . ."

argument against the law in view of its decision that the statute was improper under the principle of federalism.

We may turn to the words of the Constitution—*no person shall be deprived of his life, liberty, or property, without due process of law*. What do they mean? Bearing in mind the idea of a search for constitutional certainty, or specific guideposts, we do not find the situation at first glance too hopeful. Two or three points may be noted immediately. The word "person" is used, and not "citizen." Second, we may note the obvious implication that not all deprivations of life, liberty, or property, are outlawed. Those that occur *with* due process of law, as opposed to those that occur *without*, are apparently valid and proper. If a man commits murder, is given a fair trial, convicted, and then executed, the state deprives him of his life, but presumably with due process of law. And the same is true of such ordinary, everyday deprivations of property or liberty as those resulting from taxation, or traffic regulation. Property is taken in one instance, liberty in the other, but *with* due process of law. So the problem becomes one of determining when governmental action results in deprivation of life, liberty, or property with due process of law, and when without due process of law. In other words, what is due process of law, anyway? In attempting to answer such a question one legal scholar has recently thrown up his hands in disgust and called the phrase "that lovely limpid legalism."[3] In somewhat less facetious fashion Justice Frankfurter has spoken of the due process clauses as being expressed in the Constitution "in words so undefined, either by their intrinsic meaning, or by history, or by tradition, that they leave the individual Justice free, if indeed they do not actually compel him, to fill in the vacuum with his own controlling notions of

[3]Fred Rodell, *Woe Unto You, Lawyers!* (New York: Reynal and Hitchcock, 1939) 77.

economic, social, and industrial facts with reference to which they are invoked."[4]

The Evolution of the Due Process Symbol

Judicial interpretation of the two due process of law clauses of the Constitution has by no means remained constant from the beginning to the present time. The Fifth Amendment has been a part of our Constitution since 1791; the Fourteenth only since 1868. But since the vitalization of due process of law has been largely confined to the period of the last fifty years, the wide gap between the origins of the two amendments is unimportant. Until the eve of the Civil War, no federal statute was condemned by a majority of the justices of the Supreme Court on the ground of lack of due process of law, and, indeed, "only one case involved any serious consideration of the meaning of the term."[5] Moreover, even following the Civil War and the addition of the Fourteenth Amendment to the Constitution, it was a matter of some twenty years before the Supreme Court began to utilize the due process of law clause as a means for judicial review of the *substantive* content of legislation. According to one count, of 128 state laws invalidated by the federal courts before 1888 only one was thrown out on the ground that it involved a taking of property without due process of law.[6]

"Due process of law" is a phrase which has been known in English and American jurisprudence for centuries. While the phrase had been variously interpreted by different courts from time to time in the light of specific circumstances and problems, its importance in American constitutional develop-

[4]Frankfurter, *op. cit.* (Chap. V, n. 8), p. 13. Reprinted by permission of Harcourt, Brace and Company, publishers.

[5]Haines, *op. cit.* (Chap. I, n. 1), p. 411.

[6]*Ibid.*, p. 401, n.

ment through the close of the 1880's was largely limited to its so-called *procedural* aspect. According to this interpretation the constitutional provision of due process of law was (and is) considered as guaranteeing fair procedural treatment to persons who have dealings with certain governmental agencies. Perhaps the most striking and interesting cases in this category have been those concerning individuals who have violated the law and are accused of crimes. Here due process of law is held today to guarantee certain forms of judicial procedure in determining the question of guilt or innocence. These have come to include such guarantees as the right to be informed of the charges that have been preferred against one, the right to a fair, open trial, and the assistance of adequate legal counsel.

However, even before the Civil War there were increasing signs that the courts were becoming inclined to utilize due process of law as a means for judicial review of the subject matter of statutes. According to this *substantive* aspect of due process of law, individuals possess certain vested rights, in property and otherwise. If an attempt is made by statute to regulate or interfere with these personal rights in an adverse and unreasonable fashion, the courts may then intervene, invoke the requirement of due process of law, and declare such statutes null and void.

The complete story of these varying views of the requirements of due process of law is a long and confusing one and need not be examined in detail here.[7] It is perhaps sufficient to say that in the twenty-five-year period following the close of the Civil War the Supreme Court resisted for the most part all efforts to develop the Fourteenth Amendment as an

---

[7] *Ibid.*, pp. 410–27. See also, E. S. Corwin, "The Doctrine of Due Process of Law Before the Civil War," 24 *Harvard Law Review* (1911) 366, 460; I *Selected Essays* 203, and C. G. Haines, "The History of Due Process of Law after the Civil War," 3 *Texas Law Review* (1924) 1; I *Selected Essays* 268.

instrument for judicial supervision of state legislation dealing with economic and social problems. For instance, in 1873, in the famous *Slaughter-House Cases,* Justice Miller, speaking for the majority, denied that the due process clause of the Fourteenth Amendment was ever to be considered as limiting the exercise by the states of their police power.[8] The justice strongly intimated that the Fourteenth Amendment was designed solely to protect the Negro and could have little application to other matters. A few years later Justice Miller again spoke in a similar vein:

It is not a little remarkable, that while this provision [the due process clause] has been in the Constitution of the United States, as a restraint upon the authority of the Federal government, for nearly a century, and while, during all that time, the manner in which the powers of that government have been exercised has been watched with jealousy, and subjected to the most rigid criticism in all its branches, this special limitation upon its powers has rarely been invoked in the judicial forum or the more enlarged theatre of public discussion. But while it has been a part of the Constitution, as a restraint upon the power of the States, only a very few years, the docket of this court is crowded with cases in which we are asked to hold that State courts and State legislatures have deprived their own citizens of life, liberty, or property without due process of law. There is here abundant evidence that there exists some strange misconception of the scope of this provision as found in the fourteenth amendment. In fact, it would seem, from the character of many of the cases before us, and the arguments made in them, that the clause under consideration is looked upon as a means of bringing to the test of the decision of this court the abstract opinions of every unsuccessful litigant in a State court of the justice of the decision against him, and of the merits of the legislation on which such a decision may be founded.[9]

[8] 16 Wallace 36 (1873).
[9] *Davidson* v. *New Orleans* 96 U.S. 97, 103–4 (1878).

But in these and ensuing cases there were minority justices who were vigorously insisting upon a much broader interpretation of the due process clause, an interpretation giving the Court the power to weigh the social advantages of a particular exercise of the police power against the resulting interference with the rights of private individuals. For example, Justice Field, dissenting in the *Slaughter-House Cases,* had asserted that the Fourteenth Amendment was designed to "protect the citizens of the United States against the deprivation of their common rights by State legislation."[10] It may be noted that Justice Field was a conservative Democrat from the frontier state of California, strongly convinced of the soundness of the philosophy of individualism. It has been said of him that he "distrusted government, the less of it the better."[11]

The conservative minority in the Court gained in strength during the late 1870's and the 1880's. These were the years in which the Industrial Revolution made tremendous headway in the United States, with the result that conservative business points of view were of considerable importance and came to have an increasing influence upon government. In many ways, business interests sought special favors and positive action from legislatures. But in good part, the intent of business was to avoid government regulation. At the same time, agrarian and laboring pressure groups were also gaining in strength and began to make demands for progressive social and economic legislation. Naturally enough, the increasing power of the business class was thrown into the struggle in opposition to these demands. In this conflict the Supreme Court was destined to play an important part. When the conservative business class lost its fight in the legislative arena

[10] 16 Wallace 36, 89.

[11] Charles M. Hough, "Due Process of Law—To-Day," 32 *Harvard Law Review* (1919) 218; I *Selected Essays* 302, 308.

and found itself confronted by an increasing tide of regulatory statutes it often transferred the struggle to the calmer, more judicious, and, incidentally, friendlier atmosphere of the courts. In 1886 the Court ruled that corporations were "persons" within the meaning of that word in the Fourteenth Amendment and thus entitled to possible protection under it.[12] With this decision it was clear that Justice Miller's assertion that the Amendment was designed primarily to protect Negroes no longer carried weight. The Court still hesitated about taking the next step of actually invalidating state legislation regulating business on the ground of deprivation of business liberties and property without due process of law. But the hesitation was only momentary. In 1890 came the decisive step when the Court in the *Minnesota Rate Case* held that the regulation of railroad rates by state legislatures was subject to review by the Court under the due process clause of the Fourteenth Amendment. The Court said:

The question of the reasonableness of a rate of charge for transportation by a railroad company, involving as it does the element of reasonableness both as regards the company and as regards the public, is eminently a question for judicial investigation, requiring due process of law for its determination.[13]

Three justices dissented vigorously from this decision and continued to insist that the reasonableness of a particular governmental regulation of business remained with the legislative body for determination, and that the Fourteenth Amendment gave the courts no general power to interfere. The dissenting justices also made a significant reference to

[12]*Santa Clara County* v. *Southern Pacific R.R. Co.* 118 U.S. 394, 396 (1886).
[13]*Chicago, Milwaukee and St. Paul Ry. Co.* v. *Minnesota* 134 U.S. 418, 458 (1890).

the desirability of holding the judicial role in the governmental process within certain limits:

Due process of law does not always require a court. It merely
requires such tribunals and proceedings as are proper to the
subject in hand. . . .
It is complained that the decisions of the . . . [Minnesota
Railroad Commission] are final and without appeal. So are the
decisions of the courts in matters within their jurisdiction. There
must be a final tribunal somewhere for deciding every question
in the world. Injustice may take place in all tribunals. All human
institutions are imperfect—courts as well as commissions and
legislatures.[14]

But the interested persons who were endeavoring to transfer their fight against regulatory legislation to the judicial
arena did not worry about the fallibility of judges. They knew
only that the courts and the Constitution might be utilized
to reopen some of the disputes and that judges might well
be expected to consider some of these problems from a conservative point of view. It had taken nearly twenty years to
persuade the Supreme Court that it had the power to set
aside state legislative enactments deemed contrary to the
Fourteenth Amendment. But since 1890 the power of the
federal judiciary to review the content of state police power
measures has not been seriously questioned.

A careful search of their decisions indicates that the justices
have never succeeded in defining very precisely the words
"due process of law." The opinions on this subject are full of
vague generalizations not unlike the following: "Is this a fair,
reasonable and appropriate exercise of the . . . power of the
State, or is it an unreasonable, unnecessary and arbitrary interference with the right of the individual to his personal liberty

[14]*Ibid.*, pp. 464–65.

[or life, or property] ... ?"[15] But just where is the dividing line between reasonable and unreasonable governmental policies affecting individual rights? No matter how that line is drawn it would certainly seem that there can be no legal rule or formula which can be applied in yardstick fashion to challenged policies to obtain an answer. The best approach to the problem, then, is to examine specific decisions of the Court. It will at once be obvious that the time and circumstances of the individual cases have had an important bearing on their outcome and the resultant evolution of constitutional doctrine. It was in a due process of law case that Justice Holmes made his famous remark: "General propositions do not decide concrete cases. The decision will depend on a judgment or intuition more subtle than any articulate major premise."[16]

We may now analyze the use which the Supreme Court has made of the due process clauses during the last half century in passing on the constitutionality of state legislative enactments. According to a count of cases made by Felix Frankfurter, the Supreme Court set aside state laws 232 times under the Fourteenth Amendment between 1890 and 1938.[17] However, it will be sufficient for our purposes to examine three types of decisions in this area of constitutional law: one pertaining to the question of the validity of wages and hours legislation; another to the constitutionality of governmental attempts at price fixing; and the third to the validity of statutes affecting civil liberties.

[15]*Lochner* v. *New York* 198 U.S. 45, 56 (1905).
[16]*Ibid.*, p. 76.
[17]Felix Frankfurter, *Mr. Justice Holmes and the Supreme Court* (Cambridge: Harvard University Press, 1938) 97–139.

Due Process of Law and Wages and Hours Legislation

State statutes fixing maximum hours of labor or minimum wage levels for workers were first passed toward the end of the nineteenth century, on the basis of the state police power. More recently Congress has begun to enact wages and hours legislation, first for the District of Columbia in 1918, and later, in 1938, for all interstate business throughout the nation on the basis of the commerce power. It is nearly half a century since the Supreme Court was first asked to review state legislation of this kind under the due process clause. The most recent chapter in this development has just been written in a 1941 decision of the Court upholding the 1938 federal statute.

Shortly before the close of the last century the case of *Holden* v. *Hardy,* involving a statute of the state of Utah limiting the labor of workers in underground mines or in smelters to eight hours a day except in emergency, was appealed to the Supreme Court. The constitutionality of this progressive statute of the Mormons was attacked on the ground that it deprived both employer and worker of their freedom of contract, and thus, in effect, of their liberty and property without due process of law. This argument the Supreme Court rejected, upholding the law as a valid and reasonable exercise of the police power in view of its limitation to occupations admittedly hazardous and unhealthy. The Court said:

These employments, when too long pursued, the legislature has judged to be detrimental to the health of the employés, and, so long as there are reasonable grounds for believing that this is so, its decision upon this subject cannot be reviewed by the Federal courts.

While the general experience of mankind may justify us in believing that men may engage in ordinary employments more than eight hours per day without injury to their health, it does not follow that labor for the same length of time is innocuous when carried on beneath the surface of the earth, where the operative is deprived of fresh air and sunlight, and is frequently subjected to foul atmosphere and a very high temperature, or to the influence of noxious gases. . . .[18]

Two justices dissented, believing that the statute was unconstitutional.

A few years later, a similar case, *Lochner* v. *New York*, involving a New York statute limiting the labor of workers in bakeries to sixty hours a week and ten hours a day, came before the Court. To our surprise we find the minority position in the Utah case becoming the majority decision in this case. Justice Peckham, one of the two justices who dissented in the earlier case, was the author of the majority opinion in the *Lochner* case. In a vitriolic opinion he denied that the law could possibly have any reasonable relation to the issue of public health and condemned it in no uncertain terms as a "mere meddlesome interference with the rights of the individual" and thus contrary to due process of law.[19]

The decision was by the narrow margin of five to four, and two powerful dissenting opinions were written. That by Justice Holmes has become a classic. Adhering closely to the fundamental constitutional issue in the case, he made it clear that he thought the law in question was at least reasonably related to a perfectly valid purpose of governmental activity, the protection of health, and thus should not be considered a violation of the Fourteenth Amendment. Holmes said:

The Fourteenth Amendment does not enact Mr. Herbert Spencer's *Social Statics.* . . .

[18]169 U.S. 366, 395–96 (1898).
[19]198 U.S. 45, 61.

I think that the word liberty in the Fourteenth Amendment is perverted when it is held to prevent the natural outcome of a dominant opinion, unless it can be said that a rational and fair man necessarily would admit that the statute proposed would infringe fundamental principles as they have been understood by the traditions of our people and our law. It does not need research to show that no such sweeping condemnation can be passed upon the statute before us. A reasonable man might think it a proper measure on the score of health.[20]

Moreover, it was the opinion of the minority justices that where there are reasonable grounds for the enactment of a police power statute the Court must accept the judgment of the legislature. Justice Harlan stated in his dissenting opinion that "... the State is not amenable to the judiciary, in respect of its legislative enactments, unless such enactments are plainly, palpably, beyond all question, inconsistent with the Constitution of the United States...."[21]

But the pendulum was not yet through swinging. Just three years later in *Muller* v. *Oregon* the Court upheld an Oregon statute limiting to ten hours a day the employment of women in virtually *any* type of industrial work,[22] and then in 1917 in *Bunting* v. *Oregon* sanctioned another Oregon law, far more sweeping in its provisions than either the Utah or the New York laws and restricting the employment of all workers, men and women alike, in virtually all industrial or manufacturing establishments to ten hours a day.[23] In this last case the Court, following the approach Justice Holmes had employed in his dissenting opinion in the *Lochner* case, did not see how it could be said that the statute was unreasonable or arbitrary, in view of the admitted relation of hours of labor

[20]*Ibid.*, pp. 75–76.
[21]*Ibid.*, pp. 72–73.
[22]208 U.S. 412 (1908).
[23]243 U.S. 426 (1917).

to public health. Three justices dissented. Not the least significant thing about this case is that there was not a single reference to the previous decision in the relevant *Lochner* case—no effort to distinguish this apparently contradictory decision from that in the earlier case, no specific admission that the earlier case was here being reversed. How this silence was to be reconciled with the principle of *stare decisis* was not explained.

After *Bunting* v. *Oregon* there has been little doubt that legislation limiting the hours of employment for men and women in virtually all types of occupations is perfectly valid so far as the due process limitation of the Constitution is concerned, as long as the standards imposed by the law have some reasonable relation to public health or public safety. But there had been twenty years of uncertainty and a good deal of wobbling before the Supreme Court was able to make up its mind what meaning should be attributed to the vague words of the due process of law clauses in the face of governmental attempts to control hours of labor.

If it is permissible under the due process clauses to regulate maximum hours of labor on the ground that such regulation is necessary for the protection of public health, it would seem difficult to draw any other conclusion than that laws prescribing minimum wage levels for the same purpose are equally valid. For the relationship between the wages of workers and such social problems as public health and public morality seems about as obvious as the similar relationship between hours of labor and public health. But has the Supreme Court taken this view? Have its decisions in minimum wage cases been similar to those in maximum hours cases?

The Supreme Court made its first ruling in a minimum wage case at almost exactly the same time that it was rendering its definitive decision on the question of the control of maximum hours in the *Bunting* case. In the case of *Stettler* v.

O'Hara, the justices divided four to four and thereby upheld an Oregon minimum wage law, since a tie vote among the justices has the effect of sustaining the decision rendered by the next lower court.[24] Here that ruling had been favorable to the legislation. Justice Brandeis, a strongly liberal judge newly appointed to the Court by President Wilson, abstained from participation because he had been connected with the case as a private attorney during its earlier stages. There is not a shadow of doubt that had he participated he would have voted to uphold the legislation, and the constitutionality of minimum wage legislation would accordingly have been definitely determined by a five-to-four vote at the same time that the Court was finally sanctioning maximum hours legislation. As it was, the four-to-four favorable decision proved little, since according to the rules of the Court it did not constitute a controlling precedent.

As might have been expected, the matter was not permitted to rest at this point. Again in 1923 the issue was brought to the Supreme Court. In the meantime, President Harding had strengthened the conservative group on the Court through the appointment of several justices, and the Court by a five-to-three vote ruled in the case of *Adkins* v. *Children's Hospital* that a minimum wage law for the District of Columbia, limited to women and children, violated the due process clause of the Fifth Amendment.[25] Justice Brandeis again refrained from participation. Otherwise, the minority group would certainly have numbered four justices. The majority opinion, written by Justice Sutherland, is remarkable for its unrelenting conservatism. Every possible argument in the law's favor is swept aside. To the majority the fact that regu-

[24] 243 U.S. 629 (1917).

[25] 261 U.S. 525 (1923). Two Harding appointees, Justices Sutherland and Butler, joined the three of the four justices who had voted against the Oregon law and were still on the Court, to constitute a five-to-three majority against the statute.

lation of hours of labor had finally been declared constitutional proved nothing as to the validity of the control of minimum wages. Moreover, Justice Sutherland actually resurrected the discredited ruling in the old *Lochner* case and implied that it was still good law, the ruling in the more recent *Bunting* case notwithstanding. The fact that the law was limited to women and minors, whose good morals and health might have been supposed to constitute a somewhat special problem, carried no weight. Justice Sutherland even made this remarkable statement: "It cannot be shown that well-paid women safeguard their morals more carefully than those who are poorly paid. Morality rests upon other considerations than wages; and there is, certainly, no such prevalent connection between the two as to justify a broad attempt to adjust the latter with reference to the former."[26]

In part the Court's decision was the result of its adverse reaction to the standard by which the law provided that minimum wage levels should be fixed. Under the law these levels were to provide working women with at least the minimum wage which the administrative commission considered necessary to enable them to protect their health and morals. To the Court the use of such a standard meant that the *value* of the worker's services was being ignored as a factor in determining the wage scale, and thus the employer was being deprived of his property without due process of law. In other words, suggested the Court, there was no difference between this law and one that would require grocers to sell people enough food to enable them to live, whether they could pay the regular price for it or not. The possibility that the value of a worker's services, however great its maximum may be and regardless of the other criteria that may be considered, is at the very least equal to that sum of money which will enable him to live at a bare subsistence

[26]261 U.S. 525, 556.

level was apparently completely beyond the comprehension of the majority justices.

The dissenting justices did not take their defeat lying down. They rose to the occasion and did some of the plainest and bluntest talking to be found in the literature of Supreme Court decisions. The majority decision was too much even for conservative Chief Justice Taft and he led the attack upon it. He reminded the majority justices that "it is not the function of this Court to hold congressional acts invalid simply because they are passed to carry out economic views which the Court believes to be unwise or unsound." He recalled that the Court had actually rendered such a decision as the one in the *Bunting* case and that he had "always supposed that the *Lochner Case* was thus overruled." Finally, he could not see that the due process clause required the invalidation of minimum wage legislation at the same time that it permitted the regulation of maximum hours. "I do not feel . . . that either on the basis of reason, experience or authority, the boundary of the police power should be drawn to include maximum hours and exclude a minimum wage."[27]

Justice Holmes also wrote a separate dissenting opinion. He, too, stated: "I confess that I do not understand the principle on which the power to fix a minimum for the wages of women can be denied by those who admit the power to fix a maximum for their hours of work. . . . I perceive no difference in the kind or degree of interference with liberty, the only matter with which we have any concern, between the one case and the other."[28]

That the particular elements of time and personality may have an important influence upon a decision has never been more strikingly revealed than in this case. According to a careful study by Thomas Reed Powell, of some forty-one state

[27]*Ibid.*, pp. 562–66.
[28]*Ibid.*, p. 569.

and federal judges who passed upon the issue between 1917, the date of the first court decision on minimum wage legislation, and 1923, when the *Adkins* case was decided, thirty-two concluded that such legislation was valid, whereas only nine thought it unconstitutional. Yet because of chance, when the issue came before the Supreme Court for a final ruling those judges who were opposed to such legislation happened to have a majority of the seats and the law was invalidated by the slenderest of margins. Professor Powell himself suggests: "In the words of the poet, it was not the Constitution but a measureless malfeasance which obscurely willed it thus'—the malfeasance of chance and of the calendar. . . . The issue was determined not by the arguments but by the arbiters."[29]

For more than a decade the decision in the *Adkins* case blocked legislation in America prescribing minimum wages for workers. Then, with the coming of the depression, and the tremendous impetus it gave to the enactment of progressive social legislation, it was inevitable that the question of the constitutionality of such relatively mild legislation as a minimum wage law should be raised once more. And raised it was, with some rather startling and dramatic results, as we shall see.

In 1936, not many months before the presidential election and at a time when the Court would certainly have preferred to avoid such an embarrassing issue, the matter was returned to its doorstep in the case of *Morehead* v. *Tipaldo*. A 1933 New York statute providing for the payment of minimum wages to women and children was challenged as a violation of the Fourteenth Amendment. The standard in the New York law was somewhat different from that in the earlier District of Columbia law in that in fixing minimum wage

[29]Thomas Reed Powell, "The Judiciality of Minimum Wage Legislation," 37 *Harvard Law Review* (1924) 545; I *Selected Essays* 553, 556, 559; II *Selected Essays* 716.

scales it required that some attention be given to the value of the services rendered by the workers, as well as to the amounts necessary to enable them to protect their health. On the basis of this more flexible formula the Court, if it had chosen, might have distinguished the law from that in the earlier case and thus upheld it. But a majority of the justices were just as conservative as the majority had been in 1923 and could not see that there was any real difference in the standards.[30] The two statutes were both unreasonable and arbitrary and thus equally bad. One may agree with the Court, for the sake of argument, that the two laws could not be distinguished from each other. But even so, in the later case if the Court had wished to uphold such legislation, could it not have specifically reversed the decision in the *Adkins* case as having been originally in error, and thus have avoided the necessity of following it as a precedent? After all, the Court does occasionally reverse itself. The majority justices avoided answering this question on a technicality, by pointing out that the lawyers who had defended the law for the New York legislature had neglected to ask specifically for a reversal of the *Adkins* decision. It is difficult to believe that this oversight actually prevented the Court from otherwise reversing the previous decision.

Four justices dissented, including Chief Justice Hughes.

This decision of the Court in 1936 was clearly a strategic error. For by now public opinion had come to demand such legislation as absolutely necessary in a modern society. And in the great controversy over the Supreme Court and the institution of judicial review which was beginning to take shape and which was to culminate shortly in the Roosevelt proposal to reform the Court, the decision in this case figured as an inexcusably reactionary one. Even conservatives realized that this was true and consequently deplored the decision.

[30]298 U.S. 587 (1936).

In words which Hughes has used to describe similar decisions, this was "a self-inflicted wound," and the Court had only itself to blame.[31]

But events were now moving rapidly. The very next year a minimum wage statute of the state of Washington, passed in 1913 and presumably rendered inoperative at the time of the *Adkins* decision in 1923, was resurrected and enforced by the state. The issue of constitutionality was raised in *West Coast Hotel Co.* v. *Parrish*. The Court, as we have seen, began to shift from its generally conservative attitude of the previous decade or so. By a five-to-four vote it upheld the statute and specifically reversed the decisions in the District of Columbia and New York cases.[32] Interestingly enough, the standard in the Washington act for the fixing of the minimum wage level was very similar to the one involved in the *Adkins* case, for it did not make the concession to the employer's position present in the New York law. But such technical details had suddenly become irrelevant. Curiously, this quick reversal of a decision just one year old was made possible through a shift in position by one man, Justice Roberts. Since he maintained an unbroken silence in the writing of the various majority and dissenting opinions in both cases, one can only speculate as to the reasons for his change of mind.

It will be noted that the 1937 decision upholding minimum wage legislation concerned a statute which was limited to women and children. A decision upholding minimum wage legislation for all types of workers, including able-bodied men, had not yet been rendered. But it was not to be long delayed. In 1938 Congress, impressed by the arguments of many pressure groups that the time had come to attack both the maximum hours and minimum wage problems along national, uniform lines, passed a federal wages and hours act applicable

[31]Hughes, *op. cit.* (Chap. I, n. 21), pp. 50 ff.
[32]300 U.S. 379 (1937).

to millions of laborers, male and female, adult and child, alike. As we have already seen, this statute was based upon the commerce power and was thus limited to workers having some relation to interstate còmmerce.[33] In general, this federal statute was far more comprehensive in its regulatory effects than earlier state wages and hours laws. Naturally enough, the constitutionality of this important New Deal statute was soon challenged in the courts. But when the case finally reached the Supreme Court in 1941, it was the question of the right of Congress to pass such a statute upon the basis of the commerce power that received primary consideration. A unanimous Court dismissed the due process of law argument against the statute so curtly that the statement on this point seems like little more than a footnote to the decision. The due process issue was disposed of in these words:

> Since our decision in West Coast Hotel Co. v. Parrish, it is no longer open to question that the fixing of a minimum wage is within the legislative power and that the bare fact of its exercise is not a denial of due process under the Fifth more than under the Fourteenth Amendment. Nor is it any longer open to question that it is within the legislative power to fix maximum hours. Similarly the statute is not objectionable because applied alike to both men and women.[34]

What conclusion can be drawn concerning these cases in which the Supreme Court has endeavored to test the validity of wages and hours legislation in terms of the requirements of the two due process clauses of the Constitution? Can any

[33]How substantial this relation must be is, of course, an uncertain and crucial point, as the examination of the commerce decisions in the last chapter has made evident.

[34]*United States* v. *Darby Lumber Co.* 85 Law. ed. Advance Opinions 395, 406 (1941). But see also *Opp Cotton Mills* v. *Administrator of Wage and Hour Division* 85 Law. ed. Advance Opinions 407 (1941), decided the same day, a case in which the Court held that the procedural directions set forth in the statute are in compliance with due process of law.

other conclusion possibly be drawn than that these two clauses are sufficiently vague and ambiguous to enable any judge to read almost anything into them that he wishes to; and that in determining the constitutionality of wages and hours laws the individual justices have been enforcing not the Constitution but their own "personal economic predilections?"[34a] Or in other words, have not the justices been consciously or unconsciously influenced by the claims and counterclaims of various pressure groups, some benefited by such legislation, some feeling themselves injured? If this be so is not the Supreme Court truly an active instrument of government sharing with Congress and the state legislatures the power to legislate?

Due Process of Law and Price Fixing

There is a second series of cases which also provides an excellent opportunity to examine the attempts of the Supreme Court to give meaning to the due process clauses of the Constitution. The recent history of government regulation of American social and economic life reveals certain successive stages of control. As this progression has taken place one particular type of regulation has often been regarded as radical and extreme. This is the control or fixing by the government of the prices at which business interests sell their products or services to the public. Whether such control is necessary and wise is, of course, a controversial matter. Whether it is an indication of socialism, or of fascism, may perhaps be argued. What we are interested in is the question of its constitutionality.

The story begins in 1877 in the period following the Civil War, when modern American industrial development was

[34a]Justice Stone was the author of this phrase in his dissenting opinion in *Morehead* v. *Tipaldo* 298 U.S. 587, 633 (1936).

getting under way and was bringing in its wake a whole host of complex social problems. One result was that in large sections of agricultural America the farmer was growing increasingly distrustful of the vast power the railroads and other industrial enterprises were coming to wield in the economic life of the nation. Because of this unrest certain progressive tendencies began to be apparent in a number of state legislatures, and among other results was the enactment of the so-called "Granger" laws. One of these was an Illinois statute providing for the fixing of the maximum charges which could be made for the storage of grain by certain privately owned grain elevators in the state. It occurred to those who were opposed to this new tendency that the validity of such a statute might be challenged under the Fourteenth Amendment, and in due time the issue reached the United States Supreme Court in the case *Munn* v. *Illinois*. There a majority of the justices were inclined to uphold the constitutionality of this particular price-fixing statute, although it represented a radical tendency. As we have already seen, the Court was not yet prepared in 1877 to utilize the due process clause as a basis for the condemnation of a state statute in the economic field. Moreover, the Court was passing through one of its periodic liberal phases; after all, the farmers had good cause for their grievances, and in the light of the circumstances the control of the grain elevators' storage charges by law seemed entirely reasonable. But the justices were somewhat reluctant to admit these factors in their decision. Accordingly, they hit upon a historical justification, or apology, for their ruling and asserted that there was an ancient doctrine in the old English common law to the effect that certain private businesses by their character become "affected with a public interest." The result is, said Chief Justice Waite, that "when . . . one devotes his property to a use in which the public has an interest, he, in effect, grants to the public an interest in that use, and must submit to be controlled by the public for the common good, to the extent of the interest he has thus created."[35] Actually, this doctrine had never been much of a common-law principle. First suggested about 1670 by Matthew Hale, Lord Chief Justice of the King's Bench in England, in a treatise which was not even published until óne hundred years later, the idea had an uncertain and not very important subsequent history so far as the English common law was concerned.[36]

The Supreme Court further discovered that one of the ways in which businesses affected with a public interest had been regulated was by governmental control of the prices they charged the public for the services they rendered. Thus it remained only to determine that a grain elevator fell within this category to sanction the Illinois law in question on the basis of an ancient doctrine. The Court quickly found that there was historical evidence that grain elevators did fall into this special class. There remained a possible further objection to the statute that, granting the validity of the general idea of price control by law, this particular control violated the due process clause because it was too harsh and prevented the owners of the elevators from making reasonable profits on their investments. But the Court ruled that this last question of the reasonableness of rates was one for legislative determination and was not subject to judicial review. Chief Justice Waite even went so far as to say: "For protection against abuses by legislatures the people must resort to the polls, not to the courts."[37] But this part of the opinion as to the reasonableness of the prescribed rates was later reversed by the Court, and there has been a long subsequent history of

[35] 94 U.S. 113, 126 (1877).

[36] See Breck P. McAllister, "Lord Hale and Business Affected with a Public Interest," 43 *Harvard Law Review* (1930) 759; II *Selected Essays* 467, and Walton Hamilton, "Affectation with Public Interest," 39 *Yale Law Journal* (1930) 1089; II *Selected Essays* 494.

[37] *Munn* v. *Illinois*, 94 U.S. 113, 134 (1877).

judicial review of the reasonableness of rates and prices pre-scribed by legislative and administrative agencies of govern-ment. That, however, is another story. Our concern here is with the holding that only those private businesses that are affected with a public interest can be subjected to price fixing of any kind. Chief Justice Waite's opinion in *Munn* v. *Illinois* has often been praised by liberals in that it presumably cleared the way against the possible barrier of the due process clause and made it possible for state legislatures to regulate the rates charged by public utilities and other businesses affected with a public interest. Actually, from the point of view of those who oppose judicial interference with legislative or administrative regulation of business, the Waite opinion was an unfortunate one for it represented a considerable step forward in the development of the Fourteenth Amendment as a means for judicial interference. Where Justice Miller, speaking for the majority in the earlier *Slaughter-House Cases,* had denied altogether that the police power of the states was limited or restricted by the due process clause of the Fourteenth Amendment, Chief Justice Waite now inti-mated that, had it not been for the fact that a grain elevator was a business affected with a public interest, the attempt by a state to use its police power to regulate such a business might have been held a violation of the due process clause.

It should be obvious that the crux of the issue concerned the line between those businesses that were, and those that were not, so affected with a public interest. For the one might have its prices controlled, whereas to attempt by law to con-trol the prices of the other would amount to a deprivation of property and liberty without due process of law. From 1877 to 1934 the Supreme Court endeavored to draw such a line dividing private businesses into the two categories. For nearly fifty years after the *Munn* decision the Court was reasonably generous in approving statutes designating specific fields of

economic enterprise as businesses affected with a public interest and subjecting them to price fixing and other forms of
governmental control more drastic than those to which the
ordinary business was being subjected. Railroads, waterworks,
electric power companies, in fact, all of the so-called "public
utilities," as well as insurance companies and certain other
enterprises, were placed within the category by the courts.
All during these years the Supreme Court was attempting (to
use Justice Holmes's phrase) to prick out a line in this field
of constitutional law. It sought some sort of practical formula
by which the characteristics of a business affected with a
public interest might be easily and clearly determined. But
the Court failed in its search. In some cases it seemed as
though the presence of a condition of monopoly was the all-
important factor to the Court in deciding whether to desig-
nate a business as a public utility. In others, the designation
was made even though no condition of monopoly existed. At
times the Court spoke as though the designation depended
upon a business having been granted a charter by the government, imposing upon it the duty of serving the general public.
Again it seemed rather a matter of the history of the business
—had it been rendering a service through the years which had
come to be indispensable to the public?

After the World War a number of states developed ambitious programs of social legislation. In some states this movement included efforts to widen the public utility concept and
thereby to extend rate control in the public interest. Confronted with this tendency, a Supreme Court dominated by
conservative justices, most of whose members had been appointed by either Taft or Harding, became increasingly severe
in its treatment of such laws.[38] As the 1920's were succeeded
by the 1930's one price-fixing case after another passed before

[38]By 1927 the Court included such undeniable conservatives as Chief
Justice Taft, and Justices Van Devanter, McReynolds, Sutherland, and Butler.

the Court and one legislative experiment after another was outlawed. Three of these cases will be briefly examined.

In 1922 the state of New York passed a law limiting the surcharge on the resale of theater tickets by brokers (or "scalpers") to fifty cents per ticket. To justify such a price-fixing measure the legislature thought it necessary to declare the theater business one affected with a public interest. Naturally enough, the law was attacked as violating the due process clause of the Fourteenth Amendment and in *Tyson* v. *Banton* the Court invalidated it. For support, Justice Sutherland, who wrote the majority opinion, went all the way back to the Englishman, Lord Hale, who had originated the common-law doctrine of businesses affected with a public interest. Beginning with Lord Hale's views, Justice Sutherland made a quick journey down through many of the famous decisions on this point of law, admitted that the idea of a business affected with a public interest "it is true, furnishes at best an indefinite standard," but came nonetheless to the very definite conclusion that theaters were no such business. "It may be true, as asserted, that, among the Greeks, amusement and instruction of the people through the drama was one of the duties of government. But certainly no such duty devolves upon any American government." And if the state was to be permitted to control the admission charges to all forms of amusements, "including the lowly merry-go-round with its adjunct, the hurdy-gurdy," the justice could not see where price fixing could be stopped.[39]

Four justices dissented, including the famous triumvirate of liberals who were united in so many dissents during this conservative period—Justices Holmes, Brandeis, and Stone. Holmes's brief, sparkling, dissenting opinion finds him at his best. He makes it clear, first of all, that he has little regard for the legitimacy of the fundamental legal principle upon

[39] 273 U.S. 418, 430, 441-42 (1927).

which the majority decision was based—that only businesses affected with a public interest can be subjected to price fixing.

We fear to grant power and are unwilling to recognize it when it exists. . . . When legislatures are held to be authorized to do anything considerably affecting public welfare it is covered by apologetic phrases like . . . the statement that the business concerned has been dedicated to a public use.

I do not believe in such apologies. I think the proper course is to recognize that a state legislature can do whatever it sees fit to do unless it is restrained by some express prohibition in the Constitution of the United States or of the State, and that Courts should be careful not to extend such prohibitions beyond their obvious meaning by reading into them conceptions of public policy that the particular Court may happen to entertain. Coming down to the case before us I think . . . that the notion that a business is clothed with a public interest . . . *is little more than a fiction* intended to beautify what is disagreeable to the sufferers. The truth seems to me to be that, subject to compensation when compensation is due, the legislature may forbid or restrict any business when it has a sufficient force of public opinion behind it.

But in thus suggesting that the Court throw out the window the whole legal principle which had been so laboriously evolved since 1877, Holmes realized that he was battering his head against a stone wall. So, in rather resigned fashion, he went on to conclude:

But if we are to yield to fashionable conventions [a rather flippant reference to a doctrine of constitutional law created by the United States Supreme Court!], it seems to me that theatres are as much devoted to public use as anything well can be. We have not that respect for art that is one of the glories of France. But to many people the superfluous is the necessary, and it seems to me that Government does not go beyond its sphere in attempting to make life livable for them. I am far from saying that I think this particular law a wise and rational provision. That is not my affair. But if the people of the State of New York speaking by their authorized voice say that they want it, I see nothing in the Constitution of the United States to prevent their having their will.[40]

Before leaving this case, one sentence from the separate dissenting opinion of Justice Stone may be quoted. "To say that only those businesses affected with a public interest may be regulated is but another way of stating that all those businesses which may be regulated are affected with a public interest."[41] Not often has a Supreme Court justice so openly exposed the essential hollowness of a principle of constitutional law!

The next year a majority of the justices struck down a New Jersey statute attempting to control the fees charged by private employment agencies. Such a business was not affected with a public interest and therefore could not be subjected to price fixing, said the Court in its decision in *Ribnik* v. *McBride*. And Justice Sutherland in his majority opinion made it clear that the Court had had about enough of this radical type of legislation and was determined to put its foot down from then on. ". . . it is no longer fairly open to question that, at least in the absence of a *grave emergency,* the fixing of prices for food or clothing, of house rental or of wages . . . is beyond the legislative power."[42] Again the three liberals dissented. Justice Stone spoke for the group and again indicated its belief that there was little reason or constitutional necessity for distinguishing between ordinary governmental control of private business generally, and price fixing as a special form of control, or little reason for the insistence that price fixing be restricted to certain kinds of

[40]*Ibid.,* pp. 445–47. (Italics added.)

[41]*Ibid.,* p. 451.

[42]277 U.S. 350, 357 (1928). (Italics added.)

businesses which could be described as affected with a public interest.

Then in 1932 came the decision in the famous Oklahoma Ice case, *New State Ice Company* v. *Liebmann*. This case involved an Oklahoma statute subjecting the business of manufacturing and selling ice, not to price fixing but to a licensing system under which only those enterprises that received a permit from the state government could engage in the ice business. Like price fixing, this type of control was one that the Court had always ruled could be applied only to businesses affected with a public interest. Again, the question to be decided by the Court was whether the ice business was one that might be placed in this special category. Once more the Court ruled against the state.[43] Once more the liberals dissented (Brandeis and Stone; Holmes was now gone from the Court). This time it was Brandeis's turn to present the dissenting point of view. In a long opinion he marshaled much statistical data to prove the reasonableness and even necessity of this particular type of regulation, and also, like Holmes and Stone, indicated his belief that the public interest category was worthless as a legal principle.

The notion of a distinct category of business "affected with a public interest" . . . rests upon historical error. . . . In my opinion, the true principle is that the State's power extends to every regulation of any business reasonably required and appropriate for the public protection. I find in the due process clause no other limitation upon the character or the scope of regulation permissible.[44]

But the days of this rule of constitutional law were now numbered, and the repeated attacks upon it by liberal justices in dissenting opinions were soon to have their effect. In 1934 a New York statute came to the Court which provided for

[43]285 U.S. 262 (1932).
[44]*Ibid.*, pp. 302-3.

control of the milk business, including among other regulatory measures that of price fixing. Based as it was upon the assumption that the milk business fell within the category of businesses affected with a public interest, the statute seemingly clashed with the Court's warning in the *Ribnik* decision that the price of food could not be controlled save in "a grave emergency." It might have been argued that the depression constituted such an emergency, but that was not necessary, for in the present case, *Nebbia* v. *New York,* the majority of the Court was now ready to abandon this doctrine of law completely. Justice Roberts, a middle-of-the-roader, was assigned to write the majority opinion, perhaps to soften somewhat the Court's change of direction and, if possible, to placate the conservatives.

The meaning of the decision is inescapable. Going back to *Munn* v. *Illinois,* Justice Roberts made the belated discovery for the Court that when it had talked in that case about governmental price fixing in businesses affected with a public interest, it had not meant to identify and limit that category to the public utility classification, but had simply intended the phrase to convey the same meaning as would the words, "subject to the exercise of the police power." Thus, it became

. . . clear that there is no closed class or category of businesses affected with a public interest, and the function of courts in the application of the Fifth and Fourteenth Amendments is to determine in each case whether circumstances vindicate the challenged regulation as a reasonable exertion of governmental authority or condemn it as arbitrary or discriminatory. The phrase "affected with a public interest" can, in the nature of things, mean no more than that an industry, for adequate reason, is subject to control for the public good.[45]

The four conservative justices dissented, and in his rather bitter dissenting opinion Justice McReynolds made it clear

[45]291 U.S. 502, 533, 536 (1934).

that he and his colleagues of the minority realized that the majority opinion was sweeping away in its entirety a constitutional rule of long standing. Naturally, they deplored this new direction of doctrine.

Evaluation of the Wages and Hours and Price-Fixing Cases

During much of the period since the Supreme Court began invalidating social and economic legislation on the ground that it was without due process of law the Court has been the subject of much criticism both from within and without. It has been pointed out repeatedly that the record of the Court's activity in due process cases indicates it has often acted as a legislative agency unfettered by any requirement that it render its decisions according to rules and principles having a fixed meaning. Typical of the criticism from within the Court, which has usually taken the form of dissenting opinions, is the following excerpt from a dissent by Justice Holmes:

I have not yet adequately expressed the more than anxiety that I feel at the ever increasing scope given to the Fourteenth Amendment in cutting down what I believe to be the constitutional rights of the States. As the decisions now stand, I see hardly any limit but the sky to the invalidating of those rights if they happen to strike a majority of this Court as for any reason undesirable. I cannot believe that the Amendment was intended to give us *carte blanche* to embody our economic or moral beliefs in its prohibitions. Yet I can think of no narrower reason that seems to me to justify the present and . . . earlier decisions. . . . Of course the words "due process of law," if taken in their literal meaning, have no application to this case; and while it is too late to deny that they have been given a much more extended and artificial signification, still we ought to remember the great caution shown by the Constitution in limiting the power of the States, and should be slow to construe the clause in the Fourteenth Amendment as committing to the Court, with no guide but the Court's own discretion, the validity of whatever laws the States may pass.[46]

The same type of criticism has often come from outside the Court. An able student of constitutional law has said:

In addressing the court in due-process cases one should not commence with the usual salutation "May it please the Court." Instead, one should say "My Lords." Backed by and charged with the enforcement of the due-process clauses of the fifth and fourteenth amendments, the Supreme Court of the United States is the American substitute for the British house of lords.[47]

In the light of the concluding cases, *Bunting* v. *Oregon, United States* v. *Darby Lumber Company,* and *Nebbia* v. *New York,* it may be said that the Court has shown a change of heart toward the aspects of due process of law which we have been examining, and that such criticisms are no longer applicable. Certainly the decisions in these cases reveal a new reticence on the part of a majority of the justices, a reluctance to substitute their own judgments for those of legislators as to the wisdom of social legislation. The majority opinion in *Nebbia* v. *New York* illustrates this new tendency:

So far as the requirement of due process is concerned, and in the absence of other constitutional restriction, a state is free to adopt whatever economic policy may reasonably be deemed to promote public welfare . . . . The courts are without authority either to declare such policy, or, when it is declared by the legislature, to override it. If the laws passed are seen to have a reasonable relation to a proper legislative purpose, and are neither arbitrary nor discriminatory, the requirements of due process are satisfied. . . .[48]

[46]*Baldwin* v. *Missouri* 281 U.S. 586, 595 (1930).

[47]Albert M. Kales, "New Methods in Due Process Cases," 12 *American Political Science Review* (1918) 241; I *Selected Essays* 488. See also the Frankfurter statement above, page 142.

[48]291 U.S. 502, 537 (1934).

But a word of warning is necessary. It must be remembered that in the more recent due process decisions referred to, with the exception of that in the *Darby Company* case, three or four justices dissented and objected vigorously to the refusal of the majority to invalidate the statutes in question. Moreover, it is not without significance that just two years after he wrote the majority opinion in the *Nebbia* case, Justice Roberts weakened in his newly found liberal sentiments to a point where he was able to go through the remarkable gyrations in the New York and Washington minimum wage cases, already referred to.

So it is evident, as Justice Holmes suggests above, that it is too late to expect the Court to refrain altogether from the use of the due process clause to check the exercise of the police power. A return by the justices to the noninvolvement stand of the *Slaughter-House* decision of 1873 is too much to look for, even from the liberal Court of 1941. Justice Black is almost the only one of the present liberal justices who has shown any interest in reviving Justice Miller's interpretation of the due process clauses.[49]

There is little doubt that the Court will from time to time continue to invalidate laws on this ground. But there is perhaps considerable reason to expect that the Court will also maintain its recent reluctance to utilize the due process clauses as a means of emphasizing the symbolic over the instrumental aspect of the Constitution.

Due Process of Law and Civil Liberties

In examining the third type of due process cases—those involving legislation affecting civil liberties—it is appropriate to note a recent comment by Robert Jackson, lately attorney

---

[49]See *McCart* v. *Indianapolis Water Co.* 302 U.S. 419, 423 (1938), and *Connecticut General Life Insurance Co.* v. *Johnson* 303 U.S. 77, 83 (1938).

general of the United States and now a Supreme Court justice, on the inconsistency of judges in matters of constitutional interpretation. Jackson points out that many people think that the liberals on the Court have always been broad constructionists of the Marshall type, and the conservatives, strict constructionists of the Taney variety. Actually, he goes on to assert, neither group has been the exclusive champion or critic either of the doctrine of strict construction or of that of broad construction. In interpreting the instrumental clauses of the Constitution, such as the commerce power, conservatives have been "strict and niggardly." But they have then been "liberal to the point of extravagance" in construing such symbolic sections as the two due process of law clauses for purposes of curtailing governmental activity.[50] Similarly, it may be contended that liberal justices have often been broad constructionists in interpreting governmental powers, and strict when it has been a matter of defining the limiting clauses of the Constitution.

Such inconsistency may be shown to exist in the attitudes of the justices toward the limitation clauses alone. As already indicated, the conservatives have sought to construe due process of law broadly so as to bring about the invalidation of progressive regulatory measures in the social and economic fields, and the liberals have protested against such use of these constitutional provisions. But when attempts have been made to attack state laws endangering civil liberties, the justices have reversed their positions. In such cases the liberal justices have sought to stretch the meaning of the Fourteenth Amendment so that it might be considered to re-enact as against state action many of the specific civil liberties enumerated in the first ten amendments and there guaranteed against federal encroachment. In the same cases the conservatives have often lost their zest for a broad construction of due process of law

[50]Jackson, *op. cit.* (Chap. II, n. 11), p. xiii.

and have argued against the use of the clause to invalidate this type of statute.

To state this point in somewhat different fashion, it would be unfair to suggest that the development of the *substantive* aspect of the due process of law clauses of the Constitution has been the exclusive work of conservative justices who have sought thereby to protect property and business interests. That conservative justices have utilized the Fifth and Fourteenth Amendments to accomplish such purposes cannot be denied. But it should not be overlooked that these amendments have also been used by certain justices, in the main, liberals, to protect civil liberties against arbitrary governmental action. Moreover, as will shortly be shown, this use of due process of law has been in addition to the older *procedural* guarantee provided by the clause against arbitrary treatment of persons on trial in the courts. In other words, the more recent *substantive* aspect of due process of law has finally been made to serve liberals in striking down legislative enactments interfering with civil liberties.

The long fight to protect the fundamental civil liberties of the individual in America has been primarily waged against threatened encroachments by the state governments. It will be recalled that to many people's way of thinking the one serious defect in the original Constitution was the absence of a Bill of Rights, and early in the 1790's the first ten amendments were added to the Constitution specifically guaranteeing such civil rights as freedom of speech, press, assembly, and religious worship, and many others, against federal encroachment. It is true that similar bills of rights protecting the individual against arbitrary state action were incorporated during the same period in many state constitutions. But these guarantees could be enforced only in the state courts, and almost from the first, efforts were made to obtain the protection of federal courts against interference by the states with the civil liberties of the individual. In so far as these efforts have met with success the justices of the Supreme Court have been largely instrumental in making such a result possible.

Attempts to "nationalize" the protection of civil liberties in the United States have been made in three ways. The first of these was an unsuccessful attempt to persuade the Supreme Court that the rights enumerated in the first ten amendments were guaranteed to the individual against state as well as federal encroachment by these amendments themselves. Although it seems clear from the historical evidence that the framers of these amendments had absolutely no intention that they should apply against the States,[51] the fact that, with the exception of the First Amendment, which specifically mentions Congress, they are all worded generally encouraged the thought that they might afford protection against state action. But in the famous case *Barron* v. *Baltimore,* decided in 1833, Chief Justice Marshall destroyed this hope, stating: "These amendments contain no expression indicating an intention to apply them to the state governments. This Court cannot so apply them."[52] Thus it became impossible to argue, for example, that the words of the Eighth Amendment against the infliction of cruel and unusual punishments operated in any way directly upon the states.

The second attempt to seek federal protection of civil liberties against state encroachments was not made until the Fourteenth Amendment was added to the Constitution after the Civil War. One of the phrases of that amendment provides that "no State shall make or enforce any law which shall abridge the privileges or immunities of citizens of the United States; . . ." These words might have seemed to hold

---

[51]Charles Warren, "The New 'Liberty' Under the Fourteenth Amendment," 39 *Harvard Law Review* (1926) 431; also II *Selected Essays* 237, 240.

[52]7 Peters 243, 250.

forth considerable hope for the nationalization of civil liberties. Professor Cushman states:

There seems no doubt that as a matter of historical fact the framers of the amendment meant by "privileges or immunities of citizens of the United States" the whole body of ordinary civil rights and especially those enumerated in the Bill of Rights of the federal Constitution. They intended to place in the hands of Congress the broadest possible power to prevent the impairment of these rights, and they thought they had done so. Instead of looking to the state legislature for legislative protection of his civil liberty, the citizen, especially the freedman, would henceforth look to Congress or to the federal courts. A veritable revolution would thus be wrought in the previous equilibrium of state and national power.[53]

But this second attempt was to end in failure, too. Beginning with the *Slaughter-House Cases* the Supreme Court has fairly consistently ruled that the privileges and immunities of citizens of the United States do not include the ordinary civil rights or even those specifically set forth in the Bill of Rights.[54] For example, the right to trial by jury set forth in the Bill of Rights was definitely held not to be a privilege or immunity of a citizen of the United States, and thus the privilege or immunity clause of the Fourteenth Amendment did not re-enact this guarantee as against state encroachment. It may seem surprising that the decision in the *Slaughter-House Cases* was rendered by one of the great liberals of the period, Justice Miller, who perhaps might have been expected to favor federal protection of civil liberties against state encroachment. But the factual background of the *Slaughter-House Cases* makes it clear that it was more a matter of economic rights than of civil rights that was involved. Justice

[53]Cushman, *op. cit.* (Chap. IV, n. 6), p. 41. Reprinted by permission of F. S. Crofts and Co., publishers.

[54]16 Wallace 36 (1873); *Maxwell* v. *Dow* 176 U.S. 581 (1900).

Miller was perhaps reluctant to encourage interference by the federal judiciary with the efforts of the states to control the economic activities of their citizens.[55] Moreover, since nearly half a century was to elapse before liberal justices would exert strong pressure that the Fourteenth Amendment be utilized to invalidate state legislation endangering civil liberties, it was perhaps too much to have expected Justice Miller to favor such a policy in 1873.

The third attempt to nationalize the protection of civil liberties was based upon the due process of law clause of the Fourteenth Amendment and was destined in the end to prove successful. The argument behind this third attempt was an essentially simple one, being to the effect that when the Fourteenth Amendment forbids the states to deprive persons of their "liberty" without due process of law, the word "liberty" should be considered as including civil liberties generally and, in any case, the rights specifically enumerated in certain of the first ten amendments. Were this argument to be accepted it is clear that the Fourteenth Amendment would have the effect of re-enacting much of the Bill of Rights as against state action. What had proved impossible to accomplish under the privileges and immunities clause would instead be effected under the due process clause of the same amendment. It is probably true, as Charles Warren asserts, that when the word "liberty" was included in the Fifth and Fourteenth Amendments it was intended to suggest no more than the old English idea of the right of a person to be free from physical restraint (arrest) without due process of law.[56] But when one recalls that the whole concept of due process of law in the English tradition apparently applied only to *procedural* matters and that the application of this clause after 1890 to the

---

[55]Charles Fairman, *Mr. Justice Miller and the Supreme Court* (Cambridge: Harvard University Press, 1939) 182–86.

[56]II *Selected Essays* 237, 245.

substantive content of social and economic legislation represented a distinct addition to or growth in the original meaning, a similar expansion of the word "liberty" seems entirely possible and proper.

The attempt to persuade the Supreme Court to expand the meaning of the word "liberty" developed much more slowly than the similar attempt to obtain protection for property and business against governmental regulation through an expansion of the word "property" in the Fourteenth Amendment. Even as late as 1922 the Supreme Court was saying in the words of the conservative Justice Pitney that "neither the Fourteenth Amendment nor any other provision of the Constitution of the United States imposes upon the States any restriction about 'freedom of speech'. . . ."[57] However, two liberals, Justices Harlan and Brandeis, had previously argued in dissenting opinions that freedom of speech and of the press were protected against state action by the Fourteenth Amendment.[58] In the middle 1920's these earlier dissenting opinions became the point of view of the majority of the Court. Although the Court failed in *Gitlow* v. *New York* to invalidate the state statute in question, it announced that "for present purposes we may and do assume that freedom of speech and of the press—which are protected by the First

[57]*Prudential Insurance Co.* v. *Cheek* 259 U.S. 530, 543 (1922).

[58]*Patterson* v. *Colorado* 205 U.S. 454 (1907); *Gilbert* v. *Minnesota* 254 U.S. 325 (1920). There will be some objection to the designation of Justice Harlan as a "liberal." Such terms are, of course, relative, and there are exceptions which make it difficult to classify almost any justice as completely liberal or as completely conservative. But when one notes that Justice Harlan wrote the Court's opinion in such cases as *Champion* v. *Ames, Northern Securities Co.* v. *United States, Mugler* v. *Kansas,* and *Jacobson* v. *Massachusetts,* and that he dissented from the majority decisions in *Pollock* v. *Farmers' Loan & Trust Co., United States* v. *E. C. Knight Co.,* the *Civil Rights Cases, Standard Oil Co.* v. *United States, United States* v. *American Tobacco Co., Hurtado* v. *California, Twining* v. *New Jersey, Maxwell* v. *Dow, Plessy* v. *Ferguson,* and *Lochner* v. *New York,* the reference to him as a liberal does not seem too inappropriate.

Amendment from abridgment by Congress—are among the fundamental personal rights and 'liberties' protected by the due process clause of the Fourteenth Amendment from impairment by the States."[59] In 1931 on the ground that it deprived persons of liberty without due process of law, the Court in *Near* v. *Minnesota* for the first time flatly invalidated a state law restricting freedom of speech and the press. Chief Justice Hughes tersely stated: "It is no longer open to doubt that the liberty of the press, and of speech, is within the liberty safeguarded by the due process clause of the Fourteenth Amendment from invasion by state action."[60] It is significant to note that this was a five-to-four decision, with the strongly liberal justices, Holmes, Brandeis, and Stone, and the "moderates," Hughes and Roberts, in the majority, and the strongly conservative justices, McReynolds, Van Devanter, Butler, and Sutherland, in the minority. The dissenting justices did not necessarily deny that the Fourteenth Amendment protects freedom of speech and press but, rather, asserted that the statute in the case did not actually encroach upon these liberties. However, Justice Butler's dissenting opinion makes it quite clear that the conservatives were not overjoyed with the new principle and the use made of it by the majority. This is obvious from Justice Butler's warning words that the majority decision "gives to freedom of the press a meaning and a scope not heretofore recognized and construes 'liberty' in the due process clause of the Fourteenth Amendment to put upon the States a federal restriction that is without precedent."[61]

Near v. *Minnesota* has been followed by subsequent decisions of the Supreme Court invalidating state laws under the

[59]268 U.S. 652, 666 (1925). See Cushman, *op. cit.* (Chap. IV, n. 6), pp. 85–87.

[60]283 U.S. 697, 707.

[61]*Ibid.*, p. 723.

Fourteenth Amendment on the ground that they abridged the right of freedom of assembly, and that of the freedom of religious worship.[62] It remains to be seen how many more specific liberties will be brought within the scope of the Fourteenth Amendment and protected by the federal courts against state laws which infringe them. But the nationalization, as a matter of principle, of civil liberties and the availability of relief in the federal courts against state as well as federal legislative encroachment upon these rights would seem to be clearly established.

Meanwhile, the Supreme Court, led by its liberal justices, has been resurrecting and revitalizing the old *procedural* concept of due process to provide protection for the individual against arbitrary state treatment where no statute is involved. By way of background it is worth noting that at the turn of the present century, when the Fourteenth Amendment was being increasingly utilized to invalidate social laws in the states, the Court was very much inclined to interpret rather narrowly the protection afforded by the amendment in procedural matters. In successive decisions it held that the right to indictment by a grand jury, the right to trial by jury, and the right to be free from self-incrimination—all of which are guaranteed in federal judicial procedure by the Bill of Rights —were not necessarily available in state judicial procedure because of the Fourteenth Amendment.[63] Justice Harlan dissented in all of these cases.

In contrast to these holdings, the recent tendency toward

[62]*De Jonge* v. *Oregon* 299 U.S. 353 (1937); *Cantwell* v. *Connecticut* 310 U.S. 296 (1940).

[63]*Hurtado* v. *California* 110 U.S. 516 (1884); *Maxwell* v. *Dow,* 176 U.S. 581 (1900); *Twining* v. *New Jersey* 211 U.S. 78 (1908). It is somewhat difficult to evaluate these decisions from a liberal-conservative point of view. Some of them, at least, were conservative in that they failed to provide federal protection against state judicial procedure of a somewhat arbitrary character. But they have their liberal side in that they left the states free to experiment with new procedural forms in criminal cases.

strengthening the *procedural* aspect of due process of law is to be seen in such cases as *Powell* v. *Alabama* and *Chambers* v. *Florida*.[64] The first of these is part of the famous Scottsboro case in Alabama and involved an appeal to the Supreme Court of the decision of a state court sentencing seven Negroes to death for the crime of rape. An appeal was taken on the ground that Alabama had not provided the defendants with adequate legal counsel to defend them at their trial and that because of this inadequacy their execution would amount to a deprivation of life without due process of law. The Supreme Court sustained this argument and set aside the verdict of guilt in the state court, thereby indicating that due process of law in its *procedural* aspect does require that the state provide adequate legal counsel for a defendant who cannot himself afford to obtain such assistance. It should be pointed out that the majority decision in this case was written by Justice Sutherland, a conservative. However, Justices Butler and McReynolds, the two most persistent conservatives of this period, dissented.

Chambers v. *Florida* concerned the use by state officers of "third degree" methods to obtain a confession which resulted in a sentence of death being pronounced upon four Negroes for the crime of murder. A unanimous Court set aside this verdict of guilt on the ground of denial of due process of law. In a truly eloquent opinion Justice Black said:

Under our constitutional system, courts stand against any winds that blow as havens of refuge for those who might otherwise suffer because they are helpless, weak, outnumbered, or because they are non-conforming victims of prejudice and public excitement. Due process of law, preserved for all by our Constitution, commands that no such practice as that disclosed by this record shall send any accused to his death. No higher duty, no more solemn responsibility, rests upon this Court, than that of

[64]287 U.S. 45 (1932); 309 U.S. 227 (1940).

translating into living law and maintaining this constitutional shield deliberately planned and inscribed for the benefit of every human being subject to our Constitution—of whatever race, creed or persuasion.[65]

The civil liberties cases which have been examined indicate that on the whole it is the liberal and not the conservative justices who have taken the lead in favoring a broad construction of due process of law in so far as it operates as a symbol of restraint upon the power of state government. In the light of this situation it becomes rather difficult to characterize or classify any justice merely because he seeks to construe the Constitution narrowly or broadly. The point is, to return once more to Professor Corwin's thesis, the Constitution is both an instrument and a symbol, and in either of these aspects it is capable of being broadly or narrowly interpreted. Thus it is of significance to determine what group is at any given time interested in utilizing the instrumental Constitution broadly, what group wants the instrument curtailed, what group wants the symbol emphasized, and what group the symbol limited. Moreover, it is important to know in each of these situations what motivation is controlling each of these groups in its attitude toward the Constitution. Finally, it is of no small concern to observe how the justices of the Supreme Court respond to these group desires by sanctioning particular uses of the Constitution sympathetic to the interests of certain groups and antagonistic to those of others. In making such an observation of the Court, the varying use that has been made of the due process of law clauses is a particularly fruitful point for study.

[65]309 U.S. 227, 241. But see also *Palko* v. *Connecticut* 302 U.S. 319 (1937) for an indication that this recent liberal interpretation of the *procedural* aspect of the due process clause will not be carried beyond certain limits.

Chapter VIII

The Scope of Judicial Review: Limitations

JUDICIAL review is a much misunderstood process of government. On the one hand, many people err in the direction of exaggerating the importance of this judicial power by supposing that the courts engage in a more or less continuous process of checking the constitutionality of all governmental actions. Some people even have the impression that a bill which has passed Congress and has been signed by the president is automatically sent to the Supreme Court for approval or rejection. On the other hand, many people often make the opposite mistake of underestimating the importance of judicial review when they suppose that the invalidation of an occasional act of Congress every two or three years tells the full story of this power. Since it is obvious that both of these contradictory concepts of judicial review cannot be correct, it is desirable to give some attention to the meaning and extent of this power. Accordingly, in the present chapter we shall examine the scope of judicial review from a point of view of certain limitations governing its operation, an examination which will quickly make it clear that the process is not an automatic or continuous one. In the next chapter we shall note certain conditions pertaining to the exercise of this power which tend to broaden its scope, paying particular attention to two very important aspects of the power which are often overlooked: judicial interpretation of statutes, and judicial review of administrative rulings. The latter will make it clear that judicial review is by no means an inconsequential power merely because it operates in a sporadic rather than a continuous fashion.

It is important to note that almost without exception the extent to which judicial review has operated in practice has been controlled by the courts themselves. The initial exercise of this power in *Marbury* v. *Madison* took place in the manner in which the Supreme Court willed it, and this has been true of virtually all later developments. Occasionally Congress has exercised its power to create courts or to determine their jurisdiction in such a way as to affect the operation of judicial review. But by and large the courts have been left to themselves freely to determine the limits of this power. Accordingly, nearly all of the specific limitations which are said to govern the exercise of judicial review have been announced by the Supreme Court itself.

The "Case" or "Controversy" Limitation

In the first place, the Supreme Court has repeatedly insisted that under the Constitution it may exercise the power of judicial review only in the course of actual bona fide litigation. There must be a real "case" or "controversy" involving conflicting rights and interests of separate parties before the courts will pass upon the question of a statute's constitutionality. A collusive suit or test case will supposedly be rejected. In other words, if the Court feels that the parties in litigation are not so much concerned about their own personal antagonistic interests as they are anxious to obtain a ruling on a statute's constitutionality, it may conclude that no "case" or "controversy" is before it and refuse to render a decision.

But let the Court speak for itself. Such statements as the following one are fairly common in its decisions:

> Whenever, in pursuance of an honest and actual antagonistic assertion of rights by one individual against another, there is presented a question involving the validity of any act of any legislature, State or Federal, and the decision necessarily rests on the competency of the legislature to so enact, the court must, in the exercise of its solemn duties, determine whether the act be constitutional or not; but such an exercise of power is the ultimate and supreme function of the courts. It is legitimate only in the last resort, and as a necessity in the determination of real, earnest and vital controversy between individuals. It never was the thought that, by means of a friendly suit, a party beaten in the legislature could transfer to the courts an inquiry as to the constitutionality of the legislative act.[1]

Actually, there can be little doubt that the Supreme Court has from time to time ignored this limitation upon its power. For instance, in the famous early case, *Hylton* v. *United States,* which concerned the validity of an act of Congress, the Court accepted the case and rendered a decision even though there was evidence that it was a test case and that the government had paid the lawyers' fees on both sides.[2] Later, in the case of *Pollock* v. *Farmers' Loan and Trust Company,* there is evidence that in its original form this was a test suit.[3] This was the extremely controversial case in which the Court, for all practical purposes, invalidated the federal

[1] *Chicago and Grand Trunk Ry. Co.* v. *Wellman* 143 U.S. 339, 345 (1892). See also *Muskrat* v. *United States* 219 U.S. 346 (1911). On the limitations of judicial review, see Edward S. Corwin, "Judicial Review in Action," 74 *University of Pennsylvania Law Review* (1926) 639; I *Selected Essays* 449, and T. M. Cooley, *Constitutional Limitations* (7th ed.; Boston: Little, Brown and Company, 1903) Chap. VII.

[2] 3 Dallas 171 (1796). See Walter F. Dodd, *Cases on Constitutional Law* (2nd ed.; St. Paul: West Publishing Co., 1937) 58.

[3] 157 U.S. 429 (1895); 158 U.S. 601 (1895).

income tax. Following this decision it was necessary to add an amendment to the Constitution to enable Congress to levy an income tax, and it took nearly twenty years to overcome the ruling in that fashion.

In more recent cases in which the constitutionality of the original T.V.A. and Guffey Coal statutes was passed upon, it has been charged that the Supreme Court went out of its way to consider the issue of constitutionality. Both of these cases got into court as the result of suits brought by stockholders to obtain injunctions restraining their own companies from complying with federal policies. Consequently, it was questionable in each instance whether the opposing parties to the litigation represented adverse interests.[4] In fact, the nine justices themselves were divided on this point, and although in both cases a majority favored taking jurisdiction and passing upon the laws, dissenting justices presented powerful arguments to the effect that, had it really wanted to adhere to its tradition in this respect, the Court had available an adequate excuse in each case to justify a refusal to accept jurisdiction.[5]

Disposing of Cases on Non-Constitutional Grounds

Second, the Supreme Court has insisted many times that it will not pass upon the constitutionality of a law even where there is a "case" or "controversy" if it can possibly dispose of the case at hand without making such a ruling. If it can decide a case, see that justice is done to the litigants, and at the same time avoid the issue of a statute's constitutionality, the Court claims it will do so. In his dissenting opinion in *Ashwander* v. *Tennessee Valley Authority,* Justice Brandeis

[4] See Jackson, *op. cit.* (Chap. II, n. 11), pp. 143–44, 153.

[5] *Ashwander* v. *T.V.A.* 297 U.S. 288 (1936); *Carter* v. *Carter Coal Co.* 298 U.S. 238 (1936).

has gathered together many statements from previous Court decisions expressing this principle. He says, in part:

The Court will not "anticipate a question of constitutional law in advance of the necessity of deciding it." "It is not the habit of the Court to decide questions of a constitutional nature unless absolutely necessary to a decision of the case." . . .

The Court will not pass upon a constitutional question although properly presented by the record, if there is also present some other ground upon which the case may be disposed of.[6]

Here, too, there are instances where the Court has seemed inclined to ignore this tradition of judicial review. For instance, it is generally believed that the facts of the *Dred Scott* case were such that the Court could have readily disposed of it without passing upon the validity of the Missouri Compromise and that, in fact, it went considerably out of its way to create an opportunity to pass upon the statute.

Preferring a Favorable Interpretation of a Statute

A third and somewhat similar rule of judicial review which the Supreme Court has voluntarily established is that it will interpret a statute so as to permit its being upheld, if that is at all possible. Passages such as the following can be found in any number of Supreme Court opinions: "It is elementary when the constitutionality of a statute is assailed, if the statute be reasonably susceptible of two interpretations, by one of which it would be unconstitutional and by the other valid, it is our plain duty to adopt that construction which will save the statute from constitutional infirmity."[7] Such a policy may be "elementary," but, again, a careful examination of Supreme Court decisions will reveal a number of cases in which the Court has seemed to honor this rule more in the breach than in the observance. Indeed, as has already been pointed out,

[6]297 U.S. 288, 346–47.
[7]*United States* v. *Delaware & Hudson Co.* 213 U.S. 366, 407 (1909).

in the first of all the judicial review cases, *Marbury* v. *Madison* itself, the Court refrained from preferring a clearly legitimate interpretation of the statute in question by which it might have avoided a decision invalidating the legislation.

The Benefit-of-the-Doubt Rule

A fourth and likewise similar self-imposed rule of the Court which limits the scope of judicial review is to be seen in its repeated insistence that, even where an interpretation of a statute throwing doubt upon its constitutionality cannot be avoided, the law will still be given all possible benefit of the doubt. "This declaration [holding a law unconstitutional] should never be made except in a clear case. Every possible presumption is in favor of the validity of a statute, and this continues until the contrary is shown beyond a rational doubt."[8] Chief Justice Marshall himself sanctioned this tradition. In a famous decision invalidating a state law he said:

The question, whether a law be void for its repugnancy to the constitution, is, at all times, a question of much delicacy, which ought seldom, if ever, to be decided in the affirmative, in a doubtful case. . . . The opposition between the constitution and the law should be such that the judge feels a clear and strong conviction of their incompatibility with each other.[9]

Again it is possible to find similar passages in many other decisions. It can be argued that the Court, like Hamlet's lady, "doth protest too much." No one of these voluntary rules established by the Court has been the subject of more bitter controversy than this. It has frequently been argued that the Court's action has time and time again exposed the lack of meaning in its own rule and proves that it has not given statutes the benefit of the doubt. Critics of the Court see such a result in the many cases in which the Court invalidates a

[8]*Sinking Fund Cases* 99 U.S. 700, 718 (1879).
[9]*Fletcher* v. *Peck* 6 Cranch 87, 128 (1810).

law by a five-to-four or a six-to-three decision. How, they ask, can the Court claim that a statute is unconstitutional beyond a reasonable doubt, when three or four justices actually think it is constitutional? Does not this amount, as *The New Republic* once put it, to "the oft recurring scandal of five members of the Supreme Court solemnly adjudging that the other four hold opinions which no reasonable man can entertain?"[10]

Defenders of the Court have a ready answer to this charge. When the Court, they argue, insists that it gives a law the benefit of the doubt yet actually invalidates a law by a five-to-four vote, what has happened is that each justice has asked himself, privately so to speak, whether the law is valid beyond a reasonable doubt. If five justices, as the result of their own individual and independent thinking, come to an agreement that the law is bad, it makes no difference that the other four have arrived at an opposite conclusion. We believe in majority rule—the five must be right and the four wrong. But it may be asked whether this attempt to reconcile the Court's practice with its theory is anything more than hairsplitting? Does it minimize the importance of a dissenting opinion in a doubtful case to a point where, as Justice Holmes once suggested, it is dismissed on the assumption that one side is not doing its sums right?[11]

There is another reason for questioning the steadfastness of

[10] 11 *New Republic* (July 30, 1917) 410. Quoted disapprovingly by Robert E. Cushman in "Constitutional Decisions by a Bare Majority of the Court," 19 *Michigan Law Review* (1921) 771; I *Selected Essays* 527, 529.

[11] A former justice of the Supreme Court, John H. Clarke, rejects this attempt of the Court's friends to reply to the charge that the Court is hardly giving a statute the benefit of the doubt when there are minority justices dissenting from a decision invalidating legislation. He suggests that the attempt at a reply can carry weight only with a mind "steeped in legalistic thinking." John H. Clarke, "Judicial Power to Declare Legislation Unconstitutional," 9 *American Bar Association Journal* (October 1923) 689, 692.

the Court in giving statutes the benefit of the doubt. Quite often in invalidating a statute a justice has indicated that such a decision resulted not so much from the impropriety of the statute at hand as it did from the danger that if the law were sustained legislatures might be encouraged to go still further and pass extreme and admittedly unconstitutional laws. Hence legislatures must be discouraged even at the cost of the statute under consideration. Any number of examples of the use of this technique can be given. An illustration is Justice Sutherland's opinion in the New York Theater Ticket case already examined. As though the attempt by the government of New York to regulate the prices charged for theater tickets by scalpers was not sufficiently unreasonable and therefore clearly a violation of the Fourteenth Amendment, the justice permitted his imagination to run wild for a moment and threw in the suggestion that, the next thing the Court knew, the state would be trying to control hurdy-gurdies and merry-go-rounds.[12] The same justice did much the same thing in his majority opinion in the *Adkins* case. It would be unwise, he said in effect, to permit a legislature to tell an employer that he must pay a woman a sufficient minimum wage to enable her at least to support herself. Let such a statute be upheld and the legislature would next be telling a groceryman that he must give his customers enough food to enable them to live, whether they can pay for it or not.[13]

Justice Sutherland has by no means been alone in his use of this technique. Many other examples might be given. For instance, Justice Roberts employed the same method in his opinion in the *Butler* case. This was the case in which the Agricultural Adjustment Act was invalidated by a six-to-three vote.[14] Justice Roberts specifically sanctioned the old

[12] *Tyson* v. *Banton* 273 U.S. 418, 442 (1927).
[13] *Adkins* v. *Children's Hospital* 261 U.S. 525, 558–59 (1923).
[14] *United States* v. *Butler* 297 U.S. 1 (1936).

rule that "every presumption is to be indulged in favor of faithful compliance by Congress with the mandates of the fundamental law. Courts are reluctant to adjudge any statute in contravention of them."[15] But having said that, he went on in his opinion to indicate that the Court's decision was in part the result of a fear that if it upheld this statute Congress might soon be passing more extreme laws of a similar character.

Assume that too many shoes are being manufactured throughout the nation; that the market is saturated, the price depressed, the factories running half-time, the employes suffering. Upon the principle of the statute in question [in the A.A.A. case] Congress *might* authorize the Secretary of Commerce to enter into contracts with shoe manufacturers providing that each shall reduce his output and that the United States will pay him a fixed sum proportioned to such reduction, the money to make the payments to be raised by a tax on all retail shoe dealers or their customers.[16]

The justice gave other equally extreme examples of what Congress "might" do. It was no wonder that in his dissenting opinion Justice Stone said:

The suggestion that . . . [the power to tax] must now be curtailed by judicial fiat because it may be abused by unwise use hardly rises to the dignity of argument. So may judicial power be abused. . . .

A tortured construction of the Constitution is not to be justified by recourse to extreme examples of reckless congressional spending. . . . Such suppositions are addressed to the mind accustomed to believe that it is the business of courts to sit in judgment on the wisdom of legislative action. Courts are not the only agency of government that must be assumed to have the capacity to govern.[17]

[15] *Ibid.*, p. 67.

[16] *Ibid.*, p. 76. (Italics added.)

[17] *Ibid.*, p. 87.

Professor Thomas Reed Powell of the Harvard Law School calls this technique which Sutherland, Roberts, and other justices have used "the parade of the imaginary horribles." Of course, as Justice Stone indicates, the use of the technique has an obvious logical weakness. By its very nature almost any political power is capable of being abused. If a reasonable exercise of a power is to be declared void because to sanction it might encourage the possessor of the power to go on and use it in unreasonable fashion, the courts would find it necessary to invalidate nearly all governmental activity. Moreover, it is obvious, as Justice Holmes once suggested in a dissenting opinion by way of a reply to the use of the imaginary-horribles technique, that the Supreme Court continues to sit year after year and that it is time enough for it to call a halt when Congress or a state legislature actually attempts to adopt some of the preposterous policies which some of the justices seem so much to fear.[18]

The Issue of Statute Motivation

A fifth rule in the long list of traditions with which the Court has surrounded its exercise of judicial review is one to the effect that when a statute is seemingly valid on its face, the Court will not search for hidden, and possibly unconstitutional, motives that the legislature may or may not have had in mind when it passed the law. "No principle of our constitutional law is more firmly established than that this court may not, in passing upon the validity of a statute, enquire into the motives of Congress."[19] Or again, "If the legislation enacted has some reasonable relation to the exercise of . . . [a power] conferred by the Constitution, it cannot be invalidated because of the supposed motives which

[18]*Panhandle Oil Co.* v. *Knox* 277 U.S. 218, 223 (1928).

[19]*Hamilton* v. *Kentucky Distilleries Co.* 251 U.S. 146, 161 (1919).

induced it."[20] This tradition, like the benefit-of-the-doubt rule, may be traced back to Chief Justice Marshall, who in his opinion in *Fletcher* v. *Peck* said:

> If the title [under a contract] be plainly deduced from a legislative act, which the legislature might constitutionally pass . . . a court . . . cannot sustain a suit brought by one individual against another founded on the allegation that the act is a nullity, in consequence of the impure motives which influenced certain members of the legislature which passed the law.[21]

Again, to the layman it would seem as though there are cases in which the Court has disregarded its own rule. For example, there is a series of cases in which the Court has invalidated federal laws purporting to be exercises of the taxing power. These laws were admittedly tax measures, but the Court permitted itself to be influenced by the assertion that Congress seemed in these laws not so anxious to raise revenue as to regulate some social or economic evil by placing a heavy tax burden upon it. The most famous of these cases is *Bailey* v. *Drexel Furniture Company,* in which the Court declared a tax measure void because it felt that Congress's real purpose was an unconstitutional one—the federal regulation of child labor.[22] Much the same thing was true of the Court's decision in the first child labor case, *Hammer* v. *Dagenhart.* On its face the law in question was clearly a regulation of interstate commerce, but the Court invalidated it because it felt the commerce power was being used to accomplish an unconstitutional purpose—the prohibition of child labor. The Court's decision in the case makes its position clear:

[20]*United States* v. *Doremus* 249 U.S. 86, 93 (1919).
[21]6 Cranch 87, 131 (1810).
[22]259 U.S. 20 (1922).

The thing *intended* to be accomplished by this statute is the denial of the facilities of interstate commerce to those manufacturers in the States who employ children within the prohibited ages. The act *in its effect* does not regulate transportation among the States, but *aims* to standardize the ages at which children may be employed in mining and manufacturing within the States.[23]

Or again in *Foster-Fountain Packing Company* v. *Haydel,* the Court invalidated a state law forbidding the exportation from the state of shrimp from which the shell and head had not been removed, on the ground that it was not motivated by a valid desire to conserve natural resources, as the legislature claimed, but rather by an unconstitutional wish to favor the state's own industries.[24]

Here, too, there has been a good deal of hairsplitting in an effort to refute the argument that the Court sometimes violates one of its own rules. It is argued that there is no reason why the Court should not determine whether the "purpose" or "intent" of the legislative body has been a proper one at the same time that it claims it is not interested in "motive." But the layman may well wonder how the Court can distinguish between such concepts as purpose, intent, or motive, in determining how far it may go in trying to decide what was in a legislature's mind at the time it passed a law.[25]

Partial Validation of Statutes

A sixth self-imposed rule of the Court concerns the situation of partial constitutionality. Is a statute valid in part, and invalid in part? In that case, the Court has repeatedly said,

[23]247 U.S. 251, 271–72 (1918). (Italics added.)

[24]278 U.S. 1 (1928).

[25]See Dodd, *op. cit.* (above, n. 2), p. 51, n. for a brief discussion of this point.

if the valid part can stand by itself it will be sustained. "It is elementary that the same statute may be in part constitutional and in part unconstitutional, and if the parts are wholly independent of each other, that which is constitutional may stand while that which is unconstitutional will be rejected."[26] But it must be noted that the Court has here imposed an important qualification to the operation of this rule—the parts of a statute must be separate and independent of each other if the valid portions are to be upheld. Who is to say whether the parts of any statute are so separable? Obviously, such a determination may often be very difficult. Accordingly, taking their cue from this oft-repeated rule, in the laws they enact legislative bodies have followed the practice of specifying their desire that all valid portions are to be preserved even though other portions be invalidated by the courts.

In spite of the fact that this self-imposed rule of judicial review supposedly represents an unvarying tradition, there are cases in which the courts seem to have disregarded the express wish of a legislative body by striking down an entire statute because part of it was invalid. No better illustration can be provided than the treatment given the original Guffey Coal Act by the Supreme Court. The act as passed by Congress provided essentially for two quite different things—federal control of wages and hours in coal mining, and federal control of prices in the distribution and sale of coal. In the minds of a majority of the justices, the first part was unconstitutional. The question then arose whether the second part could be separated from the first part and allowed to stand by itself. Congress, in unmistakable terms in the statute, had anticipated and answered the question in the affirmative. But the Court ruled that Congress could not have meant what it had so clearly said, and that, since the second part of the law would not constitute a well-rounded, complete statute by

[26] *Pollock* v. *Farmers' Loan & Trust Co.* 158 U.S. 601, 635 (1895).

itself, it must fall with the first part.[27] Whereupon Congress promptly proved that it *had* meant what it had said by re-enacting the second portion as an act by itself. This second Guffey Coal Act was finally upheld by the Supreme Court in 1940.[28] Thus this episode would seem to indicate that the rule of partial constitutionality is capable of being used by the Court about as it sees fit.

Political Questions

Finally, the Supreme Court has established a tradition to the effect that it will not decide questions of constitutionality in cases presenting so-called "political questions." Here, says the Court, are certain issues of constitutionality which only the political arms of government can decide. For example, the Court has ruled that whether or not a state actually has "a republican form of government," as guaranteed by the Constitution, is a political question which it will not attempt to answer. Instead it is up to Congress and the president to settle such a point.

Clearly the category of political questions—particularly its extent—becomes a very important matter, for it is almost as though the Court in these cases renounces the power of judicial review and refuses to pass upon the constitutionality of the acts of other departments of government. Unfortunately, in so far as it offers any clear-cut, intelligible, and unvarying tradition of judicial review, this rule is hardly more satisfactory than those which have already been considered. For just what is a *political* question, anyway? Obviously the answer is up to the Court. And it has been suggested that when the Court, for reasons of strategy or otherwise, has wished to refrain from the exercise of its supervisory power over the rest of our American political system, it has

[27]*Carter* v. *Carter Coal Co.* 298 U.S. 238 (1936).
[28]*Sunshine Anthracite Coal Co.* v. *Adkins* 310 U.S. 381 (1940).

had merely to call the question at hand a political one to escape from the onus of providing an answer.[29] There is little doubt that the Court, by means of this safe exit, actually has avoided some decidedly embarrassing issues in which it was much easier to render no decision at all. For example, basing its refusal at least in part on this doctrine of lack of jurisdiction in political questions, the Court has avoided cracking such hard nuts as the legitimacy of Dorr's Rebellion in Rhode Island, the validity of the Initiative and Referendum in Oregon, the constitutionality of the Reconstruction Acts following the Civil War, and the continuing vitality of the pending Child Labor Amendment to the federal Constitution fifteen years after Congress submitted it to the states.[30]

It is obvious from the nature and variety of these cases that the extent to which judicial review has been rendered nonoperative, on the ground that certain questions are "political" in character, is quite uncertain. It is extremely unlikely that many, if any, constitutional experts foresaw the nature of the decision in *Coleman* v. *Miller,* a case attacking the pending child labor amendment to the Constitution. It was argued that because the amendment had been pending for more than a reasonable number of years, without being accepted by the necessary number of states, and also because certain state legislatures which had originally rejected the amendment had

[29]See M. Finkelstein, "Judicial Self-Limitation," 37 *Harvard Law Review* (1923) 338; I *Selected Essays* 397, and M. F. Weston, "Political Questions," 38 *Harvard Law Review* (1925) 296; I *Selected Essays* 418. The latter presents an argument that the Court has not consciously used the "political question" device to escape from embarrassing cases but has merely been observing the requirements of the constitutional principle of separation of powers in refusing to encroach upon the powers of the executive and legislative departments.

[30]*Luther* v. *Borden* 7 Howard 1 (1849); *Pacific States Telephone & Telegraph Co.* v. *Oregon* 223 U.S. 118 (1912); *Mississippi* v. *Johnson* 4 Wallace 475 (1867); *Georgia* v. *Stanton* 6 Wallace 50 (1867); *Coleman* v. *Miller* 307 U.S. 433 (1939).

later improperly ratified it, the Court should declare the pending amendment null and void. This a majority of the justices refused to do on the ground that both of the points raised against the amendment were in the nature of political questions which could be answered only by Congress.[31] In the previous decisions of the Court on the amending process there was little to suggest that the Court might dispose of the *Coleman* case in the way it did. Indeed, the Court in previous cases involving constitutional amendments had passed upon and decided the legal points raised.[32] Actually, the nine justices had great difficulty in arriving at a majority decision in *Coleman* v. *Miller,* as is shown by the fact that three separate majority opinions were written and that in the dissenting opinion two justices denied that the issue of the time element was a political question. There is no intention to criticize here the decision in *Coleman* v. *Miller,* for it was an eminently sensible one. The only purpose in this discussion is to indicate that the Court's unexpected use of the political question rule to avoid passing on the constitutional issues in the case proves that the rule is highly flexible and uncertain.

, *Conclusions*

Two conclusions may be suggested as to the operation of these traditional limitations on judicial review. In the first place, they are far from being fixed or conclusive, and seem quite capable of being used in a variety of ways. The result is, of course, that the free choice of the Court in controversial cases is considerably increased. There is apparently no rule or tradition of judicial review to which the Court has always rigidly adhered. Every one of the rules of judicial review

[31]307 U.S. 433.

[32]See *Hawke* v. *Smith* 253 U.S. 221 (1920); *Dillon* v. *Gloss* 256 U.S. 368 (1921); *Leser* v. *Garnett* 258 U.S. 130 (1922).

seems at some time to have been subject to exceptions or qualifications. Their chief significance probably lies in the conscious strategic use which the Court has made of them. They are often available as props to strengthen the particular decision which the Court has chosen to render and have frequently had no small value in enabling the Court to support the view that judicial review is subject to many limitations which have been self-imposed by the justices. There has been no period in our history in which judicial review has not been vigorously attacked by some faction or party, and it is not surprising that the Supreme Court should have endeavored to forestall as much of this criticism as possible by seeming to hold the exercise of this controversial power within specific and reasonable limits. But it is significant that many of the repeated assertions of these limiting rules have been made in opinions *invalidating legislation.*

The numerous and conspicuous departures from these rules have perhaps been inevitable. For the most part these rules are of such a character that they cannot always be followed in an absolutely consistent manner. At the same time they have been followed so often that it would be misleading to suggest that they have had no significance at all. Unquestionably there have been justices who have, for example, both consciously and conscientiously favored giving a law the benefit of the doubt. In upholding the constitutionality of a Massachusetts compulsory vaccination law which had been vigorously challenged, Justice Harlan, speaking for the majority of the Court, asserted that it was the Court's rule not to invalidate such a law unless it was "beyond all question, a plain, palpable invasion of rights secured by the fundamental law," and he went on to conclude, "Whatever may be thought of the expediency of this statute, it cannot be affirmed to be, beyond question, in palpable conflict with the Constitution."[33]

[33]*Jacobson* v. *Massachusetts* 197 U.S. 11, 31 (1905).

Moreover, in cases where it may have seemed that, in voiding certain statutes, a majority of the justices were failing to observe one or more of the traditions of judicial review, dissenting justices have often vigorously insisted that the Court should adhere to them more rigidly. For instance, Justice Holmes in his dissenting opinions repeatedly insisted that the Court be more consistent in following its rule that a challenged statute be given the benefit of the doubt. Again, as has already been mentioned, Justice Brandeis in one of his dissenting opinions strongly reminded the Court of its traditions of self-limitation and even spoke of "a series of rules under which it [the Court] has avoided passing upon *a large part of all the constitutional questions pressed upon it for decision.*"[34]

Second, in so far as adherence to these traditional limitations has actually led the Supreme Court to avoid "passing upon a large part" of the constitutional issues that have come before it, the inevitable result has been to make the operation of judicial review quite sporadic. The insistence of the Court that it will pass only upon laws as they come before it in the course of bona fide litigation has sometimes served to delay indefinitely a final decision as to a statute's constitutionality. In the *Dred Scott* case the Court invalidated a law that had been passed thirty-seven years before and which had already been repealed by Congress.[35] As recently as 1926 in the *Myers* case the Court declared unconstitutional a statute originally enacted in 1876 and still in force.[36] However, when it comes to the controversial economic and social legislation of the present era, any serious delay in the operation of judicial review is not to be expected. Important statutes such as the National Industrial Recovery Act, the Agricultural

[34]*Ashwander* v. *T.V.A.* 297 U.S. 288, 346 (1936). (Italics added.)
[35]*Dred Scott* v. *Sandford* 19 Howard 393 (1857).
[36]*Myers* v. *United States* 272 U.S. 52 (1926).

Adjustment Act, and the Wagner Act have all been passed upon by the Supreme Court within two or three years after their passage by Congress.

On the other hand, the sporadic quality of judicial review is increased by the difficulty which potential litigants sometimes experience in attempting to bring a law to the test of the Court. Occasionally Congress so words a statute, or the statute is of such a nature, as to make a test virtually impossible. This has been true, for instance, of the Reciprocal Tariff Act of 1934. Because of the way in which this legislation operates, opportunities to challenge its constitutionality in the course of litigation are almost nonexistent. The same is true of nearly all acts appropriating funds to finance governmental activities. A taxpayer may try to challenge the validity of some questionable expenditure, but it is very difficult for him to prove to the Court that the tax payments from his pocket are being used to finance the alleged improper activity. The federal Maternity Act of 1921, which made available federal funds for use by the states in reducing maternal and infant mortality and in fostering the health of mothers and infants, was never passed upon by the Supreme Court. There was some reason to doubt the constitutionality of such a use of federal funds, but attempts by the state of Massachusetts and by an individual taxpayer to test the statute failed when the Court ruled that neither plaintiff was able to show any justiciable interest in the matter. As to the individual plaintiff, the Court said: "The right of a taxpayer to enjoin the execution of a federal appropriation act, on the ground that it is invalid and will result in taxation for illegal purposes, has never been passed upon by this Court."[37]

Whether this sporadic quality of judicial review is a thing to be applauded or deplored perhaps depends upon one's

[37]*Massachusetts* v. *Mellon; Frothingham* v. *Mellon* 262 U.S. 447, 486 (1923).

attitude toward judicial review itself. To the critic of this judicial power anything that lessens its operation may represent that much gain, whereas the champion of judicial review may oppose any condition that makes the operation of this power less complete than it might be. Both, however, might well feel that because the practice of judicial review has been neither complete nor entirely lacking its status is rather unsatisfactory.

In any case we have seen that judicial review does have certain limitations as to scope. We may now observe certain generally unrecognized aspects of this power which serve strongly to offset any minimizing tendency resulting from the power's limitations.

Chapter IX

The Scope of Judicial Review: Judicial Interpretation of Statutes and Review of Administrative Rulings

In the century and a half that has passed since the days of the Constitutional Fathers the Supreme Court of the United States has declared acts of Congress unconstitutional in some seventy-five cases.[1] During this same period Congress has passed slightly fewer than twenty-five thousand public acts.[2] It is thus apparent that Congress has suffered relatively few reversals at the hands of the Supreme Court. In fact, it is not even technically correct to say that seventy-five statutes have been invalidated, for in most of these cases only part of an act was annulled. For instance, in *Marbury* v. *Madison* the Court invalidated but one minor section of the Judiciary Act of 1789. According to one analysis of the situation the Court has declared void in their entirety only eight federal statutes. On the other hand, some eighty-four different provisions of law

---

[1]It is rather difficult, for technical reasons, to be absolutely accurate in determining the total number of these cases. See *Provisions of Federal Law Held Unconstitutional by the Supreme Court of the United States,* prepared by W. C. Gilbert of the Legislative Reference Service, Library of Congress (Washington: Government Printing Office, 1936) 1–91, for an analysis of cases in which federal laws have been invalidated and a further list of questionable cases.

[2]Charles G. Haines, "Judicial Review of Acts of Congress and the Need for Constitutional Reform," 45 *Yale Law Journal* (1936) 816; I *Selected Essays* 844, 855, n.

have in some respect been invalidated.[3] In any case, these invalidated laws constitute a very small percentage of the total output of congressional legislation. The fierce battles that have been fought over the Supreme Court and its power of judicial review make one inclined to wonder whether the whole controversy has not been a tempest in a teapot.

The Numerous Courts Exercising Judicial Review

Such a conclusion would be based upon a wholly inadequate concept of the extent of judicial review. This power of the judiciary in the United States is a far more extensive phenomenon than the mere invalidation of acts of Congress by the Supreme Court. In the first place, this judicial power is exercised by virtually all American courts. In addition to the Supreme Court there are ten federal circuit courts of appeals and some eighty-six federal district courts which share this power. Nor is the process of judicial review confined solely to the field of national government. The courts of forty-eight states review the acts of forty-eight state governments, legislative and executive departments alike, for compliance with the requirements of state constitutions as well as with those of the federal Constitution. Moreover, federal courts may invalidate state laws, and even provisions in state constitutions, if they violate the national Constitution. And state courts may invalidate federal laws, although only for violation of the national Constitution and not for violation of state constitutions. Consequently there is, as a rule, no lack of opportunity for a private litigant to get a case into court and then to raise the issue of constitutionality.

Of course, it is true that virtually all of the decisions of lower federal and state courts having to do with the validity

[3]*Provisions of Federal Law Held Unconstitutional, op. cit.* (above, n. 1), pp. 91–95.

of laws under the federal Constitution are ordinarily appealed to and reviewed by the Supreme Court, so that in the final analysis the definitive power of judicial review rests with that one Court. Nonetheless, the lower courts often exercise a rather wide discretion in the use they make of the power of judicial review. This is particularly true during the period, often quite long, between the appearance of a new constitutional problem and its settlement by a final decision of the Supreme Court. The Judiciary Act of 1937 has speeded up the process of carrying appeals of constitutional issues to the Supreme Court, but the lower courts still necessarily retain considerable, even though temporary, power to check the legislative department of government. Robert Jackson has pointed out that in 1935 and 1936, when the constitutionality of the New Deal was being argued in the courts, some sixteen hundred injunctions restraining the enforcement of acts of Congress were granted by more than one hundred federal judges, who "assumed the power to nullify acts of Congress."[4] These numerous and often conflicting decisions seriously hampered and curtailed the administration of national policies for a matter of years during a critical period. Although final decisions, many of them favorable to the government, were eventually rendered by the Supreme Court, one may raise the question as to how much momentum in the nation's program was lost during this period when the lower courts vied with one another in exercising their power of judicial review.

The Effect of a Decision Invalidating Legislation

In the second place, it should be remembered that one decision invalidating a law may well have the practical effect of bringing to an end efforts to enforce other similar laws, federal or state, and it may also deter Congress and many state

[4] Jackson, *op. cit.* (Chap. II, n. 11), p. 115.

legislatures from passing further legislation in the same field. When in 1923 the Supreme Court, after considerable vacillation, declared void a federal statute prescribing minimum wages for women and children in the District of Columbia, the decision had the practical effect of rendering inoperative many similar laws which had been enacted by the states.[5] Or, to refer to a Supreme Court decision invalidating a state law, it has been pointed out that the decision in *Ribnik* v. *McBride,* annulling a New Jersey statute regulating employment agencies, automatically determined "the constitutionality of similar statutes in perhaps twenty other states."[6]

Moreover, the enactment of new statutes is strongly influenced by the potential threat of judicial invalidation. Hardly a major bill comes before Congress for consideration without the issue of constitutionality being thoroughly debated. This issue often figures as prominently in the discussion of these bills as does any other single topic. Probably this is as it should be, but the situation is somewhat anomalous. The uncertainty which may well mark previous Supreme Court rulings as to similar laws usually results in members of Congress advocating all possible points of view. Consequently the issue of constitutionality is apt to remain a rather perplexing one. It has occasionally been suggested that since the courts insist upon acting as guardians of the Constitution, they might as well act as the keepers of the constitutional consciences of all legislative and administrative offices. President Roosevelt perhaps had some such thought in mind when at the time of the congressional debate over the first Guffey Coal Act he urged a congressional committee to give favorable consideration to the bill even though it might have reasonable doubts about the bill's constitutionality. He was, of course, bitterly criticized for such "flouting" of the

[5] *Adkins* v. *Children's Hospital* 261 U.S. 525 (1923).
[6] 277 U.S. 350 (1928). Dodd, *op. cit.* (Chap. VIII, n. 2), p. 97.

Constitution. But he might have answered his critics, if he had chosen, by pointing to an experience that occurred to President Taft. That chief executive, who later became chief justice of the United States and who was a very able student of constitutional law in his own right, vetoed in 1913 the Webb-Kenyon Act on the ground that it was unconstitutional. Congress proceeded to repass the law over his veto, and when the Act was later challenged before the Supreme Court it was upheld.[7]

Significance of Particular Decisions

In the third place, it may well be asserted that the decisions of the Supreme Court invalidating federal statutes, while few in number, have profoundly affected the course of the nation's social policies. Even granting that most of the seventy-five cases in which federal legislation has been voided have concerned statutory provisions of minor importance, and that only a handful of cases remain in which any great issue was at stake, the effect of judicial invalidation of congressional acts has been very important. This has been particularly true of the period since the World War, although one can point to such decisions in the earlier period as that in the *Dred Scott* case, which helped to bring about the Civil War, and later the income tax decision in *Pollock* v. *Farmers' Loan and Trust Company,* which held back for a generation the development of an equitable federal tax program. But in the post-World War period one can hardly deny that the invalidation of the child labor laws, an important portion of the Federal Corrupt Practices Act, the National Industrial Recovery Act, the Agricultural Adjustment Act, the Railway

[7]See *Clark Distilling Co.* v. *Western Maryland Ry. Co.* 242 U.S. 311 (1917). For an argument that judicial review has had but a limited effect upon legislative debate and activity see Oliver P. Field, "Judicial Review as an Instrument of Government," I *Selected Essays* 733, 740–45.

Workers' Pension Act, the Farm Mortgage Relief Act, the Bituminous Coal Act, and the Municipal Bankruptcy Act has definitely affected the program of the national government. It is true that one or two of these decisions have later been reversed by the Supreme Court and that others have been qualified and restricted as to effect, but in the meantime they have operated to curb important federal policies. Edith Abbott, sister of the late Grace Abbott who was head of the federal Children's Bureau under the first child labor law, has commented in very strong terms on the recent reversal of *Hammer* v. *Dagenhart*. One may not approve her intense and somewhat embittered criticism of the Court, but one cannot deny that she is right about the widespread and lasting effect of *Hammer* v. *Dagenhart*. She comments as follows:

Hammer v. Dagenhart is overruled! But what of the army of children who have come and gone from the mills and factories and lumber yards, the millions of weary days of work, and the lost vision of an education to do a proper share of the world's work? These children, many of them now living as unemployed workers, should indict the Supreme Court of these United States for their stunted minds and broken lives. My sister once said in a frequently quoted address that you could not make up to children deprived of proper food and proper education for one year by giving them a substitute some other year. Nor can the Supreme Court make compensation to the children whose deprivations and sufferings were caused by a judicial decision now said to have been wrong.[8]

Judicial Review of Administrative Rulings

Finally, judicial review in practice has included the review by the courts of the rulings of administrative agencies which are made in the course of statute interpretation and enforcement. Defining the scope of judicial review broadly enough

[8]104 *New Republic* (March 24, 1941) 408.

to include this last process is perhaps a controversial matter, for it will be argued that judicial review in its proper technical sense is concerned only with the testing of governmental acts for compliance with the higher law of a constitution. There need be no quibbling about the definition of terms. But certainly, in any discussion of the work of the United States Supreme Court there is too great a tendency to give a disproportionate attention to the cases in which statutes have been invalidated outright, and relatively little attention to the cases in which statutes are merely interpreted and applied. Undoubtedly the former type of case is ordinarily more spectacular than the latter. Moreover, considered individually, they are apt to be more significant. A *Schechter* decision invalidating the N.I.R.A. or an *Adkins* decision outlawing minimum wage legislation is of profound importance because of the way in which it necessarily curtails the economic policies of the nation or the states. One such decision is admittedly a more serious matter than a single decision of the Supreme Court perhaps interpreting a minor provision of the Wagner Act preparatory to applying that statute to a particular situation. Nonetheless, it has sometimes been suggested that this power of the courts to give meaning to the cold, brief words of a technical statute is at least as significant in its influence upon the law under which we live as is the power of the courts to destroy completely an occasional statute by ruling that it violates the Constitution. It will be recalled that within his concept of the term "judicial supremacy" Professor Haines includes both of these aspects of judicial power.[9] If one is primarily interested in the total power of the Supreme Court to participate in the governing process, it is a serious mistake to give attention solely to the outright invalidation of statutes. Since 1936 the Court has not invalidated a single federal law, and state laws have been declared void in

[9] See above, page 24.

only a handful of cases. Yet the work of the Court continues to be highly controversial at numerous points. Much of this controversy is centered about the exercise of judicial power in the interpretation of statutes and the reviewing of the work of administrative agencies, two functions, which, as will shortly be shown, are closely related to each other.

In recent years Congress has found it increasingly necessary to word its great statutes in broad, general terms, leaving many of the specific details to be added within broadly defined limits by the officers called upon to enforce them. These latter include the members of both the administrative and the judicial departments of government. Moreover, at one time or another, each has been vigorously attacked for the manner in which it has filled in such details. Recently, the great administrative commissions of the national government have been bearing the brunt of such criticism. Such New Deal creations as the Securities Exchange Commission and the National Labor Relations Board, in particular, have been widely condemned for the way in which they have implemented the statutes which Congress has charged them with enforcing. But in their day, the courts, too, have been repeatedly attacked on the same ground. Particularly, the charge of "judicial legislation" has been hurled against the courts. This phrase has been employed to convey an improper connotation in the sense that judges have endeavored to *make* law where it was only intended that they *enforce* law. Whether the suggestion of impropriety in this process is justifiable is a controversial matter. That judges do in fact "legislate" is undeniable.

In the remainder of this chapter we shall examine, first, the extent to which the courts and the administrative departments and commissions do necessarily participate in the lawmaking process. Second, the troublesome problem which results from the rivalry between administrative and judicial agencies in this process will receive our attention. The relative roles which these two divisions of our government are to play in the implementation of statutes and, more specifically, the exact relationship that should exist between them constitute one of the most substantial and controversial political issues of the day. Only the broad outline of the problem can be here examined.[10]

Participation of Courts and Administrative Agencies in the Lawmaking Process

That the judiciary does in fact help make law has already been illustrated.[11] This discussion might be extended almost indefinitely, for there is hardly an important national statute that has not been given much of its real meaning through the operation of judicial power. For instance, the original Sherman Act of 1890, as worded by Congress, seemed to outlaw all combinations or trusts held to be in restraint of interstate commerce. Congress clearly used the word "every" in indicating the types of "combination" it had in mind. The only discretion which the courts were presumably to exercise in enforcing the statute was to make a factual finding as to whether a combination charged with violating the act really had been restraining trade. But after the passage of many years, marked by much uncertainty on the part of the individual justices, the Supreme Court came finally to the somewhat surprising conclusion that the word "every" in the statute was synonymous with the word "unreasonable," and that, accordingly, only unreasonable combinations in restraint of trade were improper under the statute. Reasonable combinations in restraint of trade were all right. Needless to say,

[10]See J. Roland Pennock, *Administration and the Rule of Law* (New York: Farrar & Rinehart, Inc., 1941) for a full discussion of this problem.

[11]See above, Chapter I.

this decision in *Standard Oil Company* v. *United States* resulted in a storm of controversy in which the Court was charged with having indulged in "judicial legislation."[12]

The role of the administrative agents in the implementation and enforcement of the Sherman Act has been almost as controversial as that of the courts. When Congress passed the Sherman Act it turned the work of enforcement over to one of the already existing executive agencies, the Department of Justice, rather than to a new and independent administrative commission. In fact, the first of this latter type of agency had only just been established three years before in 1887, when Congress set up the Interstate Commerce Commission. But for our purposes distinction between the old type of "executive" department and the newer "administrative" commission is unimportant and may be ignored.[13] Both play much the same part in the process we are examining. In any case, it is undeniable that the Department of Justice has had much to do with the implementation of the Sherman Act. In large part it has been up to that agency to determine whether a particular situation fell within the terms of the legislation and called for administrative efforts to enforce the act. The point needs little elaboration for in so far as the Department of Justice under succeeding administrations has sought alternately to limit or to expand the enforcement of the act as against the great variety of situations to which it might possibly be applied, it has been helping shape the *legislative* character of this national policy. For example, the applicability of the antitrust laws to labor union activities has always been a troublesome point. It is fair to say that Congress has never made its intentions in this respect abso-

[12]See *United States* v. *Trans-Missouri Freight Ass'n* 166 U.S. 290 (1897); *Standard Oil Co.* v. *United States* 221 U.S. 1 (1911).

[13]See Pennock, *op. cit.* (above, n. 10), pp. 3ff., for a discussion of the distinction between the terms "executive" and "administrative."

lutely clear. Accordingly, in so far as the Department of Justice has either refrained from attempts to apply the legislation to labor unions or, on the other hand, has assumed that they are subject to the control of such legislation it has been participating in the determination of legislative policy.

Another illustration will serve to show the manner in which administrative agencies and the courts find it necessary to interpret and implement statutes by rulings of their own, and will also introduce our second problem—the relative roles which these two agencies of government play in this process. When Congress enacted the National Labor Relations Act its purpose was twofold. In the first place, it guaranteed the right of workers to bargain collectively with their employers and encouraged them to form labor unions so that the process of collective bargaining might be facilitated. Second, it listed certain labor practices which were henceforth to be regarded as "unfair," and it forbade employers to continue them. Then Congress created a special administrative agency, the National Labor Relations Board, and charged it with the enforcement of the act.

Specific though the statute is as to the two main purposes it is to accomplish, it remains essentially a broad general statement of policy with many specific details to be filled in by the National Labor Relations Board during the process of enforcement. Let us take one example. Section 2 of the Wagner Act defines the word "employee" (with whom the employer is compelled to bargain collectively) as including "any individual whose work has ceased as a consequence of or in connection with any current labor dispute or because of any unfair labor practice." In other words, no worker ("employee") is to lose his status or privileges under the act just because he participates in a strike. Otherwise an employer could simply announce that any workers out on strike were fired and they would then lose the benefits provided by the

Wagner Act to employees. Now it happened that in the summer of 1936 the Fansteel Metallurgical Company became involved in a dispute with some of its workers. On its part it refused to bargain collectively with their union, hired a labor spy, tried to segregate the union president from his fellow workers, and generally violated the unfair labor practices section of the statute. Thereupon the workers engaged in a sitdown strike, and, as a consequence, the company fired them. Somewhat later these dismissed workers complained to the board and asked it to use its power to order their reinstatement to their jobs, on the ground that the act prevents an employer from dismissing his employees during the course of a labor dispute.

Unfortunately there was a factor present in the case which the wording of the statute did not seem to cover. This was the factor that a sit-down strike presumably violated state law in the state where this strike had occurred, and thus in the course of the "labor dispute" the workers had been guilty of using unlawful methods. How did this affect the situation? Did the Wagner Act continue to guarantee their status as employees all during the dispute, or did the use of illegal methods by the workers during the dispute cancel the protection provided them by the statute? Clearly the act did not say. Here was an instance where a rule would have to be promulgated by the agency administering the law. Accordingly the board made a careful study of the facts of the controversy and, no doubt considerably influenced by the admitted fact that both sides had violated laws during the controversy, concluded that the workers did retain their status as employees in spite of their improper tactics. So it ordered the Fansteel Company to reinstate them. Naturally the company balked at that and appealed the ruling of the board to the courts. Eventually the case reached the Supreme Court and there, in a seven-to-two decision, the justices reversed the ruling of the board and declared that it had erred in the detail which it had added to the original statute.[14] Instead, said the Court, it should have ruled the other way to the effect that the use by the workers of illegal methods during a labor dispute did result in a surrender of their privileged status as employees under the statute.

An evaluation of the roles of the National Labor Relations Board and of the Supreme Court in interpreting the Wagner Act in this case shows that each of these agencies was exercising a considerable measure of discretionary power. Obviously neither agency could be absolutely certain what Congress had really intended at this point, for it is doubtful if Congress had given the matter any thought. All either could do was to guess as to which interpretation of the act Congress would prefer. *The New York Times,* perhaps anticipating that the charge of "judicial legislation" would be made against the Court, editorialized as follows upon the decision in the *Fansteel* case: "It may surely be laid down as a sound principle of legislation that nothing should be left to judicial decision that the legislative body itself can reasonably be expected to clarify."[15] In other words, *The Times* was suggesting that Congress should have anticipated just this sort of situation when it was enacting the statute and have made clear what its intention was. Or having failed that, it should now amend the act so as to make it more specific and thus spare both the National Labor Relations Board and the Supreme Court the necessity of adding these details in controversial cases.

Reasonable though these suggestions may seem, they are something less than completely realistic. Congress cannot possibly word an original statute to make it so clear that it will cover every possible later development which may arise

[14]*N.L.R.B.* v. *Fansteel Metallurgical Corp.* 306 U.S. 240 (1939).
[15]*The New York Times,* March 1, 1939.

under it. It is asking too much to expect Congress to foresee the future completely, and should Congress make the attempt, its statutes would inevitably become so lengthy and so loaded down with technical details that they would lose much of their value. When a statute which vitally affects the interests of workers and employers alike to the extent that the Wagner Act does is being passed, it is highly desirable to keep it as simple and as intelligible as is humanly possible under the circumstances.

The second, and possibly implied, suggestion in *The Times* editorial is merely the old answer to the charge that the courts have been guilty of "judicial legislation." If a legislative body does not like the way in which the courts have read certain ideas into one of its statutes, it is absolutely free to amend the statute and prove the courts wrong by saying just exactly what it had meant originally, or at least what it does mean now. For example, it has long been argued that the failure of Congress to amend the Sherman Antitrust Act to the effect that it intended the law to cover reasonable trusts as well as unreasonable ones, proves that Congress was not dissatisfied with the Court's ruling in the *Standard Oil* case that only unreasonable trusts were covered by the act.

Such an argument unquestionably has much merit, but it does overlook a particularly important factor in the legislative process—the matter of timing. Except during an extreme crisis, Congress does not legislate easily. For better or for worse, we have deliberately chosen to make our national legislative process an exceedingly difficult and complex one. Overwhelmed as it is by the restraining effect of numerous checks and balances, our legislative system is simply not conducive to the easy and frequent passage of a variety of laws. The original Wagner Act was passed in 1935 only after a great deal of discussion and controversy. In a sense it took an unusual and fortuitous combination of circumstances to make

possible the passage of such a law at all. The same is true of
the more recent federal wages and hours act. Since the passage
of these two statutes numerous proposals for their amendment have been suggested. Some of the proposed amendments would undoubtedly change these laws in a direction
favorable to business, others would strengthen the legislation
from labor's point of view. Some would benefit the North,
some the South. Some are favored by the American Federation of Labor, some by the Congress of Industrial Organiza-
tions, and some by the United States Chamber of Commerce
or the National Association of Manufacturers. Thus there is
apt to be a sharp contrast in the attitudes and arguments
which interested pressure groups will present to Congress
under such circumstances. Accordingly, in view of clashing
interests such as these, and in view of the intricacies of the
legislative process, it is not surprising that Congress is slow
to revise an important statute. Therefore to argue that every
time Congress is displeased with any particular twist given to
one of its statutes by an administrative agency, or by the
courts in the course of the law's enforcement, it can easily
amend the law to make its intent clear, is to ignore one of
the important realities in the legislative process.

Of course, if one pays attention solely to the *theory* of democracy, it can be argued that when Congress enacts a
statute it does so because majority public opinion favors
such action; that when administrative agencies or the courts
add certain details to this statute while enforcing it, public
opinion will react one way or the other; and that if majority
public opinion is displeased it will quickly bring sufficient
pressure on Congress to secure legislation repudiating these
additions. But between such theory and the realities of the
political process there is a wide gulf. Can one assume that
when the Supreme Court in the *Standard Oil* case interpreted the Sherman Act so as to restrict it to unreasonable

trusts, the public approved such action, or even knew what was going on? It is perhaps true that an intelligent and vigorous public opinion in a democracy may go so far as to favor the regulation of monopoly, but it is not easy to persuade it to concern itself with the technicalities of that regulation. Thus the failure of Congress ever to repudiate that particular bit of judicial legislation simply proves that there has never existed a sufficiently strong positive pressure in the country at large, or in the halls of Congress, to force through such legislative action.

This state of affairs would seem to be inevitable. It is not that the democratic system is at fault. It is only that government is a complicated affair coping with almost hopelessly technical problems. Occasionally sufficient public opinion will take shape, and sufficient congressional majorities can be rallied to put through such great pieces of legislation as the Sherman or Wagner Acts. But once these statutes are passed it is likely to be a case of the "moving finger" of legislation, "having writ, moves on." The moment is gone, public opinion is diverted elsewhere, legislative coalitions dissolve and new ones take their place. It is only rarely that the scene can be reconstructed, the actors returned to their places on the stage, and an applauding audience restored to its seats. Once in a while this can be done. But to assume that the legislature is capable of following closely the work of the innumerable courts and administrative agencies to which it may have entrusted the interpretation and enforcement of its statutes, and capable furthermore of ratifying or repudiating the more or less continuous legislative rulings of these bodies, is to assume the impossible.

So it is perhaps inescapable in our governmental system that administrative and judicial bodies must remain free to exercise no small "power to govern," with little restraint from the legislative body except in so far as the statute it provides,

by way of a starting point, serves to hold administrative body
and court, alike, within certain limits. In this respect we shall
do well to recall our earlier discussion of constitutional principles. How can this participation of administrative and
judicial agencies in the legislative process be reconciled with
the principle of separation of powers? The answer is, in the
strict sense, it cannot. But we must also recall that this principle is by no means a strict one and that it is often counter-
balanced by the rival principle of checks and balances. Occasionally a congressional statute granting to an administrative
agency wide discretionary power by way of policy determination is challenged as to constitutionality by reference to the
symbolic principle of separation of powers. But, in this field
of constitutional interpretation at least, the courts have shown
a strong preference for the instrumental values of the Constitution and such statutes have seldom been invalidated, at least
on the ground that Congress has improperly attempted to
delegate away its legislative powers. In this matter, as is so
often true, we cannot do better in seeking a realistic answer
than to refer to the words of Justice Holmes. In a dissenting
opinion in a case in which the majority of the justices invalidated an act of the Philippine territorial legislature on the
ground that it attempted improperly to bestow executive
power upon certain members of the legislative branch contrary to the principle of separation of powers contained in the
Philippine Organic Act, he spoke as follows:

The great ordinances of the Constitution do not establish and
divide fields of black and white. Even the more specific of them
are found to terminate in a penumbra shading gradually from
one extreme to another. . . . It is said that the powers of Congress
cannot be delegated, yet Congress has established the Interstate
Commerce Commission, which does legislative, judicial and
executive acts, only softened by a *quasi;* . . . It does not seem to
need argument to show that however we may disguise it by

veiling words we do not and cannot carry out the distinction between legislative and executive action with mathematical precision and divide the branches into watertight compartments. . . .[16]

Relationship between Court and Administrative Agency

We may now turn to the matter of the rival roles played by administrative agency and court in the process of statute implementation. It is clear from an examination of the *Fansteel* case that the National Labor Relations Board and the Supreme Court had contradictory ideas as to the meaning of the Wagner Act at the point involved in the case. Moreover, because of the undeniable element of choice which each agency possessed in making its interpretation, it seems reasonable to suppose that both were influenced by certain outside considerations and pressures. The N.L.R.B. was generally sympathetic to labor. It undoubtedly concluded that since both sides had been guilty of illegal conduct, it was not unreasonable to interpret the statute so as to return both sides to the *status quo* which had prevailed before the dispute began. The Supreme Court, speaking through Chief Justice Hughes, was apparently primarily influenced by its traditional high regard for the sanctity of private property. Here the workers had committed an offense against private property, and this fact led the Court to prefer an interpretation of the Wagner Act which would penalize the workers for their offense by denying them a privilege otherwise extended by the law. The fact that during the dispute the employer had also been guilty of violating the law seemingly carried little weight with the Court.

From a point of view of constitutional procedure the Supreme Court occupied a superior position to the N.L.R.B. and consequently its point of view as to the disputed issue

[16]*Springer* v. *Philippine Islands* 277 U.S. 189, 209–11 (1928).

prevailed. At the same time, a strong argument can be advanced in support of the board's ruling in the case. In view of its exclusive concern with the labor problem and the Court's general concern with a wide variety of legal problems it is probable that the N.L.R.B. was better qualified to weigh the pros and cons of the dispute and then to make a proper ruling under the relevant statutory provisions. Perhaps in spite of this advantage it erred in its final judgment and the Supreme Court did well to reverse it. At the same time it would seem to be a sound principle that the courts should be generally slow to substitute their judgment as to the meaning of a statute for that of the special tribunal charged with the enforcement of the statute in the first instance. In a recent case in which the Supreme Court was reviewing an order issued by an administrative agency under a federal statute, Justice Stone made a very pertinent observation concerning the relationship that ought to prevail between administrative agency and court:

. . . in construing a statute setting up an administrative agency and providing for judicial review of its action, court and agency are not to be regarded as wholly independent and unrelated instrumentalities of justice, each acting in the performance of its prescribed statutory duty without regard to the appropriate function of the other in securing the plainly indicated objects of the statute. Court and agency are the means adopted to attain the prescribed end, and so far as their duties are defined by the words of the statute, those words should be construed so as to attain that end through coördinated action. Neither body should repeat in this day the mistake made by the courts of law when equity was struggling for recognition as an ameliorating system of justice; neither can rightly be regarded by the other as an alien intruder, to be tolerated if must be, but never to be encouraged or aided by the other in the attainment of the common end.[17]

[17]*United States* v. *Morgan* 307 U.S. 183, 191 (1939).

In contrast with Justice Stone's plea for "coördinated action" between administrative agency and court, of late there has been a strong tendency to attack the administrative agency's record in the work of statute enforcement. It is asserted that these agencies are often prejudiced in favor of the claims of particular pressure groups, that in conducting hearings they fail to observe the traditional rules of judicial procedure which are designed to safeguard the rights of all interested parties, that they act as prosecutor, judge, and jury, and that accordingly their orders and rulings are often arbitrary and improper. If such a view were to prevail it would subordinate the administrative agency to the superior power of the courts. Indeed, such criticism recently culminated in the introduction of a bill in Congress providing for a considerable measure of judicial supervision over the activities of administrative agencies. This was the Logan-Walter bill around which a storm of controversy raged and which was finally passed by Congress, only to be killed by a presidential veto. In the first place, this bill would have authorized the courts to play a part in the preparation of the rules and regulations by which the various administrative agencies of the federal government conduct hearings, issue rulings, and go about their business generally. Second, it would also have subjected the rulings of these latter agencies in specific cases, arising under the statutes they enforce, to a greater measure of judicial review and possible alteration or reversal by the courts. Would it be wise to establish this increased judicial authority?

Without attempting to discuss all of the details of the problem or the need for some such legislation, we may comment upon certain aspects of the situation which are pertinent to our subject. One point to be made here is that the Logan-Walter bill would have granted little entirely new authority to the courts; it would merely have increased an already existing power to review the work of administrative agencies. This is particularly true of the Supreme Court, which has for fifty years and more claimed the authority to scrutinize the correctness of administrative rulings in cases brought to it on appeal. Our brief examination of the collaboration, if not co-operation, between administrative and judicial agencies in the interpretation and enforcement of the Sherman and Wagner Acts has shown that there is nothing novel in the proposal that courts be permitted to exercise supervisory powers over administrative agencies. In fact, that part of the work of the Supreme Court which involves review of the rulings of administrative agencies has increased in recent years until it has assumed substantial proportions. During the 1939 term of the Court thirty-four of its opinions, or 24 per cent of the total number handed down in the course of the year, pertained to litigation which had originated before administrative tribunals.[18] Consequently the debate over the Logan-Walter bill was centered about the question of the desirable degree of such judicial supervisory power.

Second, it is obvious from much of the discussion occasioned by the proposed Logan-Walter bill that what is obviously needed is a more adequate understanding and appreciation of the character and caliber of the administrative agencies in our national government. There are now dozens of these administrative agencies enforcing scores of federal statutes ranging over a wide field. Many of these statutes are extremely technical and deal with such difficult and diverse subjects as radio broadcasting, stock exchange practices, railroad consolidations, fair trade and business practices, supervision of aviation, the fixing of minimum wages and maximum hours, and the development of national defense, to mention only a very few of the more important and obvious

[18]*Annual Report of the Attorney General of the United States, 1940* (Washington: Government Printing Office, 1940) 47.

ones. Consequently it is not surprising that many of the members of these agencies are technical experts eminently qualified for service in their respective fields. To cite but one example, Mr. Joseph Eastman, for many years the outstanding member of the Interstate Commerce Commission, is generally recognized as one of the leading authorities on railroad problems, either within or outside government circles. Moreover, a factor which must not be overlooked in any discussion of this problem is the presence of lawyers in the important administrative offices of the national government. In view of the legal talents possessed by many of these officers it is somewhat curious to see how much difference a mere title or a name makes. For example, it is quite obvious that the work of many of the commissioners identified with the numerous independent administrative agencies of the national government is at certain points not unlike that of a judge. They are called upon to interpret and apply statutes in specific situations involving private individuals and corporations. Many of them are able lawyers and might perhaps bear the title of "judge." Had Congress chosen to organize the National Labor Relations Board as a special "court," and it could conceivably have done so without any undue distortion of the meaning of that word, at least as to the "quasi-judicial" aspects of the Board's duties, the powers and duties of the office would have remained very much the same, but it is quite likely that its treatment at the hands of the public would have been somewhat different. The suggestion here intended is not that the American people should be persuaded to look upon a labor board member with the same feeling of awe and reverence that one views a judge, but rather that they see through the impressive trappings of the courts and the judicial robes of judges to find there an aspect of our governmental system that is not materially different from much of the machinery which we have erected within our administrative division of government. Perhaps the courts have the best of it when it comes to the employment of proper procedural forms with a view to protecting the rights of individuals under the law. But even this may at least be questioned, and it is of some significance that there is a tendency within our judicial system, particularly in state and local government, to develop special courts and special modes of procedure which often involve dispensing with many of the external and traditional aspects of judicial procedure. Of course, it must be conceded that the internal organization of many of the independent administrative commissions is far from satisfactory and that remedial legislation on this subject may be needed. There is strong argument that the quasi-judicial powers should be segregated from the more definitely administrative duties of these agencies and perhaps vested in separate tribunals.[19] However, the reorganization of these commissions is a highly controversial topic, and it is quite certain in any case that quasi-judicial power will continue to be exercised by such agencies at some point in the administrative process. Thus the problem of judicial review by the courts of such exercise of power will presumably not be solved by the mere internal reform and reorganization of the administrative agencies.

It is of further significance to note the successful records enjoyed by some of the administrative agencies in avoiding reversals at the hands of the Supreme Court. For example, the National Labor Relations Board has achieved an amazingly good record. According to one count, in the first four years of its existence, of the twenty-four cases carried from its rulings to the Supreme Court, that tribunal sustained the board in nineteen instances, modified its rulings in three, and

[19]See Robert E. Cushman, "The Problem of the Independent Regulatory Commissions," *Report of the President's Committee on Administrative Management* (Washington: Government Printing Office, 1937).

reversed it in only two.[20] Likewise, the record of the N.L.R.B. and the other administrative commissions, collectively, as to Supreme Court reversals may readily be compared with the similar record of federal district and circuit courts of appeals. Although they are presided over by "judges," their decisions have been very frequently overridden by the Supreme Court. For example, during its 1937 term the Supreme Court reviewed and disposed of on their merits nineteen cases coming from the Third Circuit Court of Appeals, at the time a notoriously reactionary court. The Supreme Court reversed its decisions in every one of these nineteen cases. Moreover, the record of the other nine circuit courts was not too good. In the same year the percentage of reversals by the Supreme Court in cases disposed of on their merits was not below 50 per cent for a single circuit court.[21]

The *1938 Annual Report of the Attorney General of the United States* contained a very interesting study of the opinions of the Supreme Court which reviewed decisions of the lower federal courts involving rulings of administrative agencies over a period of ten years. This study showed that the administrative agencies have had a much better record in avoiding reversals at the hands of the Supreme Court than have the lower courts. During this period the Supreme Court disposed of 257 cases falling within the above category. The decisions of the lower courts were sustained in 139 cases, or 54 per cent, and reversed in 117 cases, or 46 per cent. But the original rulings of the administrative agency were affirmed in 166 cases, or 64 per cent, reversed in 89 cases, or 35 per cent,

[20]*Time* (March 25, 1940) 21.

[21]*Annual Report of the Attorney General of the United States, 1938* (Washington: Government Printing Office, 1938) 31. Of course, the Supreme Court refused to review a great many circuit court decisions and thereby, in effect, affirmed them. The figures given pertain only to cases actually reviewed and disposed of on their merits.

and modified in 2 cases.[22] Thus, so far as the judgment of the Supreme Court carries weight, it would seem that the administrative agencies have been more nearly correct in their enforcement of law than have the lower federal courts. The figures for the 1939 term are even more impressive. In that year the Supreme Court sustained 76 per cent of the administrative orders which it considered, but affirmed decisions of the lower courts involving administrative orders in only 41 per cent of such cases. The percentage of affirmances of lower court decisions in all cases reviewed, other than those involving administrative orders, was only 39.[23]

Of course, much the same comment may be made concerning these data as can be made on the infrequency of Supreme Court decisions invalidating federal statutes outright. If the administrative agencies have such a good record in avoiding reversal of their rulings by the Supreme Court, why should there be any opposition to judicial review of administrative rulings? The answer to this question is much the same as that to the similar question pertaining to the judicial review of statutes. The Supreme Court may sustain more administrative rulings than it reverses, but some of the reversals have occurred in important cases, and the results have profoundly affected and altered the course of national policy. For example, it has been pointed out that the numerous reversals which the rulings of the Federal Trade Commission have met at the hands of the Court have been of very great importance:

The Federal Trade Commission has jurisdiction over unfair competitive trade practices. The legislative history of the act shows that Congress hoped to build up an administrative law of unfair competition by the decisions of a body of independent experts. This, however, the courts did not permit. In an early case

[22]*Ibid.*, p. 43.

[23]*1940 Report of the Attorney General, op. cit.* (above, n. 18), p. 47.

involving the Commission's power the Supreme Court held that "It is for the courts, not the commission, ultimately to determine as a matter of law what they [the words 'unfair method of competition'] include." Instead of permitting the concept of unfair competition to be developed by an administrative process of trial and error, the Court has kept it fairly rigidly confined to common law precedents.[24]

Conclusions

Accordingly, it is desirable to raise the issue of the respective roles to be played by administrative agency and court in the business of interpreting and applying to particular situations the doubtful language of a statute. It cannot be denied that some such agency must often exercise a very considerable measure of discretionary power in preferring a certain interpretation. But the division of this power between an administrative body and a court is not easily arranged. There is no need to suggest that judges be deprived of all opportunity to check the work of administrators. After all, a judge may very well be something of a technical specialist himself and have good reason to check an administrator as to the meaning of a statute. But we do need to remember that a judge is apt to approach the task of interpreting a law in much the same fashion as does the administrator. In both instances, personal prejudices, impersonal technical considerations, the weight of tradition, and the influence of public opinion will combine in varying amounts to determine the result. Whether a better mixture of these forces will occur in the mind of a judge or in the mind of an administrator is not easily ascertained. But in view of the respective functions performed by these two agencies in the total governmental process it is probably reasonable to argue that a court as a general rule should be

[24]Cushman, *op. cit.* (above, n. 19), p. 227. The case referred to is *Federal Trade Commission* v. *Gratz* 253 U.S. 421 (1920).

slow to override an administrative agency. In the following words Professor Hart of the Harvard Law School has made a strong plea for greater judicial deference to the findings of administrative agencies:

Statutes dependent upon administrative enforcement, even more than most statutes, are skeletons which take on flesh and blood only by the creative process called interpretation. . . . The main burden of creation of this law of the statute falls inescapably upon the [administrative] agency; hosts of cases which never reach the courts are decided in accordance with it. Enlightened judicial action must take this law into account, aiding its creation where possible, avoiding its unnecessary or unintended disruption, distinguishing between needed correction or guidance and *the mere disturbing substitution of a preference.*[25]

It may well be, then, that the scope of judicial power as it extends to the supervision of the work of administrative agencies in interpreting and applying statutes should be, and can be, narrowed somewhat. But even if such a tendency should actually develop, it is clear that the power of the American courts, usually referred to by the phrase "judicial review," will still remain very much broader and more significant than the mere outright invalidation of an occasional act of Congress. Moreover, whatever aspect of judicial power is considered, it would seem clear that the Supreme Court is a true instrument of government wielding political power, rather than a mere judicial automaton coldly and impartially following Law. And if the automaton version of judicial review may be discarded, it would seem wise at this point to give further attention to the *human* side of the Court.

[25]Henry M. Hart, Jr., "The Business of the Supreme Court at the October Terms, 1937 and 1938," 53 *Harvard Law Review* (1940) 579, 624. (Italics added.) Reprinted by permission of the author and of the *Harvard Law Review.*

Chapter X

Personality and Judicial Review

About twenty years ago a very successful corporation lawyer made the following remarks before a branch meeting of
the American Bankers' Association: "The business man in
America today feels that he is doing business with a minion
of government looking over his shoulder with an upraised
arm and a threatening scowl. . . . Are we to go into a state
of socialism, or are you men, and men like you, prepared to
get out, take off your coats, and root for good old-fashioned
Anglo-Saxon individualism?"[1] A short time before, the
president of the American Bar Association in his presidential
address before that body stated: ". . . there never has been a
time when the business of the country occupied a higher
moral plane; never a time when the voluntary code which
governs the conduct of the banker, the manufacturer, the
merchant, the railway manager, has been finer in tone or more
faithfully observed than it is today; and yet never before
have the business activities of the people been so beset and
bedeviled with vexatious statutes, prying commissions, and
governmental intermeddling of all sorts."[2]

[1]Quoted by Charles Beard in "Historiography and the Constitution,"
The Constitution Reconsidered, edited by Conyers Read (New York: Columbia University Press, 1938) 163.

[2]*Report of the Fortieth Annual Meeting of the American Bar Association*
(Baltimore: The Lord Baltimore Press, 1917) 198.

These two men were being very frank and sincere about their fundamental economic and political philosophies. Soon after they revealed their ideas, both of these men, Pierce Butler and George Sutherland, were appointed to the United States Supreme Court. During the years they served on that Court federal laws were declared unconstitutional in twenty-six cases and, in view of their fundamental antipathy toward legislative activity by government, it is hardly surprising that neither of these justices dissented from the majority decision in a single one of these cases.

In the years before he was appointed to the Supreme Court in 1916 another future justice was actively involved in public affairs and frequently spoke out in such a manner as to make his social philosophy quite clear. Among this man's statements one finds remarks such as the following:

". . . the end for which we must strive is the attainment of rule by the people, and that involves industrial democracy as well as political democracy. . . . Industrial democracy will not come by gift. . . . if the situation is such that a voluntary organization like a labor union is powerless to bring about the democratization of a business . . . the State must in some way come to the aid of the workingmen if democratization is to be secured. . . . nothing could be more revolutionary than to close the door to social experimentation."[3]

There is a very brief story that is told of another justice of the Supreme Court which leaves no doubt about his attitude toward the activities of government. He was asked one day by his secretary, "Don't you hate to pay taxes?" The secretary was rebuked with the hot response, "No, young feller. I like to pay taxes. With them I buy civilization!"[4]

[3]*Industrial Relations,* 64th Congress, 1st Session, *Senate Documents,* Vol. 26, 7659–62 (1916); Albert Lief, *Brandeis* (New York: Stackpole Sons, 1936) 313.

[4]Frankfurter, *Law and Politics, op. cit.* (Chap. V, n. 8), p. 78.

These two members of the Court were Justices Brandeis and Holmes. Like the statements of their colleagues mentioned above, the words they spoke made quite clear their positive and specific social philosophies. In view of their attitude toward governmental activity it is not surprising that from the thirty-five decisions *invalidating* federal legislation during his service on the Court, Justice Brandeis dissented twenty-one times, or that Justice Holmes dissented from fourteen of the thirty-five decisions striking down federal legislation during his period of service.[5]

Professor (now Justice) Frankfurter was once led to observe: "The history of the Supreme Court is not the history of an abstraction, but the analysis of individuals acting as a Court who make decisions and lay down doctrines, and of other individuals, their successors, who refine, modify, and sometimes even overrule the decisions of their predecessors. . . . *In law also men make a difference.* . . . There is no inevitability in history except as men make it."[6] No student can pursue the study of constitutional law without conceding that there is a considerable degree of truth in Justice Frankfurter's conclusion. Time and again it has been evident that the development of constitutional law has depended as much, if not more, upon the personalities of the justices who have made it as it has upon the force of fixed legal principles or precedents, or upon any compelling word of the Constitution itself. The importance of personality as against precedent in the evolution of the law has been recognized by many writers, including a number of judges. Jerome Frank points out that "a century ago a great American judge, Chancellor Kent, in a personal letter explained his method of arriving at a decision.

[5]All of the data on the decisions of these four justices is from *Provisions of Federal Law Held Unconstitutional, op. cit.* (Chap. IX, n. 1), p. 131.

[6]Frankfurter, *Mr. Justice Holmes, op. cit.* (Chap. VII, n. 17), pp. 8–9 (Italics added.) Reprinted by permission of the President and Fellows of Harvard College.

He first made himself 'master of the facts.' Then (he wrote) 'I saw where justice lay, and the moral sense decided the court half the time; I then sat down to search the authorities. . . . I might once in a while be embarrassed by a technical rule, but I *almost always found principles suited to my view of the case. . . .*'[7] Learned Hand, one of the greatest of present-day federal judges, has made the same point in these words: "The words . . . [a judge] must construe are empty vessels into which he can pour nearly anything he will."[8]

Justice Cardozo once said: ". . . the duty of a judge becomes . . . a question of degree, and he is a useful judge or a poor one as he estimates the measure accurately or loosely. He must balance all his ingredients, his philosophy, his logic, his analogies, his history, his customs, his sense of right, and all the rest, and adding a little here and taking out a little there, must determine, as wisely as he can, which weight shall tip the scales."[9] In fairness it must be pointed out that he also said: "Of the cases that come before the court in which I sit, a majority, I think, could not, with semblance of reason, be decided in any way but one. The law and its application alike are plain."[10] But he was speaking then as a member of the highest New York state court, which is largely concerned with cases in the field of private law. It is doubtful whether later, as a member of the Supreme Court of the United States, in view of its greater concern with controversial cases in the field of public law, he would have placed the percentage of "certain" cases at so high a level.

[7]Jerome Frank, *Law and the Modern Mind* (New York: Coward McCann, Inc., 1930) 104, n. (Italics presumably by Frank.) Reprinted by permission of the publishers.

[8]Learned Hand, "Sources of Tolerance," 79 *University of Pennsylvania Law Review* (1930) 1, 12. Quoted by Frankfurter, *Law and Politics, op. cit.* (Chap. V, n. 8), p. 102.

[9]Cardozo, *op. cit.* (Chap. I, n. 19), pp. 161–62. Reprinted by permission of the Yale University Press.

[10]*Ibid.,* 164.

Still another federal judge, in the following seriocomic words, denies the compulsion of legal principles upon his decisions: "I, after canvassing all the available material at my command, and duly cogitating upon it, give my imagination play, and brooding over the cause, wait for the feeling, the hunch—that intuitive flash of understanding which makes the jump-spark connection between question and decision, and at the point where the path is darkest for the judicial feet, sheds its light along the way."[11]

It is entirely possible that a careful examination of the personalities and the economic and social backgrounds of the eighty men who have served on the Supreme Court would prove to be as valuable and realistic an approach to the American Constitution as the more usual law school approach which lays so much emphasis upon the study of cases, the rule of *stare decisis,* and of fixed legal principles Benjamin Cardozo once wrote: "There is in each of us a stream or tendency . . . which gives coherence and direction to thought and action. Judges cannot escape that current any more than other mortals. All their lives, forces which they do not recognize and cannot name, have been tugging at them—inherited instincts, traditional beliefs, acquired convictions; and the resultant is an outlook on life, a conception of social needs, a sense in [William] James's phrase of 'the total push and pressure of the cosmos,' which, when reasons are nicely balanced, must determine where choice shall fall." And again, "Deep below consciousness are other forces, the likes and the dislikes, the predilections and the prejudices, the complex of instincts and emotions and habits and convictions, which make the man, whether he be litigant or judge. . . . The great tides and currents which engulf the rest of men, do not turn

---

[11]Joseph C. Hutcheson, "The Judgment Intuitive: The Function of the 'Hunch' in Judicial Decision," 14 *Cornell Law Quarterly* (April 1929) 274, 278.

aside in their course, and pass the judges by."[12] Justice Frankfurter has further expressed his conclusions in these words, ". . . the work of the Supreme Court is the history of relatively few personalities . . . the fact that they were *there* and that others were not, surely made decisive differences. To understand what manner of men they were is crucial to an understanding of the Court."[13] Certainly, any wise present-day lawyer preparing a case for presentation to the Supreme Court gives as much thought to the individual justices, their likes, prejudices, and personal idiosyncrasies, as he does to legal arguments or precedents favorable to his side of the case.

Unfortunately, when it comes to the justices of the past, this approach to the Constitution is not always an easy one for the simple reason that we know relatively little about these men, particularly of their careers before they came to the Court and of their general nonlegal backgrounds. Of late years a few good biographies of such justices as Marshall, Taney, Field, Taft, and Miller have appeared.[14] But even these have sometimes left something to be desired, for the task of the biographer who would tell the life story of a great judge and show the proper relationship between his general background and his work as a judge is not a simple one.

[12]Cardozo, *op. cit.* (Chap. I, n. 19), pp. 12, 167–68. Reprinted by permission of the Yale University Press.

[13]Frankfurter, *Law and Politics, op. cit.* (Chap. V, n. 8), p. 113. Reprinted by permission of Harcourt, Brace and Company, publishers.

[14]Albert J. Beveridge, *The Life of John Marshall* (Boston: Houghton Mifflin Company, 1916); Carl B. Swisher, *Roger B. Taney* (New York: The Macmillan Company, 1935), and *Stephen J. Field* (Washington: The Brookings Institution, 1930); Charles Fairman, *Mr. Justice Miller and the Supreme Court* (Cambridge: Harvard University Press, 1939); Henry F. Pringle, *The Life and Times of William Howard Taft* (New York: Farrar & Rinehart, Inc., 1939).

The Importance of Personality in the Appointment of Justices

On the other hand, this approach is by no means completely precluded because of the absence of pertinent data and information. Here and there bits of evidence are available, the pieces may be fitted together and the effect of personality upon the judicial process determined. For one thing, there is plenty of evidence that more than one President of the United States has appreciated the importance of personality in the judicial process and before making his appointment has carefully considered the qualifications, legal and otherwise, of the various candidates for a vacant judicial office. Professor Haines says that Washington "exercised peculiar care" to name only supporters of the new Constitution and "ardent Federalists" to the Supreme Court. "Thus Washington himself 'initiated the system of appointing political adherents, and political adherents only to places on the Supreme bench. That system has seldom been departed from.' "[15]

When at the turn of the nineteenth century, President Adams named John Marshall chief justice, he could not have foreseen that Marshall would hold fast to the reins of the Court for thirty years and more, nor could he have foreseen the exact rulings that Marshall would make in such crucial cases as *Marbury* v. *Madison, McCulloch* v. *Maryland,* and *Dartmouth College* v. *Woodward.* But he did know that Marshall had been active in Federalist party politics, he understood the character of his man, and was certainly aware of the importance of Federalist control of the judiciary. Beveridge, in his *Life of John Marshall,* reports that "doubtless

[15]Haines, *op. cit.* (Chap. I, n. 1), pp. 345–46. His quotation is from W. D. Coles, "Politics and the Supreme Court of the United States," 27 *American Law Review* (March–April 1893) 183. Reprinted by permission of the University of California Press.

the President's choice of Marshall was influenced by the fact that his 'new minister, Marshall, did all to [his] entire satisfaction.' "[16] Many a similar example might be provided from the list of nineteenth-century appointments. For instance, Haines points out that "Jefferson, Madison, and Monroe appointed only Democrats . . ." and later says, "For twenty-eight years the appointments continued to be adherents to the Democratic party with one exception. . . ."[17] Nor were Republican presidents of the second half of the nineteenth century any less politically minded in the making of their judicial appointments.

One or two examples from our own century may be examined at greater length. When Theodore Roosevelt named Oliver Wendell Holmes, Jr., to the Supreme Court in 1902 there can be no doubt that he knew fully what he was doing. He appreciated the significance of the great economic changes that were taking place in the life of this country and he knew that the Court was being, and would continue to be, called upon again and again to resolve many a troublesome and complex constitutional problem growing out of these changes. So he wrote his friend, Henry Cabot Lodge, ". . . I should like to know that Judge Holmes was in entire sympathy with our views, that is, with your views and mine . . . before I would feel justified in appointing him. . . . I should hold myself as guilty of an irreparable wrong to the nation if I should put . . . [in this vacancy] any man who was not absolutely sane and sound on the great national policies for which we stand in public life."[18]

Again in 1906, when Roosevelt was about to appoint Judge Lurton to the Supreme Court, we find the president writing his friend Lodge in similar, outspoken fashion:

[16]Beveridge, *op. cit.* (above, n. 14), II, 553-54.

[17]Haines, *op. cit.* (Chap. I, n. 1), pp. 350-51.

[18]Quoted in Frankfurter, *Law and Politics, op. cit.* (Chap. V, n. 8), p. 67.

Nothing has been so strongly borne in on me concerning lawyers on the bench as that the *nominal* politics of the man has nothing to do with his actions on the bench. His *real* politics are all-important. In Lurton's case, Taft and Day, his two former associates, are very desirous of having him on. He is right on the Negro question; he is right on the power of the federal government; he is right on the Insular business; he is right about corporations; he is right about labor. On every question that would come before the bench, he has so far shown himself to be in much closer touch with the policies in which you and I believe than even White because he has been right about corporations where White has been wrong.[19]

A decade later, it is entirely clear that the progressive Woodrow Wilson of the prewar "New Freedom" years knew his man when he named Louis Brandeis to the Court in 1916. In a letter to Senator Culbertson concerning his reasons for making the Brandeis appointment Wilson wrote as follows:

. . . I need hardly tell you that I named Mr. Brandeis as a member of . . . [the Supreme Court] only because I knew him to be singularly qualified by learning, by gifts, and by character for the position. . . .

I have tested him by seeking his advice upon some of the most difficult and perplexing public questions about which it was necessary for me to form a judgment. . . .

Mr. Brandeis has rendered many notable services to the city and State with which his professional life has been identified. He successfully directed the difficult campaign which resulted in obtaining cheaper gas for the city of Boston. It was chiefly under his guidance and through his efforts that legislation was secured in Massachusetts which authorized savings banks to issue insurance policies for small sums at much reduced rates. And some gentlemen who tried very hard to obtain control by the Boston

[19]*Selections from the Correspondence of Theodore Roosevelt and Henry Cabot Lodge*, II, 228. Quoted by Odegard and Helms, *op. cit.* (Chap. II, n. 2), pp. 168–69.

Elevated Railway Co. of the subways of the city for a period of 99 years can probably testify as to his ability as the people's advocate when public interests call for an effective champion.[20]

The intensive and bitter fight, of an almost unprecedented character, which conservatives immediately waged in an effort to defeat the confirmation of Brandeis by the Senate only serves to indicate that they, too, knew their man and were entirely aware of the importance of personality in the judicial process. Then again, the conservative Harding, to whom in the two and a half years of his presidency there came the opportunity to fill four vacancies, named a solid phalanx of conservatives to the high bench. He who would profess surprise or alarm at Franklin Roosevelt's policy of naming only liberals to the Court would do well to remember Harding's action.

Of course, there are exceptions. Not every president has always been consistent in the type of man he has appointed to the Supreme Court. For instance, President Wilson, to whose lot fell the naming of such undeniably progressive justices as Brandeis and Clarke, appointed Justice McReynolds, who proved to be one of the most conservative men in the entire history of the Court. Likewise, such conservative presidents as Coolidge and Hoover appointed to the Court the great liberal justices Stone and Cardozo.

But lest there be any lingering doubt about the extent to which presidents have realized that constitutional law is shaped by the men they name to the Court and not by the other men whom they might have named but did not, nor by abstract constitutional principles, listen to what former President Taft had to say during the 1920 presidential campaign.

Mr. Wilson is in favor of a latitudinarian construction of the Constitution of the United States, to weaken the protection it should afford against Socialist raids upon property rights. . . .

[20] 64th Congress, 1st Session, *Senate Documents,* Vol. 17, 239–41 (1916).

He has made three appointments to the Supreme Court. . . . Four of the incumbent Justices are beyond the retiring age of seventy, and the next President will probably be called upon to appoint their successors. There is no greater domestic issue in this election than the maintenance of the Supreme Court as the bulwark to enforce the guarantee that no man shall be deprived of his property without due process of law. . . .[21]

To which statement Justice Frankfurter, then of the Harvard Law School, immediately replied in the columns of *The New Republic* as follows: "Mr. Taft deserves our gratitude for his candor in recognizing that the Supreme Court involves *political* issues to be discussed like other *political* issues."[22] Of course, the ending of this story is that Harding, and not the "dangerous" Cox, was elected president in 1920; just as Taft predicted, four vacancies did develop, and who should turn up in one of them as chief justice but the safe Mr. Taft himself. And later, in 1938, Mr. Frankfurter in turn was appointed to the Supreme Court.

Another indication that the appointment by presidents of specific personalities to the Court has vitally affected the course of constitutional interpretation is to be seen in the efforts which justices themselves have made to deny certain presidents the opportunity to make appointments by holding on to their positions when they might otherwise have resigned. This is the sort of practice on the part of justices which is not always apparent or readily proved. Nevertheless, there is sufficient evidence to indicate that its occurrence has not been infrequent. For example, it is said of Justice Duval that during the last years of his service on the Court he was so deaf that he could not hear the arguments of counsel and that he remained on the Court only because of the hope that

[21]Quoted by Frankfurter, *Law and Politics, op. cit.* (Chap. V, n. 8), p. 37, from an article by Taft in the October, 1920, *Yale Review.*

[22]*Ibid.*, p. 39. (Italics added.)

he might prevent President Jackson from naming his successor.[23] Justice Miller wrote of Justice Hunt that "he will not resign while Hayes is president because Conklin[g] does not want Hayes to appoint his successor."[24] Fairman, Miller's biographer, writes of another of Miller's colleagues, Justice Clifford, as follows:

Justice Clifford had been eligible to resign with full salary since August 1873. While it would perhaps be too much to say that his decision to remain on the bench was determined by his desire to hold on until there should be a Democratic president to choose his successor, this seems to have been a considerable factor. . . . he was the sole remaining appointee of a Democratic administration. . . .[25]

More recently, Taft's biographer, Henry F. Pringle, has brought to light further evidence on this point. He reveals that at Taft's last presidential conference with the newspaper correspondents before he gave way to the liberal Wilson, Taft stated that, "above all other things . . . he was proudest of the fact that six of the nine members of the Supreme Court, including the Chief Justice, bore his commission.

"'And I have said to them,' Taft chuckled, 'damn you, if any of you die, I'll disown you.'"[26]

Later, Taft as chief justice apparently feared to let the "progressive" Hoover appoint his successor, for in 1929 he wrote, "I am older and slower and less acute and more confused. However, as long as things continue as they are, and I am able to answer in my place, I must stay on the court in

[23]Cortez A. M. Ewing, *The Judges of the Supreme Court, 1789–1937* (Minneapolis: The University of Minnesota Press, 1938) 70.

[24]Fairman, *op. cit.* (above, n. 14), p. 378. This and the following excerpt are reprinted by permission of the President and Fellows of Harvard College.

[25]*Ibid.*, pp. 378–79.

[26]Pringle, *op. cit.* (above, n. 14), II, 854. Only one Taft justice did die during the eight years of the Wilson administration. One other Taft justice resigned—he to run for the presidency.

order to prevent the Bolsheviki from getting control. . . ."[27]

Finally, there can be little doubt that the aged and conservative justices of the Franklin D. Roosevelt era deliberately held on to their posts to prevent that president from making any appointments. Robert Jackson has spoken quite bitterly, but probably truthfully, about this situation which lasted until 1937, as follows:

> When the Roosevelt administration opened in 1932 [*sic*], this conservative bloc in the Court had been holding on for four years in fear of that radical Hoover! It continued the same strategy against Roosevelt and had prevented any vacancy during his first four years. It had become on average the most aged Court in our history. But there was little doubt that the conservatives had determined that so long as they were able to answer in their places they would give neither Mr. Roosevelt nor the rising generation a chance at the judgment seat before which the policies of a democracy were to be arraigned.[28]

There is a tradition nurtured by many historians and political scientists to the effect that try as presidents may to influence the Court and the development of constitutional law by naming certain men as justices they have invariably been fooled.[29] This tradition is a rather doubtful one. Many a president who has consciously tried to influence future decisions of the Supreme Court by the naming of certain men of known views has had very little cause for any "disappointment." This tradition of the frustration which has met presidential attempts to exercise a hand in the shaping of things to come has probably been fathered by the undeniable fact that some justices have dissatisfied their appointers by their decisions in isolated cases. For example, Justice Frankfurter

[27]*Ibid.*, II, 967. Letter to Horace Taft, November 14, 1929.

[28]Jackson, *op. cit.* (Chap. II, n. 11), pp. 185–86. Reprinted by permission of Alfred A. Knopf, Inc., publisher.

[29]See Warren, *op. cit.* (Chap. V, n. 2), I, 21–22.

points out that Justice Holmes disappointed Theodore Roosevelt by deciding "against the government in the Northern Securities Case, Roosevelt's pet litigation."[30] But in the final accounting, Roosevelt would have been ungrateful, indeed, had he continued to hold this decision against Holmes, in view of the numerous decisions of that judge in other cases, decisions which must time and again have proved immensely satisfying to him.

The Requirement of Judicial Temperament

This suggestion that presidents have often deliberately sought justices for the Supreme Court with known political and economic views is not easily reconciled with the more conventional belief that presidents look for the "judicial temperament" which it is supposed only a few men have and which is considered a *sine qua non* in those men who are called upon to serve as judges. Perhaps there are a few men who truly have a judicial temperament, if by that phrase is meant the ability to decide the case at hand in reasonably intelligent and satisfactory fashion with only a minimum of reference to one's own interests and prejudices. Justice Holmes, for example, was unusually successful in submerging his own conservative economic and social views in an adherence to a sort of general principle in constitutional cases. This principle was one which led him to insist that the benefit of the doubt in cases involving the constitutionality of statutes should always be strongly on the side of the legislature.

Justice Cardozo likewise possessed such a judicial temperament. On the other hand, such an undeniably great judge as Brandeis did not possess this quality. Justice Brandeis was too much the advocate, too much the reformer, too much the social scientist, ever to have been accused of possessing a cold impartiality or devotion to abstract legal justice. Fortunately,

[30]Frankfurter, *Law and Politics, op. cit.* (Chap. V, n. 8), p. 19.

there was, and is, room on the Supreme Court for a Brandeis as well as a Holmes, granting that a Holmes is a rarer phenomenon and thus one to be more highly prized than a Brandeis. Incidentally, the secret of Justice Holmes's greatness as this rare type of judge has perhaps never been better expressed in a few words than by Archibald MacLeish: "Mr. Justice Holmes was a man of the world, who was also a philosopher, who was incidentally a lawyer. The result was that he was a very great judge."[31]

In view of the remarkable personal detachment which he maintained during his judicial career, it is perhaps safe enough to ignore the private life and personal social views of a Holmes. But unfortunately there have not been many such justices in the history of the Supreme Court. How, then, shall we approach the problem of understanding the force of personality in law, whether the personality be that of a "liberal" Brandeis, or a "conservative" McReynolds?

Important Personality Factors

One method which has been much in vogue of late years is to look to the judge's economic background. What have his past business relations been? Is he a wealthy man interested in the continued sanctity of private property? Or is he primarily a libertarian, who places the integrity of the individual man above all else? There can be no doubt that the many observers who have emphasized this approach to the problem, among whom Charles A. Beard has perhaps been most eminent, have rendered a service in pointing the way to an understanding of individual justices and the diverse forces that helped shape and influence their legal rulings. But this method, which emphasizes the "economic" in man so much,

[31]*Ibid.* (Foreword by Mr. MacLeish), p. xvii. Reprinted by permission of Harcourt, Brace and Company, publishers.

has its limitations, and there is a danger in utilizing it to the exclusion of other possible approaches.

If it be granted that a judge does not always rule the way he does in a case because the available legal precedents compel him to rule that way and no other, then what factors other than the economic may have influenced him? Obviously, there is a whole host of possibilities, some quite simple, others rather complex. He may have taken a strong personal dislike to the lawyer on what proves to be the losing side. He may be physically, or even in some cases mentally, ill and thus unwilling or unable to understand the somewhat involved and sophisticated arguments which one side has elected to present. Or he may simply be a man of limited intellectual talents. Again, he may have strong family ties or deep religious feelings which are bound to influence him in certain fields of the law. For example, we may recall Dicey's illustration of the development of the rules of equity on a married woman's property rights, a development which was largely brought about by judges who were members of the upper class and were keenly aware of the need for progress in this aspect of family law.[32] Or again a judge may be a self-made man and have little patience with the other man who has fallen by the wayside in the struggle of life. He may be a bitter partisan, intensely antagonistic toward the policies of an administration of an opposite political faith from his own. He may be an elderly man who has reached the age at which he is likely to feel that the only good lies in the past and that modern ways are evil ways. Or he may be strongly conditioned by his past residence in a particular section of the country with its peculiar economic and social views. Or he may have been a law school professor, a man of theory and broad social views, convinced that government and law are destined to play an ever-increasing role in man's life.

[32]Dicey, *op. cit.* (Chap. I, n. 16), pp. 369–93.

So we might go on, almost indefinitely. In other words, it is not the political scientist or the historian alone who can tell us what factors may have influenced a judge, although they do have important stories to tell. It is as much the task of the economist, the sociologist, and the psychologist, the latter particularly. Unfortunately, these men have but started their studies in the field of law and government, and as yet we know little about the possible answers they may be able to provide. No doubt in time they will overdo their approach, too. Efforts will probably sooner or later be made to psychoanalyze in retrospect every justice from John Marshall to Hugo Black! But granting that here as elsewhere ridiculous extremes are possible, there is more than one Supreme Court case where the psychologist may well be able to provide some very pertinent information as to what was motivating a certain justice at a particular moment.

The Previous Training of Justices

However, without wandering into the difficult, technical, and uncertain fields of psychology or psychiatry, such things in the background of a judge's career as his party membership and activity, his business interests, his wealth, his legal training, or his previous judicial experience are all capable of relatively easy ascertainment and analysis. It is obvious, for instance, that the character and caliber of a judge's previous legal training and experience may have been of very great importance in governing his attitude on the bench. Moreover, there has been a very wide variation in the legal qualifications of Supreme Court justices. Some, such as Mathews, Fuller, Butler, and Roberts, have been brilliant practicing attorneys who have enjoyed great financial success and have been much sought after by rich corporations demanding the very best of legal talent. Others, such as Frankfurter, Douglas, and Stone, have been teachers of law in the great universities. Still others, such as Holmes and Cardozo, have been career men, judges during a good part of their lives, men who have perhaps come up through the ranks of the lower courts to reach at last the goal of every judge's dreams. Finally, others, such as Sutherland and Black, have been members of Congress, practicing politicians. And let no one hasten to conclude that this last type of background has made the poorest judges. Far from it. Some judges with this background have at least been realists, aware of the significance of the tremendous forces and counterforces that are constantly contending for position in our modern society.

Of course, a great many judges have had a varied background. When Hughes was appointed Chief Justice in 1930 he had been Governor of New York, a member of the United States Supreme Court, Republican nominee for the presidency, Secretary of State, and a highly successful practicing attorney. Stone and Douglas, in addition to being teachers of the law, had held important administrative positions with the federal government. Sutherland, besides having been a United States senator, had been a successful attorney and had served as president of the American Bar Association.[33]

Unquestionably, one of the most serious shortcomings of more than one Supreme Court justice has been his narrow training and experience, concentrated almost wholly in the study and pursuit of the technicalities of the law. The result of this rather limited background has been, as one writer puts it, that "for every Brandeis familiar with economics, for every Holmes versed in literature, for every Cardozo learned in philosophy, there are a dozen judges who regard such learning as esoteric if not irrelevant."[34] Recently, President Roose-

[33]See Ewing, op. cit. (above, n. 23), for valuable statistical data on the qualifications of the Supreme Court justices.

[34]Henry Steele Commager, "Constitutional History and the Higher Law," The Constitution Reconsidered, op. cit. (above, n. 1), p. 243. Reprinted by permission of the Columbia University Press.

velt has apparently endeavored in his judicial appointments
to seek federal judges of broader academic and intellectual
background than that which the practicing attorney sometimes possesses. For example, in selecting circuit and district
court judges, he has gone to the law school faculties, and the
dean or a professor from one great law school after another
has been named to the federal judiciary. In a short time President Roosevelt has so honored the deans of the Yale University, University of Pennsylvania, Ohio State University,
University of Virginia, and University of Iowa law schools.
Needless to say, there has been among the practicing lawyers
not a little grumbling about this tendency, and considerable
talk about the president's filling the courts with theorists, or
impractical idealists.

But the tendency is likely to continue. In the case of the
Supreme Court, particularly, it is becoming increasingly clear
that this tribunal has ceased to be a court in the old common-
law sense which decides for the most part technical cases involving the petty legal quarrels of private litigants. Instead it
has tended to become through the years a great public-law
court confining its attention more and more to broad fundamental constitutional issues where a technical knowledge of
the law is only one of many sources of knowledge which may
be drawn upon in seeking a wise decision. This has been
particularly true since the enactment by Congress in 1925 of
the "Judges' Law" by which the Supreme Court was em-
powered to refuse jurisdiction in many of the petty types of
cases which it had previously been hearing.[35] When it comes
to such problems as control of collective bargaining between
capital and labor or the prohibition of child labor under the
commerce clause, the fixing of prices, the prescribing of mini-

[35]See Felix Frankfurter and J. M. Landis, *The Business of the Supreme
Court* (New York: The Macmillan Company, 1927), Chap. VII for a discussion of the Judges' Bill.

mum wage and maximum hour levels, or the protection of the freedom of speech or of the press under the due process clauses, technical legal considerations alone cannot provide wise decisions.

A Supreme Court made up of justices who have had formal training in economics or sociology as well as the law, or who have had practical experience as politicians, businessmen, or labor leaders, and not simply as attorneys, might well profit from this broadened background of its members. It is true that many of our greatest justices, from the time of Marshall and Taney to Holmes and Brandeis, have achieved a good part of their fame because they succeeded in combining several additional academic or professional qualities with their legal training and experience. But there is a definite need to make certain that the number of such justices shall increase rather than diminish.

The Factor of Age

The importance of the age of a judge and its effect upon his decisions is another matter which warrants examination. Figures relating to the age of Supreme Court justices are relatively easy to obtain, although there is likely to be considerable controversy as to what they prove. However, if one is inclined to agree that the older a man grows the more conservative he is likely to become, the statistics are revealing. Professor Cortez Ewing has prepared figures and tables showing the average age of the justices by decades since 1789. During the first decade the figure was fifty-three, and during the first seven years of the 1930's it was sixty-nine. The increase during this period of fifteen decades has been almost continuous. It is also interesting to note Professor Ewing's figures on the ages of justices at the time of appointment. During the first forty years of the Court's history, four justices were less than forty years old at the time of appointment and twelve were under fifty. None was over sixty, and only seven were over fifty. During the forty-year period ending with 1937, no justice was under forty-five when appointed to the Court, and only one was under fifty. On the other hand, five were over sixty and ten were over fifty-five. It may be noted that the average age of presidents on assuming office has fallen from fifty-eight during the first forty-year period, to fifty-three during the forty-year period ending with 1937, so that it is by no means true that all national officeholders have been increasing in age during our history.[36] It is probably more than a coincidence that the Court, which during the 1930's struck down more important federal legislation than did any previous Court during a similar period, was on the average the most aged in our history.[37]

Personality and Supreme Court Traditions

Before leaving the subject of personality and judicial review we may examine a number of traditions and customs pertaining to the Supreme Court which are sometimes considered as holding the force of personality in the Court's work to an absolute minimum.[38] One of these is that no man shall seek office on the Supreme Court. Appointment to the Court is, of course, a very great honor, and it is said that the office must seek the man and not the man the office. It is impossible to say to what extent this theory is violated in practice, for this is just the sort of human information concerning the average justice which is most difficult to obtain. But we do have enough information available to warrant the conclusion that there has been more than a little maneuvering, both successful and unsuccessful, for seats on the Supreme Court. One or

[36]Ewing, *op. cit.* (above, n. 23), pp. 63–76.

[37]Jackson, *op. cit.* (Chap. II, n. 11), p. 185.

[38]S. P. Orth and R. E. Cushman, *American National Government* (New York: F. S. Crofts & Co., 1935) 525–27.

two examples may be given. In his recent biography of Justice Miller Professor Fairman makes it clear that Miller made a vigorous campaign for the office. "Miller had no false modesty ... and ... he longed for an opportunity to wield public power. . . . [In furthering his campaign for a seat on the Supreme Court] senators and representatives from Iowa and the congressional allies they enlisted, the state bar, the Governor and the legislature, all went into action, and *presently the candidate himself went on to Washington to see that nothing was left undone.*"[39] Professor Fairman also points out that when Justice McLean died in 1861 Noah H. Swayne of Ohio "lost no time in registering his claim" to the vacant seat. He wrote to his close friend, Secretary of the Treasury Chase: " 'Intelligence of the death of Judge McLean reached here this morning. [Swayne was a fast worker!] My friends will name me to the President as one of those from whom a selection is to be made to fill the vacancy upon the Bench of the Supreme Court, thus created. If you can deem it proper to give me your friendly support you will lay me under a lasting obligation.' "[40] Swayne got the appointment.

Later, in 1864, when Chief Justice Taney died, Fairman reports that Chase, who had just resigned from the office of Secretary of the Treasury, "became an active candidate" for the Court vacancy. There is even some evidence that Lincoln was persuaded to give the appointment to Chase in return for the latter's agreement that he would withdraw as a candidate in the impending presidential election.[41]

There is no doubt, too, that the conservative and tradition-loving Taft had set his heart upon winding up his public

---

[39]Fairman, *op. cit.* (above, n. 14), p. 44. (Italics added.) This and the following excerpt are reprinted by permission of the President and Fellows of Harvard College.

[40]*Ibid.*, pp. 43–44.

[41]*Ibid.*, pp. 99, 100–1.

career as Chief Justice. Following the election in 1920 he went to see Harding in Marion, and when the latter generously suggested that he might appoint Taft to the Supreme Court, Taft bluntly told him that his dignity and past record made it possible for him to accept only the chief justiceship. Later Taft reported that he had written Harding as follows: "I told him in the note that many times in the past the Chief Justice [White, whom Taft, himself, had appointed as chief justice and who was obviously about ready to retire] had said he was holding the office for me and that he would give it back to a Republican administration. . . ."[42] The genial Harding could hardly fail to be overwhelmed by this campaign, and, of course, the appointment was a logical one for him to make. But when Chief Justice White did finally retire, Harding waited some forty days before making the appointment. All during this time Taft's agent was seeing the proper people, such as Attorney General Daugherty, and leaving no stone unturned to make certain that the office would go to Taft. Taft wrote letters to him constantly and advised him as to the strategy he should employ, such as how an objection to the appointment based upon Taft's advanced age was to be met.[43]

A second commonly accepted tradition is that Supreme Court justices must lead cloistered lives and, above all, avoid any semblance of activity in politics. Again there are any number of examples that can be cited to prove the elastic character of this tradition. Chief Justice Marshall remained the politician all of his life and was always fully aware of the political implications of his decisions. Needless to say, they usually hewed very closely to the Federalist party "line." There are also many examples of nineteenth-century Su-

[42]Pringle, op. cit. (above, n. 14), II, 955. Letter to Helen H. Taft, December 26, 1920.

[43]Ibid., II, 956–59.

preme Court justices who remained more or less active in politics after their appointment to the Court. Justice McLean, appointed to the Court by Jackson, retained his interest in politics and was frequently mentioned as a presidential candidate. "He maintained that a judge was under no obligation to refrain from the discussion of political affairs and steadfastly defended the propriety of his candidacy."[44] Justices Miller, Chase, and Field, all Lincoln appointees, likewise continued political activity of one sort or another after they went on the Court, and the latter two would have been receptive candidates for the presidency at various times.[45] Indeed, it is said of Chase that "he was a perennial aspirant for the presidential chair, and apparently would have been willing to accept the nomination from any party that offered it."[46]

In more recent times, Charles Evans Hughes was fully aware of the existence of a campaign to secure for him the Republican nomination for the presidency in 1916, and did nothing really to discourage it, although the tradition was, and supposedly is, that a member of the Supreme Court is absolutely unavailable for any political office, even the highest in the land. And when the nomination was finally offered to him he had no hesitancy about leaving his high judicial office for the political arena. Or to refer to the Taft letters once more, we find that all during his service as chief justice, Taft maintained a close watch over Republican politics and did not hesitate to extend political advice to the presidents of the 1920's.[47]

[44]*Dictionary of American Biography* (New York: Charles Scribner's Sons, 1933), XII, 127, 128.

[45]See the Chase and Field items in the *Dictionary of American Biography*, IV, 27, 32; VI, 372, 375. See also, Fairman, *op. cit.* (above, n. 14), and Swisher, *Stephen J. Field* (above, n. 14).

[46]Swisher, *Field, op. cit.* (above, n. 14), p. 125.

[47]See Pringle, *op. cit.* (above, n. 14), II, 951–1079.

A third tradition is that a justice immediately upon appointment to the Court converts his personal wealth or estate into noncommercial securities of a harmless sort. It is doubtful whether such a practice has much effect. In the first place, any type of investment—even the ownership of a government bond or of real estate—might conceivably embarrass a judge in a controversial case. But it is of more consequence to point out the folly of supposing that a mature man upon appointment to the Supreme Court can effect even a superficial break with his past customs and prejudices merely by revising his investment list. For example, the great corporation lawyers who have upon occasion been appointed to the Court undoubtedly complied with this traditional requirement, but they hardly thereby shed their prejudices in certain areas of law pertaining to the activities of corporations. There is no desire here to condemn such men for their inability to make a clean break with their past lives. The only purpose is to suggest that the so-called tradition, itself, has little to do with the realities of human nature or the process of judicial review.

Finally, there is a tradition that supposedly requires a justice to refrain from sitting in any case "with which he has been previously connected as counsel or in which he has any direct personal interest."[48] Admittedly, this tradition is scrupulously followed. Brandeis remained out of the *Adkins* case because he and a member of his family had had previous connection with the adjudication of the issue involved. Former attorneys general, such as McReynolds and Murphy, have refrained from participating in any case in which the interest of the Department of Justice dated back to the period of their connection with that office.

But the tradition has its obvious limitations. Few, if any, justices have considered themselves obliged to remain silent

[48]Orth and Cushman, *op. cit.* (above, n. 38), p. 526.

merely because the character of a case is such that it touches one of their strong previous interests. Some of the Court's former corporation attorneys have served in cases affecting the rights of corporations. Justice Butler did not feel that his long business affiliation with certain railroads disqualified him from service in railroad valuation or rate cases. On the contrary, he regarded himself as an outstanding expert in that field of law and he readily asserted his leadership in the rendering of these decisions. Probably this attitude was entirely realistic and sound.

It should be made clear at this point that the presentation of such material does not necessarily imply any criticism of these justices for their conduct, or any suggestion that they have been departing from firmly established and well-tested traditions. Rather, the intent is to show that many of these traditions fall somewhat short of the meaning usually conveyed by that word. In other words, there is an urgent necessity to realize that the courts, from the nation's supreme tribunal down to the lowest police court, resemble the legislative and executive divisions of government in that they are all a part of the *political* process and are manned by ordinary human beings possessed of about the same talents and the same disabilities, the same hopes and fears, as other public officers. A Taft as president or a Hughes as a presidential candidate is regarded as fair game for anyone to attack, and his personal prejudices and inadequacies are thoroughly scrutinized and debated. But a Taft or a Hughes as chief justice is often regarded as a demigod, above the mundane level of human frailties and by some mysterious process divested of all those human qualities that make up a personality. We must remember, "In law also men make a difference."

Chapter XI

Judicial Review under Fire

A GREAT deal of ink has been spilled over the proposal of President Roosevelt in 1937 for the reorganization of the Supreme Court. For months the country as a whole engaged in one of the most spirited and bitter debates in its entire political history. At that, the controversy proceeded to an indecisive conclusion. The proposal was defeated, but that the Court was not unimpressed by what had occurred is suggested by the fact that no federal law has since been invalidated. Accordingly it was said, and with some justification, that the president had lost the battle but won the war.

The Recurrence of Controversy

Whatever else may be said about the confusing outcome of this particular controversy over judicial review, one thing is certain: this was not the first time in our history that the issue had been publicly debated or a specific check upon the Supreme Court attempted. In fact, there has been no period in our history when the Supreme Court has been without its critics, or judicial review free from proposals for change. At almost the very beginning of our present political system, the court of John Marshall was time and again the center of bitter and acrimonious debate. Later, upon the eve of the Civil War, the *Dred Scott* decision aroused the fury of a considerable part of the country and brought down upon the Court such a measure of condemnation that there is some reason to wonder whether the Court and its power could have survived unchanged had not the War intervened and submerged all such issues in the broader problem of preserving the Union. It is not always remembered that this decision so angered Northerners, and Republicans particularly, that the new president, Abraham Lincoln, devoted part of his first Inaugural Address to a strong criticism of the Supreme Court. The new president did not directly challenge the institution of judicial review but he asserted:

. . . the candid citizen must confess that if the policy of the Government upon vital questions affecting the whole people is to be irrevocably fixed by decisions of the Supreme Court, the instant they are made in ordinary litigation between parties in personal actions the people will have ceased to be their own rulers, having to that extent practically resigned their Government into the hands of that eminent Tribunal.[1]

The Republican platform of 1860 referred to the "dogma" of the *Dred Scott* decision as a "dangerous political heresy."[2] Several Northern state legislatures denounced the decision, and that of Maine went so far as to adopt the following declaration:

Whereas, such extra-judicial opinion subordinates the political power and interests of the American people to the cupidity and ambition of a few thousand slaveholders, . . .
Therefore—
Resolved, that the extra-judicial opinion of the Supreme Court in the case of Dred Scott is not binding in law or conscience upon the government or citizens of the United States and that it

[1] James D. Richardson, *Messages and Papers of the Presidents* (Washington: Government Printing Office, 1897), VI, 9.

[2] Beard, *American Government and Politics, op. cit.* (Chap. IV, n. 7), p. 188.

is of an import so alarming and dangerous as to demand the instant and emphatic reprobation of the country.

Resolved, that the Supreme Court of the United States should, by peaceful and constitutional measures be so reconstituted as to relieve it from the domination of a sectional faction. . . .[3]

Toward the end of the nineteenth century another controversy arose over the Court's chameleonlike handling of the income tax issue which had finally culminated in its incredible five-to-four ruling in the *Pollock* case invalidating a considerable portion of the income tax law. This time the Democratic party, under William Jennings Bryan, took the lead in attacking the Court. The Democratic platform of that year suggested that the Court be reconstituted so that the decision might be reversed.[4] In the words of Charles and Mary Beard, ". . . the Supreme Court was criticized for its income tax decision in language as shocking to the new guardians of the sacred covenant as that employed by Republicans in the Dred Scott affair had once been to leaders of the Democracy."[5] But no reforms were attempted, for Bryan's defeats in 1896 and 1900 naturally prevented any action.

Then, in our own century, before the New Deal era, a variety of unpopular Court rulings in controversial cases, particularly in those bearing upon the problems of labor, resulted in new controversies over judicial review. These struggles were marked by specific proposals for reform advanced by the Roosevelt Progressive party in 1912 and the La Follette Progressive movement in 1924. Neither group was able to effect any change. Finally, there was the controversy over the power of the Supreme Court occasioned by the stream of

[3]*Ibid.,* pp. 187–88.

[4]*Ibid.,* p. 189.

[5]Beard, *Rise of American Civilization, op. cit.* (Chap. III, n. 4), II, 339. Reprinted by permission of The Macmillan Company, publishers.

anti-New Deal decisions which flowed from the Court in 1935 and 1936.

It is important to note that in this continuing controversy over judicial review all political parties have sooner or later added their voices to the chorus of criticism, and no one party has been consistently the Court's champion or critic. "Every American political party at some time has sheltered itself behind the Supreme Court and at others has found in the court's decisions obstructions to its purposes."[6] In part this has been due to the fact that the Court itself has shifted its position and has trodden first upon the toes of one party's traditional principles and then upon those of another. But in fairness to the Court it must also be pointed out that our political parties have indulged in some chameleonic adventures too. One may compare, for instance, the criticism of the Court occasioned by Chief Justice Marshall's famous decisions, which gave such an impetus to the movement for political centralization, with the criticism of the Court's decentralizing decisions of the 1930's. In both instances the censure came largely from the Democratic party. Conversely, it is just as easy to point to the Republican party, which for half a century and more called itself the party of Union and extolled the great decisions of Marshall, and then more recently started singing the theme song of state rights and became the chief defender of the Court's conservative decentralizing opinions.

A large part of the controversy which the Court's decisions have from time to time occasioned, has been recriminatory in character. In other words, it has been the disappointed litigant who has most often been the Court's chief critic. That is only natural. But it by no means follows that these

---

[6] Felix Frankfurter, "Supreme Court, United States," *Encyclopaedia of the Social Sciences, op. cit.* (Chap. I, n. 12), XIV, 474, 480. Reprinted by permission of The Macmillan Company, publishers.

critics of the Court and of judicial review have not had
honest intellectual grounds upon which to base their attacks.
It is personal defeat which has sometimes led these people
to experience a growing apprehension and distrust of the
Court's power as they have seen how it was exercised in
their own cases. Thus it will not do to set down all of the
critics of judicial review as nothing more than frustrated men
unwilling to accept defeat in litigation gracefully. There has
been a good deal of sincerity and honest conviction in such
criticism, however much one may question the wisdom of
some of the proposals for change.

We may now proceed to an examination of the specific
proposals which have been made for the alteration of the
Supreme Court, or the reform of judicial review. The list is
a long one, for it is doubtful whether any possible change in
the existing system has been overlooked by the Court's perennial critics.

Impeachment of Judges

It is not surprising that an attempt by Congress to impeach
and remove from office a Supreme Court justice should have
been one of the first methods employed in seeking to curb
the power of the judiciary, for it was one of the most obvious
means available. It will be remembered that the Federalist
party lost control of the presidency and Congress in the election of 1800. At the same time it managed to retain considerable influence over the federal judiciary due to the foresight
the party had shown during the Adams administration in
placing strong and loyal party members in important judicial
offices. Not unexpectedly, the activities of some of these Federalist judges became a more or less constant source of irritation to the Jeffersonian Democrats who were in power
after 1800. This irritation led, in 1805, to an attempt to remove
from office via the impeachment route one of the leading

Federalist justices of the Supreme Court, the irascible Samuel Chase. The House took the necessary step of impeaching Chase and then, according to schedule, he was tried by the Senate. There the vote for conviction, while reaching majority proportions, fell short of the required two thirds, and the attempt ended in failure.[7] Historians have usually applauded this result. Chase had certainly cut a rather sorry figure as a justice, but it must be remembered that the Constitution limits the grounds for impeachment of federal officers to "treason, bribery, or other high crimes or misdemeanors."[8] Chase had almost certainly not been guilty of any such offense, and the attempt to use this method of removing him from office was rather clearly a partisan one. There is evidence that had the attempt been successful Chief Justice Marshall would have been the next to go under the axe.

The Chase episode reveals the tentative attitude which prevailed toward the power of judicial review in those days. Chief Justice Marshall himself apparently made an amazing proposal that Congress should be conceded the power to reverse Supreme Court decisions in return for an agreement by Congress not to exercise its impeachment power over the judiciary.[9] But with the failure of the impeachment proceedings against Chase nothing further came of this Marshall formula for compromise.

Thus ended the one and only serious attempt by Congress to exercise a check over the Supreme Court through the use of its impeachment power. Had the case turned out differently there is no telling to what extent the judiciary might have become subordinate to Congress. It may be noted that several federal judges in the lower courts have been impeached, and a few convicted and removed from office. But

[7]Hockett, op. cit. (Chap. III, n. 14), pp. 313–14.

[8]Constitution of the United States, Art. II, sec. 4.

[9]Beveridge, op. cit. (Chap. X, n. 14), III, 177–78.

for the most part these cases have not involved any quarrel between the legislative and judicial branches of government over the issue of judicial review.

It should also be noted in passing that the Constitution, in addition to the impeachment provision, speaks cryptically of federal judges holding office for life "during good Behavior,"[10] the obvious implication being that a judge may be removed for bad behavior. But what constitutes good or bad behavior? Presumably a judge who has not actually committed such a serious offense as treason, bribery, some other high crime, or even just a misdemeanor, might be considered guilty of bad behavior. May not Congress then remove a judge for mere bad behavior in a manner entirely different from the regular impeachment process? No such attempt has ever been made nor has the question ever been answered. However, it is interesting to note that Representative Sumners, chairman of the House judiciary committee, has recently sponsored a bill providing a new method for removing all federal judges, save those of the Supreme Court, for bad behaviour. Upon the adoption of a resolution by the House the chief justice would appoint a special panel of three circuit judges to try a federal judge indicted by the House for bad behavior. In October, 1941, this bill passed the House by a very narrow margin and is now in the Senate.

Congressional Abolition of Courts

A second proposal that is sometimes made for curbing the power of the federal judiciary is that Congress exercise its unquestioned right to abolish federal courts. That this can be done with any but the Supreme Court is clear, for the Constitution definitely gives Congress such authority.[11] As

[10]Constitution of the United States, Art. III, sec. 1.
[11]*Ibid.*

for the Supreme Court, while Congress may not abolish it, it might, as seats on that tribunal became vacant, abolish justiceships one by one until nothing was left of the Court but the name. As a matter of fact, Congress has abolished certain federal courts. For example, in 1911, the entire system of so-called circuit courts was abolished. Likewise, Supreme Court justiceships have been abolished, although not to the point suggested above. However, in 1861 as part of the attack upon the Court resulting from its *Dred Scott* decision, Senator Hale of Maine introduced a resolution in Congress: "That the Committee on the Judiciary be instructed to inquire into the expediency and propriety of abolishing the present Supreme Court of the United States, and establishing, instead thereof, another Supreme Court, in pursuance of the provisions of the Constitution, which, in the opinion of Congress, will meet the requirements of the Constitution."[12]

Senator Hale's colleagues were not ready to accept such a drastic proposal, and its constitutionality would have been debatable, although the transfer of the Supreme Court justices to other judicial positions to make possible the creation of a new Court might have constituted a valid procedure. The outright abolition of federal courts and Supreme Court justiceships for the purpose of destroying the power of judicial review would be difficult because it is far too drastic a remedy. It would be like throwing the baby out with the bath! After all, the normal judicial function is an inevitable one and we do need courts.

Congressional Curtailment of Court Jurisdiction

The same conclusion is inevitable in regard to a third proposal—that Congress may by law reduce the jurisdiction of the federal courts. Again there is no question that the Consti-

[12]*Congressional Globe*, 37th Congress, 2nd Session, p. 26; December 9, 1861. Quoted by Fairman, *op. cit.* (Chap. X, n. 14), p. 40.

tution does give Congress complete power to determine the classes of cases which the federal judiciary, including the Supreme Court, may hear.[13] But to make extensive reduction in such jurisdiction merely for the purpose of denying the federal courts any opportunity to exercise the power of judicial review would be much too extreme a method. It would amount to the same thing as abolishing courts altogether.

Another version of this proposal is that Congress simply withdraw the jurisdiction of the federal courts in those specific instances where the constitutionality of a federal law is challenged. This has been done in at least one case. In 1868 Congress passed a law rescinding a certain type of appellate jurisdiction which it had granted to the Supreme Court in the preceding year. This change was made for the rather obvious, and to the Court not unwelcome, purpose of preventing that tribunal from passing upon the constitutionality of the Reconstruction Acts.[14] However, it would probably prove rather difficult in practice for Congress to word legislation to accomplish such a purpose generally. Since a request that a court declare a law unconstitutional can be raised in almost any case where a statute is being applied, it would virtually be necessary for Congress to abolish all types of jurisdiction in order to get rid of judicial review by this method.

Congress might try to leave judicial jurisdiction untouched but forbid the courts to exercise the power of judicial review in any case where it has taken jurisdiction. But such an attempt would almost certainly itself be declared unconstitutional by the courts. The Supreme Court would probably rule that while Congress may deny the courts certain types of jurisdiction altogether, it cannot grant jurisdiction and

[13]Constitution of the United States, Art. III, secs. 1–2.

[14]*Ex parte McCardle* 7 Wallace 506 (1869). See Fairman, *op. cit.* (Chap. X, n. 14), pp. 140–42.

then try to tell the courts how to handle cases arising under such jurisdiction. Of course, there is nothing to prevent the effecting of such an arrangement by means of a constitutional amendment. We may presumably settle the problem of judicial review any way we wish by that method. But, as will be pointed out shortly, the adoption of any proposal for the reform of judicial review which involves or necessitates amending the Constitution is apt to present practical difficulties.

The Attack upon Five-to-Four Decisions

An altogether different type of suggestion has pertained to the number of justices who must agree with one another before a court invalidates a statute. In place of the usual simple majority rule which most courts have followed in this respect, it has from time to time been argued that a larger majority be required. It has been suggested that in the case of the Supreme Court a two thirds vote, or even seven out of nine, be necessary to declare a congressional statute void. Several attempts have been made to secure the adoption of some such plan by act of Congress, by constitutional amendment, or by persuading the Supreme Court itself voluntarily to alter its majority rule in this respect. As early as 1823 a resolution was introduced in Congress to require the agreement of at least seven judges before legislation could be invalidated. Many similar proposals were made in subsequent years but none was successful. In the present century Senator Borah and former Supreme Court Justice Clarke advocated this type of reform.[15] In 1937, at the time of the controversy over the Roosevelt plan to reorganize the Court, Senator O'Mahoney proposed a constitutional amendment prohibiting the invali-

[15]See Haines, *op. cit.* (Chap. I, n. 1), pp. 469–75. See also John H. Clarke, "Judicial Power to Declare Legislation Unconstitutional," 9 *American Bar Association Journal* (October 1923), 689, 692.

dation of federal or state laws by any inferior court, and
requiring the concurrence of two thirds of the justices of the
Supreme Court in a decision invalidating such legislation.[16]
Such suggestions certainly have some merit and are particularly relevant in the light of the Court's own insistence
that statutes be upheld unless they are unconstitutional beyond a reasonable doubt. Moreover, the analogy of the jury
system wherein an unusual majority for conviction is required before a presumption of innocence can be overcome
has much significance here. But, admittedly, such a change
might have unfortunate results in some cases. It might even
prove difficult if not impossible to continue the enforcement
of a statute where only a minority of the justices have approved it.[17] However, it would hardly be possible under such
circumstances to attack a statute as a "minority law," for it
would of necessity have been passed originally by a majority
in each branch of Congress.

Of course, this plan would leave untouched the seven-to-
two, eight-to-one, and unanimous decisions in which laws are
held unconstitutional. And some of the controversies over
Supreme Court rulings have centered about such cases. For
example, the *Dred Scott* decision was by a seven-to-two vote.
Thus a two thirds requirement would not necessarily bring
to an end all argument over the exercise of the power of
judicial review, although it would probably prevent many of
the most serious controversies. It may also be pointed out
that although some of the proponents of this reform have
argued that it could be forced upon the courts by means of
law it is probable that a constitutional amendment would be
necessary before the courts would agree to follow any such
rule.

[16]Jackson, *op. cit.* (Chap. II, n. 11), p. 353.
[17]See Charles Warren, *Congress, the Constitution, and the Supreme Court*
(Boston: Little, Brown and Company, 1925), Chap. VI.

Congressional Overriding of Decisions

An alternate proposal sometimes offered in lieu of the one just described is that Congress be given the power to re-enact a statute which has been invalidated by the courts. In his 1924 campaign for the presidency Senator La Follette supported this proposal. Likewise, Senator Wheeler sponsored such an amendment during the 1937 controversy over judicial review.[18] In the latter instance the proposal was worded to require a two thirds vote for repassage in Congress and was modified to provide that a national election intervene between the adverse judicial ruling and a repassage of the law by Congress. This modification would presumably have given the people an opportunity, however indirect, to pass upon the disputed law before Congress took action. Again, this is a plan which has certain attractive features. It would be quite consistent with the democratic principle, even though in practice it might amount to a new way of amending the Constitution. But it has its disadvantages, too. For one thing, it ignores the great importance of the element of timing in the legislative process, a matter which has already been discussed. It is possible that years might pass before the Supreme Court invalidated a law, and then it would perhaps be two or three years more before Congress could act upon the question of repassage. In many instances it might be impossible to recapture the conditions and circumstances that surrounded the original enactment of the law, with the result that this new congressional power might seldom be exercised. Moreover, in these controversies over progressive social laws it should be remembered that the advantage usually lies with those who would prefer no law at all rather than with those who are trying to persuade the legis-

[18]Jackson, *op. cit.* (Chap. II, n. 11), pp. 352–53.

lature to act. As a matter of practical politics, it is far easier to kill a proposed bill than it is to bring about its enactment, or re-enactment. It should also be remembered that this suggested reform is usually couched in terms of a two thirds vote in Congress. This is of great importance, for there is not often a two thirds vote available in Congress for any statute, that has significant social or economic implications. Of course, the proposal could be modified to permit re-passage of a law by simple majority vote, but so worded it would probably receive less support. That the proposal in either form would take a constitutional amendment for adoption is obvious.

Increasing the Membership of the Court

A suggested reform with which we have lately been made familiar involves the use of the admitted power of Congress to increase the personnel of the Supreme Court. Have the justices rendered an unpopular decision invalidating a statute? Then let Congress enlarge the Court and the president appoint a sufficient additional number of progressive justices to secure a new and more favorable kind of decision. This proposal, as advanced by President Roosevelt in 1937, aroused a great deal of controversy, and the arguments, pro and con, have been worn so threadbare that it hardly seems necessary to say more on the subject here. Two or three comments may, however, be made.

In the first place, chance sometimes makes possible what lawmakers are reluctant to do. Presidents Washington, Jackson, Lincoln, Taft, and Franklin Roosevelt all had the opportunity to appoint at least five justices and thereby to reconstruct the Supreme Court. In addition to Taft and Franklin Roosevelt, four other presidents since the Civil War, Grant, Cleveland, Harrison, and Harding, have appointed four justices and have thus had opportunities to exert considerable influence on the Court. Many of these men were aware of the significance of their opportunities and to greater or less degree consciously appointed justices who could be counted on to render decisions according to a particular constitutional "line." On the other hand, nine presidents since the Civil War have been able to appoint, at the most, three justices and have thus for the most part been denied the opportunity to change the character of the Court in any substantial fashion.[19] So the question cannot be avoided; if and when such a new "line" does become desirable, and yet aged justices hang on to their jobs tenaciously, and chance or destiny seem reluctant to co-operate in bringing about the reconstruction of the Court, would it be unwise for Congress to make possible what chance will not?

One of the strongest arguments against the proposal is that once such a step is taken a precedent is created, and following each important shift in the political control of Congress and the presidency there would be a tendency to pack the Court with new appointees. However, it can be argued that the precedent has already been established. The size of the Supreme Court has been changed several times. The Supreme Court originally consisted of six members. The number was reduced to five in 1801, increased to seven in 1807, then to nine in 1837 and to ten in 1863. In 1866 it was reduced to seven and finally fixed at nine in 1869. In every instance of increase or decrease in the number of justices there is at least some evidence that the change was designed to affect the Court's decisions. For example, Professor Haines says of the change in 1837 by which the justices were increased from seven to nine that it was done "in order to make Democratic control secure."[20] Likewise the changes of the

[19]Charles Fairman, "The Retirement of Federal Judges," 51 *Harvard Law Review* (1938) 397; I *Selected Essays* 885, 889.

[20]Haines, *op. cit.* (Chap. I, n. 1), p. 351.

period 1863 to 1869, when the size of the Court fluctuated between seven and ten members, seem to have been strongly influenced by considerations much more political in character than the mere question of the most efficient size of the Court.[21] However, precedent or no precedent, the truth is that political circumstances seldom combine to permit alteration in the size of the Court. Even control of the presidency and overwhelming majorities in both Houses of Congress by one political party are not always sufficient to make such a change possible, as Franklin Roosevelt discovered.

The Nuisance Value of Attempted Reforms

In the second place, it may be pointed out that while the formal attempt to alter the Supreme Court in 1937 failed, the mere making of the attempt was not without its effect. Mr. Roosevelt was not successful in his proposal. But the Court was certainly not left untouched and perhaps the president succeeded, consciously or unconsciously, in altering the course of judicial review.

This is as good a place as any, then, to make what seems to be a rather important point. It may be said of the whole list of varying proposals for reforming judicial review that, since it is almost wholly a story of failure, there is little reason to consider it. But this would be a badly mistaken position.

If it is true in fact that the Supreme Court is a political instrumentality of our government, then the problem of subjecting the justices to at least a minimum of political pressure is important. Because of the appointive character and life tenure of their offices, the usual sort of popular control that operates in the case of the president and Congress is here lacking. Appointment of justices by the president and their confirmation by the Senate do undoubtedly provide some

[21]Swisher, *Stephen J. Field, op. cit.* (Chap. X, n. 14), pp. 115–16.

opportunity for the voice of democracy to express itself. On the other hand, although the appointment of a justice may be democratically influenced by the prevailing political ideas or mores, once in office a justice may remain there twenty-five years or more. Long before his tenure is finished, the times may have moved forward, leaving him far behind as a hopeless reactionary. Or, of course, there is the possibility that the country will turn for a while in a strongly conservative direction so that justices appointed during a previous progressive period will seem radical in their point of view. In either case, this question suggests itself: How can democracy exert pressure on such official ? We have seen that many of the formal proposals advanced at one time or another for exercising political control over the judiciary are in some way faulty, and are all difficult to put into practice. But perhaps their great significance lies in their nuisance value. A mere threat to impeach a justice, or periodic talk about changing the Supreme Court's jurisdiction, or a rare proposal to increase or decrease the Court's size, may be all that is necessary to make certain that the justices occasionally acquaint themselves with the spirit of their times and get on with the work of expounding a "Constitution." In fact, the history of the Court would seem to show that such pressures have been effectively employed upon the justices in more than one instance.

Compulsory Retirement of Judges

Another proposal sometimes urged by way of solving the problem of the elderly justice who grows increasingly reactionary with his advancing years is that judges be compelled to retire at seventy, or seventy-five. Unquestionably, many Supreme Court justices have prolonged their periods of service on that Court beyond their years of usefulness.

Charles Evans Hughes once remarked: "It is extraordinary how reluctant aged judges are to retire and to give up their accustomed work. They seem to be tenacious of the appearance of adequacy."[22] Hughes seemed to favor seventy-five as possibly a good age for compulsory retirement. Yet he himself failed to retire when he reached that age in 1937. In a very careful study he made of this matter Professor Fairman strongly favors seventy as the age for compulsory retirement, with the provision that a president, with the consent of the Senate, might reappoint the exceptional justice for an additional limited period of eight years. Fairman lists many justices who stayed on the Court after their faculties had begun to decline. For example, he refers to Justice Field's participation at the age of seventy-eight in the majority decision in the controversial five-to-four income tax case in 1895 and is led to comment: "No rationalization can justify a system whereby the powers of government in a matter of such high moment are finally determined by a mind so somnolent and prepossessed as Justice Field's had become by that time." And he concludes that "voluntary retirement, in any real sense, is very rare indeed."[23] Congress in 1937, partly as a result of the controversy over the more drastic Roosevelt Court plan, did strengthen already existing legislation so that now a justice who reaches seventy and has ten years of service may retire on full salary. The full effects of this legislation remain to be determined. Several justices have retired since 1937, but all delayed their departures until they were well beyond seventy, and only one was very prompt to avail himself of the new opportunity.

[22]Hughes, *op. cit.* (Chap. I, n. 21), p. 75. Reprinted by permission of the Columbia University Press.
[23]I *Selected Essays* 885, 910, 912.

Recall of Judges and Decisions

Still another proposal for judicial reform calls for the giving of a referendum check to the voters over judicial decisions, or even a recall check over judges themselves. Theodore Roosevelt toyed briefly with the referendum proposal in his Progressive party period. The idea has little to commend it. The initiative, referendum, and recall have been tried widely as to legislative and executive officials in state and local government. The evidence as to their effects is at best inconclusive. There is little reason to suppose that the exercise of these direct checks over judges or their decisions would be any more effective.[24]

Bringing the Constitution Up to Date

Last, but by no means least in the list of judicial reforms, is the suggestion that the Constitution be amended so as to make more positive and specific the powers of the legislative and executive departments of government. These suggestions range all the way from the mere rewording of a few of the more ambiguous sections of the Constitution such as the commerce and due process of law clauses, to the proposal that the Constitution be completely rewritten by a new constitutional convention. This type of suggestion is often advanced by persons who have been disturbed at some of the more straightforward suggestions for the curbing of judicial power itself, and who are inclined to feel that the main trouble lies not so much with our judges as with the inadequacies of the Constitution they are asked to interpret. This point of view has considerable justification. But with-

[24]See Haines, *op. cit.* (Chap. I, n. 1), pp. 482–88 for a discussion of proposals for the recall of judges and judicial decisions.

out desiring to challenge the soundness of this attitude and certainly without wishing to suggest that the Constitution is not in part outmoded or could not be changed with profit, we shall find it desirable to examine two possible objections to this particular solution.

The first concerns the complexity of the amending process and the undeniable fact that it is possible formally to amend our Constitution in any important respect only with the greatest of difficulty. There is little doubt that the Constitutional Fathers made a mistake at this point. Whichever of the four amending methods is employed, the requirements are all in terms of two thirds and three fourths majorities. Two of the methods are so difficult to invoke that they have never been used. It is true, of course, that it has been possible to amend the Constitution twenty-one times. But the first ten amendments were added immediately after the Constitution went into operation and were virtually part of the original document. Of the remaining eleven, three were adopted at the close of the Civil War, were the equivalent of the treaty of peace ending the war and, as in the case of most such treaties, the defeated states had little choice but to accept them. Of the remaining eight, at least two were of minor importance.

So the plain truth is that we do not have in the United States a very strong or significant tradition in favor of amending the Constitution. In part, the Supreme Court itself is responsible for this somewhat unfortunate state of affairs. The Court's responsibility can be traced back to Marshall's ruling in *McCulloch* v. *Maryland*. In its decision, it will be remembered, the Court sanctioned the general principle of the flexibility of the Constitution, and the specific idea of implied powers. In so ruling, the Court was in effect saying that it is not usually necessary to amend our Constitution in order to make it adequate to the needs of new and changed conditions. Instead, said the Court, this Constitution is a broad outline of our governmental system, "intended to endure for ages to come, and, consequently, to be adapted to the various *crises* of human affairs."[25]

This was an entirely legitimate point of view for the Court to have taken. In fact, Chief Justice Marshall has usually received only the highest praise for the vision and statesmanship he revealed in his opinion. We are probably far better off with a flexible Constitution which it has been possible to adapt to the needs of changing times, than we would be with a much-amended constitution which by now would almost certainly have achieved the deadening prolixity of a code of laws. But at the same time it must be remembered that it was the Supreme Court that encouraged the American people to accept the idea of flexibility in our Constitution. Accordingly, it is a bit late to argue that the Court has not been at fault in its periodic failure to make necessary adaptations in the Constitution, and that the need, instead, is to modernize the language of the Constitution by formal amendment.

A second difficulty with the amendment suggestion lies in finding the proper wording for additions to the Constitution. It is easy enough to say that we must give Congress greater and more specific power to control agricultural production or the relationship between a businessman and his workers. But to word such a grant of power briefly and in the accustomed style of constitutional language is not so simple. And in any case it must be remembered that the Supreme Court still retains the right to speak the last word, even following the successful amendment of the Constitution, for its power of interpretation extends to the amendments, themselves. There is no wish here to suggest that the Supreme Court would deliberately seek to frustrate the will of the people

[25]*McCulloch* v. *Maryland* 4 Wheaton 316, 415 (1819).

as clearly expressed through the adoption of positive amendments to the Constitution. But when we recall such subsequent steps as the necessary interpretation of the amendments by the Court, the possible application to statutes, passed under the authority of the new constitutional provisions, of the due process of law objection, and the final need of judicial interpretation of these statutes, themselves, it is clear that modernizing the Constitution would by no means bring to an end controversy over the judicial function in the governmental process.

Chapter XII

The Power to Govern

Non *sub Homine sed sub Deo et Lege.* We may refer
once more to this famous aphorism of the English common
law with which we began our discussion. If we are to reach
any sound conclusion to our study, a first requirement would
seem to be our recognition of the importance of a variable
human factor in the operation of law. Law is not entirely a
matter of certainties. The presence of a considerable measure
of flexibility in a legal system is inevitable. This is particularly
true of American public law. We have seen that our national
Constitution, for all of its admitted greatness, remains at
many points a vague, ambiguous document which can only
be given meaning by the men who interpret and apply its
words. The principles of this Constitution which have taken
shape over a period of a century and a half are little more
than informal rules of the "game," in the formulation of
which Congress, president, and Supreme Court have all
played parts.

It is easy to sympathize with and understand the motivation of those persevering people who spend their lives
searching after a law that is certain, a government that abides
by fundamental principles of justice and is uncontaminated
by the arbitrariness and caprice of the human factor. But if
it be acknowledged that life is far too complex for any such

ideal political arrangement, and that the Supreme Court both in passing upon the constitutionality of legislation and in interpreting statutes may often choose between two or more possible rulings, then what is to be our final judgment on judicial review?

It may be pointed out at once that the American people have never found such a final judgment an easy thing to make. Certainly there has never been any shortage of arguments both for and against judicial review. Some of these arguments have been impressive in an intellectual sense; others have carried weight because they seemed to rest upon practical political considerations. Individually, many of these arguments continue to be fairly convincing. But when all of the arguments, pro and con, are marshaled, the result is a somewhat inconclusive one and there has usually been a strong temptation to avoid a decisive verdict in either direction. An examination of a few of the more significant arguments that have been advanced for and against judicial review will tend to explain why any final decision in the matter is difficult to make.

The Case for Judicial Review

To begin with, it should be emphasized that even though it be conceded that judges do in fact exercise discretionary power in determining matters of constitutional and legislative policy, there will still be disagreement as to the validity or desirability of judicial review. Defenders of the power are still inclined to argue that the Constitution, for all of its uncertainty, remains nonetheless a constitution, and that therefore judges are better qualified, both in terms of technical training and lack of political bias, to determine the meaning of its clauses. But this argument can, of course, be challenged by a contrary line of reasoning: the lack of preciseness and technical terminology in the Constitution indicate that it is more of a political than a legal document. Such phrases as "interstate commerce" and "due process of law" have no fixed meaning in any sense of law. Consequently, should not the terms of the Constitution be interpreted by political officers directly responsible to the people, rather than by judges trained in the technicalities of the law and appointed to office for life? Professor Haines has pointed out that the issue is "whether it is a lawyer's interpretation of the Constitution or the people's interpretation that is to prevail," and he refers to Theodore Roosevelt's assertion: "I contend that the people, in the nature of things must be better judges of what is the preponderant opinion than the courts, and that the courts should not be allowed to reverse the political philosophy of the people."[1] In other words, it is the president and congressmen who are elected by the people and who are directly responsible to them. Consequently, if the interpretation of the Constitution is a flexible matter involving the conscious selection of certain policies and the rejection of others, does not the principle of democracy require that such power be exercised by elective officers?

Turning to more specific arguments, pro and con, we find that defenders of the Court's power to invalidate acts of Congress have traditionally advanced two claims in support of their position. One of these is that the Court protects the civil liberties of the people against congressional encroachment, and the other is that judicial review protects the power of the states by preventing Congress from violating the principle of federalism. A good example of the first argument is to be found in the assertion of the famous historian of the Supreme Court, Charles Warren, that " . . . Congress, or one of its branches, has violated the provisions of the Bill of Rights at least ten times since the year 1867; and at least ten

[1] I *Selected Essays* 844, 882.

times has the Supreme Court saved the individual against congressional usurpation of power."[2] Perhaps the most effective attempt to answer this argument has been made by Professor Edgerton of the Cornell Law School, now himself a federal judge. In a very careful study of all the cases in which federal laws have been declared void he denies the existence of a single bona fide decision protecting an individual's civil liberties against adverse federal action. He points out, interestingly enough, that in the very case in which the right of judicial review was first asserted by the Supreme Court the Court refused to protect a helpless individual against arbitrary action by officers of the federal government.[3] His final summary of the judicial review cases invalidating federal action is significant:

Of the pre-New Deal cases in which the Supreme Court annulled acts of Congress, one group protected mistreatment of colored people; another group protected businesses or business methods hurtful to the majority; another . . . protected owners of business at the direct expense of labor; another protected owners of business against taxation; another protected the recipients of substantial incomes, gifts, and inheritances against taxation; and other cases protected the interests of property owners in other ways. Not many cases of any importance fall outside these categories. A few decisions were approximately neutral in their incidence as between different social groups. . . . There is not a case in the entire series which protected the "civil liberties" of freedom of speech, press, and assembly; on the contrary, over the protest of Holmes and Brandeis, the Espionage Act was not merely upheld but extended by the Court. There is not one which protected the right to vote; on the contrary, congressional attempts to protect the voting rights of Negroes were defeated by the Court. There is not one which protected the vital

[2]Warren, *op. cit.* (Chap. XI, n. 17), p. 150. Reprinted by permission of Little, Brown and Company, publishers.

[3]*Marbury* v. *Madison.* 1 Cranch 137 (1803).

interests of the working majority of the population in organizing or in wages; on the contrary, congressional efforts to protect those interests were frustrated by the Court.[4]

The second claim that the Supreme Court has prevented Congress from encroaching upon the powers of the states may likewise be challenged. Bearing in mind the uncertain line which the Constitution draws between national and state powers, we find that there is at best but a handful of cases in which federal statutes have been invalidated because of a reasonably clear-cut invasion of state power. It may be that the mere existence of judicial review has served to dissuade Congress from the enactment of laws in fields reserved to the states, but this is rather doubtful. One needs to remember that the members of Congress are all elected to the national legislature from the states and that many of them have always shown an intense loyalty to the states they represent and have bitterly opposed all efforts to undermine the position and power of the states. Justice Holmes perhaps had in mind some such thought when he observed: "I do not think the United States would come to an end if we lost our power to declare an Act of Congress void."[5]

In a sense, both of these arguments in favor of judicial review are based upon the fundamental assumption that Congress is a body which cannot safely be trusted to refrain from abusing the powers that have been given to it; whether in the direction of destroying civil liberties, or undermining the position of the state governments.

This argument that judicial review alone prevents Congress from extreme and arbitrary exercise of its powers has

[4]Henry W. Edgerton, "The Incidence of Judicial Control over Congress," 22 *Cornell Law Quarterly* (1937) 299, 346–48; I *Selected Essays* 793, 842–44. Reprinted by permission of the author and of the *Cornell Law Quarterly*.

[5]Holmes, *Collected Legal Papers* (Chap. II, n. 7), pp. 295–96. Reprinted by permission of Little, Brown and Company.

never been more effectively answered than by certain members of the judiciary itself, who from time to time have indicated their confidence in the good faith and essential trustworthiness of legislators in our democracy. For example, over a century ago Justice Johnson of the Supreme Court spoke as follows:

The idea is utopian, that government can exist without leaving the exercise of discretion somewhere. Public security against the abuse of such discretion must rest on responsibility, and stated appeals to public approbation. Where all power is derived from the people, and public functionaries, at short intervals, deposite it at the feet of the people, to be resumed again only at their will, individual fears may be alarmed by the monsters of imagination, but individual liberty can be in little danger.

. . . if there is one maxim which necessarily rides over all others, in the practical application of government, it is, that the public functionaries must be left at liberty to exercise the powers which the people have intrusted to them.[6]

Or again nearly a century ago Chief Justice Black of the Pennsylvania Supreme Court spoke straight to the point in a remarkably wise passage.

The great powers given to the legislature are liable to be abused. But this is inseparable from the nature of human institutions. The wisdom of man has never conceived of a government with power sufficient to answer its legitimate ends, and at the same time incapable of mischief. No political system can be made so perfect that its rulers will always hold it to the true course. In the very best a great deal must be trusted to the discretion of those who administer it. In ours, the people have given larger powers to the legislature, and relied, for the faithful execution of them, on the wisdom and honesty of that department, and on the direct accountability of the members to their constituents. There is no shadow of reason for supposing that

[6] *Anderson* v. *Dunn* 6 Wheaton 204, 226 (1821).

the mere abuse of power was meant to be corrected by the judiciary.

There is nothing more easy than to imagine a thousand tyrannical things which the legislature may do, if its members forget all their duties; disregard utterly the obligations they owe to their constituents, and recklessly determine to trample upon right and justice. But to take away the power from the legislature because they may abuse it, and give to the judges the right of controlling it, would not be advancing a single step, since the judges can be imagined to be as corrupt and as wicked as legislators. . . . What is worse still, the judges are almost entirely irresponsible . . . while the members of the legislature, who would do the imaginary things referred to, "would be scourged into retirement by their indignant masters."[7]

The Case against Judicial Review

Those who have been inclined to attack judicial review have not been content merely to refute the arguments advanced by the Court's friends in favor of the retention of this power. They have gone on to advance positive arguments of their own as to why the power should be abolished or curtailed. For one thing they point out that judicial review has tended to destroy the compromise element in American politics. It is argued that the legislation passed by Congress is largely the result of pressures and counterpressures exerted by important economic and social elements within the body politic. Congress presumably weighs the conflicting interests and claims of all of these groups and seeks to formulate legislative policies that will represent an expedient middle course between opposing demands. Accordingly, the argument continues, when the Supreme Court invalidates an act of Congress it merely proves that it has been sensitive to a different combination of pressures from that influencing Con-

[7]*Sharpless* v. *Mayor of Philadelphia* 21 Pa. 147 (1853). Quotation from report of the case in Dodd, *op. cit.* (Chap. VIII, n. 2), pp. 47, 49–50.

gress. Such a decision may very well upset a delicate compromise solution which the legislature, elected along democratic lines, has succeeded in arranging. Justice Jackson, when
attorney general, stated this argument in the following words:

After the forces of conservatism and liberalism, of radicalism
and reaction, of emotion and of self-interest are all caught up in
the legislative process and averaged and come to rest in some
compromise measure such as the Missouri Compromise, the
N.R.A., the A.A.A., a minimum wage law, or some other legislative policy, a decision striking it down closes an area of compromise in which conflicts have actually, if only temporarily,
been composed. Each such decision takes away from our democratic federalism another of its defenses against domestic dis-
order and violence. The vice of judicial supremacy, as exerted
for ninety years in the field of policy, has been its progressive
closing of the avenues to peaceful and democratic conciliation
of our social and economic conflicts.[8]

Mr. Jackson goes on to strengthen his point by a further
analysis of the *Dred Scott* decision invalidating the Missouri
Compromise. He argues convincingly that in this one instance, at least, the operation of judicial review virtually
destroyed any further possibility of compromising the slavery
issue along political lines and thus did much to bring on
the Civil War.

Of course, the Court's defenders will not accept all of the
implications of this argument. Some will deny the suggestion
inherent in it that the Court is itself subject to the influence
of pressure groups and is sometimes inclined to support a
compromise policy resulting from these influences and differing from the one formulated by Congress. Others may
agree that in the realistic sense this is not an essentially incorrect or unfair description of the process of judicial review,

[8]Jackson, *op. cit.* (Chap. II, n. 11), p. 321. Reprinted by permission of
Alfred A. Knopf, Inc., publisher.

but will insist that the Court is as good an agency as Congress, if not a better one, to effect such compromises between divergent pressure groups. The Court has perhaps made errors, as in the *Dred Scott* decision. But Congress, too, has sometimes blundered in its efforts to create and preserve a condition of equilibrium in the body politic. For example, it can be argued that in invalidating such federal statutes as the National Industrial Recovery Act and the original Agricultural Adjustment Act, when it was confronted with a tendency on the part of Congress to surrender to individual pressure groups, such as labor or the farmer, the Court was merely returning our national policy to the middle of the road.

A second argument against judicial review has been expressed in the following words by Professor Haines:

Judicial review in a certain sense encourages a disrespect for law. A citizen who feels aggrieved by the enforcement of a law is warranted in resisting its enforcement in the hope that the law may eventually be declared void. Those who can afford to take chances in contesting a law can hold up its effective enforcement for many years until the final court of appeal puts its stamp of approval or disapproval on the law.[9]

That this is a very real danger has been made evident by such episodes as the extensive refusal of businessmen and employers to comply with the requirements of the Wagner Act during the period from its enactment in 1935 to the decision of the Supreme Court upholding it in 1937. These men were no doubt sincere in accepting the advice of the American Liberty League's three-score lawyers that the act was surely unconstitutional, but that hardly excused their lack of respect for the nation's law and certainly did much to render the enforcement of the statute very difficult.

[9]Haines, *op. cit.* (Chap. I, n. 1), pp. 480–81. Reprinted by permission of the University of California Press.

Again, however, advocates of judicial review will hardly let this argument pass without challenge. After all, it is the technical right of any interested party under our American political system to doubt the validity of a statute and to violate that statute preparatory to raising the point of unconstitutionality in the course of the litigation occasioned by the violation. Moreover, it may be argued that any unwillingness to obey a statute, or any lack of respect for law, while perhaps unfortunate, is only temporary, since sooner or later the Supreme Court will render a decision bringing to an end any uncertainty as to the validity of a given statute.

The Indecisive Verdict

Enough arguments have perhaps now been examined to indicate the difficulty of establishing any completely convincing case either for the retention or the abolition of judicial review. If the premises be accepted that the Supreme Court does in fact have a considerable power of choice in many of the decisions it renders, and that the principle of democracy requires that such power of choice be granted only to elective officers, it is likely that the case against judicial review is the stronger one. Nonetheless, we hesitate to accept such a conclusion. In the first place, it is clear that the power of the judiciary to scrutinize the activities of forty-eight state governments should be preserved. It is worth noting that Justice Holmes, having stated that he did not necessarily fear the consequences of the abolition of judicial review of acts of Congress, went on to add the words, "I do think the Union would be imperiled if we could not make that declaration [holding legislation unconstitutional] as to the laws of the several States."[10] In view of the complexities of our federal system of government, and the uncertainties and idiosyncra-

[10]Holmes, *op. cit.* (Chap. II, n. 7), p. 296.

sies of the laws being ground out by forty-eight state legislatures, not to mention more than ten thousand local legislative bodies such as city councils, it is entirely possible that the complete abolition of judicial review would effect thoroughgoing changes in our political system. We may hope that the Supreme Court of the future will be slower to use the Fourteenth Amendment to invalidate social legislation enacted by the states, but we can hardly avoid the conclusion that the Court, particularly in recent years, has rendered many desirable decisions thwarting unwise action by state officers. Professor Edgerton, for example, would not deny that there have been many conspicuous decisions protecting civil liberties against serious encroachment by state governments.

In the second place, we have seen that the courts must exercise considerable discretionary power in interpreting statutes and reviewing the rulings of administrative agencies. In so far as judicial review is defined to include this aspect of the power of the courts, its abolition is neither desirable nor likely. Here, as elsewhere, there is perhaps a need for the courts to show a greater humility in the exercise of power, but that judges must finally wield much discretionary power in the implementation of statutes is inescapable.

Even as to the power of the courts to invalidate federal legislation outright, much less imposing though the arguments in its favor may be, the American people seem inclined to favor its retention. Granting that the Supreme Court passes upon the wisdom as well as the constitutionality of legislation, and granting further that it has sometimes acted as the agent of minority groups harboring selfish aims, people continue to believe that the Court serves as a kind of balance wheel in the body politic. Admittedly, one of the most serious problems in a democracy is to strike a balance between the rights of the majority and those of minorities, between the rights of the present generation and those of future generations. It is possible that a present majority may by its actions endanger the fundamental rights of present minorities or of future majorities and minorities. It is because of such dangers that many people feel that the justices of the Supreme Court serve a useful function as a sort of council of elder statesmen in acting as a brake upon the majority and in slowing down the political process until the wisdom of questioned policies can be further considered. Of course, this sort of reasoning is not easily reconciled with Justice Jackson's thesis that the Supreme Court, far from serving as a balance wheel, has interfered with the making of compromise settlements between opposing forces in our society along democratic lines. Moreover, as Mr. Jackson pointed out, before his appointment to the Court, "In no major conflict with the representative branches on any question of social or economic policy has time vindicated the Court."[11] It must be admitted that historical evidence tends to support this assertion.

On the other hand, it should be noted that some of the great liberal scholars of the law have come to the conclusion that judicial review is worth retaining. Many years before he was appointed to the Supreme Court, Benjamin Cardozo stated:

The great ideals of liberty and equality are preserved against the assaults of opportunism, the expediency of the passing hour, the erosion of small encroachments, the scorn and derision of those who have no patience with general principles, by enshrining them in constitutions, and consecrating to the task of their protection a body of defenders. By conscious or subconscious influence, the presence of this restraining power, aloof in the background, but none the less always in reserve, tends to stabilize and rationalize the legislative judgment, to infuse it

[11]Jackson, *op. cit.* (Chap. II, n. 11), x.

with the glow of principle, to hold the standard aloft and visible for those who must run the race and keep the faith. . . . Great maxims, if they may be violated with impunity, are honored often with lip-service, which passes easily into irreverence. The restraining power of the judiciary does not manifest its chief worth in the few cases in which the legislature has gone beyond the lines that mark the limits of discretion. Rather shall we find its chief worth in making vocal and audible the ideals that might otherwise be silenced, in giving them continuity of life and expression, in guiding and directing choice within the limits where choice ranges. This function should preserve to the courts the power that now belongs to them, if only the power is exercised with insight into social values, and with suppleness of adaptation to changing social needs.[12]

Equally impressive are the following words of Justice Frankfurter, also written before he was appointed to the Supreme Court:

The Supreme Court is indispensable to the effective workings of our federal government. If it did not exist, we should have to create it. I know of no other peaceful method for making the adjustments necessary to a society like ours—for maintaining the equilibrium between state and federal power, for settling the eternal conflicts between liberty and authority—than through a court of great traditions free from the tensions and temptations of party strife, detached from the fleeting interests of the moment. But because, inextricably, the Supreme Court is also an organ of statesmanship and the most powerful organ, it must have a seasoned understanding of affairs, the imagination to see the organic relations of society, above all, the humility not to set up its own judgment against the conscientious efforts of those whose primary duty it is to govern. . . .[13]

[12]Cardozo, *op. cit.* (Chap. I, n. 19), pp. 92–94. Reprinted by permission of the Yale University Press.

[13]Frankfurter, *Law and Politics, op. cit.* (Chap. V, n. 8), pp. 52–53. Reprinted by permission of Harcourt, Brace and Company, publishers.

Finally, one simple but important fact needs to be remembered. Although the Supreme Court since the beginning has been the subject of almost continuous controversy and attack, the power of judicial review has not only not been abolished but has not even been altered or curtailed in any formal way. That this has been the outcome of the recurring struggles over the Court's power strongly suggests the existence of powerful political factors favoring the retention of judicial review which have always tended to outweigh the impressive intellectual arguments for its abolition.

Conclusions

Nonetheless, although formal alteration of judicial review has never been possible it is erroneous to conclude that the Supreme Court has not been affected by the storms that have raged about it. The evidence clearly indicates that the exercise of the power of judicial review has often been influenced by pressure brought to bear upon the Court. The men who have served upon the Court have frequently been influenced by the expressions of unmistakable displeasure which their decisions have sometimes evoked from the American people.[14]

The conclusion to be drawn from this final point is obvious. Judicial review is a firmly established part of the American political process, and attempts to remove it are likely to end in failure. At the same time this particular aspect of our political process is by no means beyond the influence of public opinion and popular control. Accordingly, it should be recognized that the Court is, on the whole, subject to many of the same forces and influences that the other officers of government are, and that when a case presenting a great

[14]On this point see Frank J. Goodnow, *Social Reform and the Constitution* (New York: The Macmillan Company, 1911) Chap. VIII, particularly p. 359.

"constitutional" issue arises, in all likelihood powerful and contending pressure groups have merely transferred their struggles from legislative to judicial halls.

Judges must therefore possess a continuing awareness of the great social and economic issues of the day so that they may not lose touch with the spirit and desires of the present. It is probably desirable that judges be relieved from the constant and direct responsibility to popular opinion which is the necessary lot of the legislator or chief executive, but nonetheless it is clear that theirs is no ivory tower, no strictly technical or procedural pursuit. Thus it seems proper that a majority which finds its desires being frustrated through the exercise of judicial power should endeavor to exert pressure upon judges to see things its way. Such pressure has always been forthcoming in our history and has, more often than not, been successful. And if it may be said of judicial review that it must be a desirable institution, else the people would have shown a greater interest in curtailing it, so it may likewise be said that exerting pressure upon the Supreme Court cannot be wrong, else the people would not so often have attempted it. Justice, as well as citizen, must recognize that the Supreme Court is an instrument of government which shares with president and Congress the power to govern.

Selected Bibliography

Books

Beard, Charles A., *An Economic Interpretation of the Constitution of the United States* (New York: The Macmillan Company, 1913).

The classic presentation of the thesis that the Constitutional Fathers were motivated by economic considerations. The book has been the subject of much controversy but has had a very widespread influence.

Beard, Charles A., *The Supreme Court and the Constitution* (New York: The Macmillan Company, 1912).

A strong argument that the Constitutional Fathers intended to establish judicial review.

Boudin, L. B., *Government by Judiciary* (New York: William Godwin, Inc., 2 vols., 1932).

The most famous and substantial attack upon judicial review. Vitriolic and not always dependable; nonetheless a valuable treatise.

Cardozo, Benjamin N., *The Nature of the Judicial Process* (New Haven: Yale University Press, 1921).

A brilliant little study by the famous judge. A profound, philosophic analysis of the work of the courts.

Corwin, Edward S., *The Doctrine of Judicial Review* (Princeton: Princeton University Press, 1914).

An early collection of essays by one of the great scholars in the field of constitutional law.

Corwin, Edward S., *The Twilight of the Supreme Court* (New Haven: Yale University Press, 1934).

A later study based upon lectures delivered at the Yale School of Law. Perhaps the best expression of this great scholar's theories.

Cushman, Robert E., *Leading Constitutional Decisions* (7th ed.; New York: F. S. Crofts & Co., 1940).

A short collection of Supreme Court cases by one of the most careful scholars in the field. The introductory notes to the cases are exceptionally well done and very useful.

Dicey, A. V., *Law and Public Opinion in England* (New York: The Macmillan Company, 1905).

A series of lectures delivered at the Harvard Law School by the great English legal scholar. A pioneer analysis of the influence of public opinion in the growth of the law.

Ewing, Cortez A. M., *The Judges of the Supreme Court, 1789–1937* (Minneapolis: The University of Minnesota Press, 1938).

A statistical study of Supreme Court personnel. A convenient assembly of much valuable data.

Fairman, Charles, *Mr. Justice Miller and the Supreme Court* (Cambridge: Harvard University Press, 1939).

One of the most recent biographies of a Supreme Court justice. Exceptionally well done; it should set a pattern for further writing in this field.

Frank, Jerome, *Law and the Modern Mind* (New York: Coward-McCann, Inc., 1930).

An early study of the nonlegal motivation of the judge. A pioneer work in stressing psychological influences.

Frankfurter, Felix, *Law and Politics* (Edited by Archibald MacLeish and E. F. Prichard, Jr.; New York: Harcourt, Brace and Company, 1939).

A collection of the speeches and writings of the great legal scholar and judge. A valuable although somewhat discursive presentation of his philosophy.

Frankfurter, Felix, and James M. Landis, *The Business of the Supreme Court* (New York: The Macmillan Company, 1927).

The definitive treatment of the jurisdiction and procedure of the Supreme Court. The approach is historical. Very technical and somewhat difficult to use.

Gilbert, W. C., *Provisions of Federal Law Held Unconstitutional by the Supreme Court of the United States* (Washington: Government Printing Office, 1936).

A valuable collection of data on the decisions of the Supreme Court invalidating federal laws.

Haines, Charles G., *The American Doctrine of Judicial Supremacy* (2nd ed.; Berkeley: University of California Press, 1932).

The second edition of this classic is perhaps the most valuable single volume on the Supreme Court. The approach is both historical and analytical.

Hughes, Charles E., *The Supreme Court of the United States* (New York: Columbia University Press, 1928).

A valuable and remarkably frank exposition of the work of the Supreme Court by a great judge. Very readable.

Jackson, Robert, *The Struggle for Judicial Supremacy* (New York: Alfred A. Knopf, Inc., 1941).

A highly critical analysis of the work of the Supreme Court with particular emphasis upon the New Deal years. Somewhat hurried and superficial but nonetheless one of the most stimulating volumes on the subject.

McLaughlin, Andrew C., *A Constitutional History of the United States* (New York: D. Appleton-Century Company, 1935).

Already a classic. The approach and point of view are conservative. This is a storehouse of information on the development of the American constitutional system.

Pennock, J. Roland, *Administration and the Rule of Law* (New York: Farrar & Rinehart, Inc., 1941).

A recent, very readable, and intelligent volume on a difficult but extremely important subject.

Pringle, Henry F., *The Life and Times of William Howard Taft* (New York: Farrar & Rinehart, Inc., 2 vols., 1939).

The chapters on Taft's judicial career are necessarily somewhat secondary. Nonetheless, along with Fairman's *Miller,* this is one of the best biographical studies of a Supreme Court justice.

Read, Conyers (Editor), *The Constitution Reconsidered* (New York: Columbia University Press, 1938).

A recent valuable collection of essays on the Constitution and related subjects. The separate items were originally read as papers at the 1937 convention of the American Historical Association.

Selected Essays on Constitutional Law, compiled and edited by a committee of the Association of American Law Schools (Chicago: The Foundation Press, Inc., 5 vols., 1938).

An extremely useful collection of articles from the law reviews and law quarterlies on all subjects within the field of constitutional law.

Warren, Charles, *The Supreme Court in United States History* (Boston: Little, Brown and Company, 3 vols., 1922).

The classic work on the subject. The author is one of the most conservative students of the Supreme Court. The study is very careful and complete. Extremely useful.

Articles

Clarke, John H., "Judicial Power to Declare Legislation Unconstitutional," 9 *American Bar Association Journal* (November 1923) 689.

A retired justice of the Supreme Court examines the origin of judicial review and considers the question of its reform.

Corwin, Edward S., "The Constitution as Instrument and as Symbol," 30 *American Political Science Review* (December 1936) 1071.

A very thoughtful article on the dual character of the Constitution. Read originally as a paper at the Harvard Tercentenary celebration.

Corwin, Edward S., "The Doctrine of Due Process of Law before the Civil War," 24 *Harvard Law Review* (1911) 366 and 460; also I *Selected Essays* 203.

A valuable article treating the origins of due process of law and its significance in this country before 1860.

Corwin, Edward S., "Marbury v. Madison and the Doctrine of Judicial Review," 12 *Michigan Law Review* (1914) 538; also I *Selected Essays* 128.

An examination of the origins of judicial review which considers the precedents for, and the steps that led to, Marshall's decision in *Marbury* v. *Madison*.

Cushman, Robert E., "Constitutional Decisions by a Bare Majority," 19 *Michigan Law Review* (1921) 771; also I *Selected Essays* 527.

A thorough consideration of the controversy over five-to-four decisions. The author is inclined to oppose any change in this respect.

Edgerton, Henry W., "The Incidence of Judicial Control over Congress," 22 *Cornell Law Quarterly* (1937) 299; also I *Selected Essays* 793.

A very valuable, pioneer article on the effects which the operation of judicial review has had upon different social and economic interests.

Fairman, Charles, "The Retirement of Federal Judges," 51 *Harvard Law Review* (1938) 397; also I *Selected Essays* 885.

A thorough article presenting much historical and statistical data on the retirement of judges and offering a proposal for reform.

Field, Oliver P., "Judicial Review as an Instrument of Government," I *Selected Essays* 733—a reprint of Chap. XII of *The Effect of an Unconstitutional Statute* (Minneapolis: University of Minnesota Press, 1935).

A stimulating essay discussing certain shortcomings in the operation of judicial review particularly on the procedural side.

Haines, Charles G., "The History of Due Process of Law after the Civil War," 3 *Texas Law Review* (1924) 1; also I *Selected Essays* 268.

A companion article to the one by Corwin cited above. Presents a critical analysis of the widening scope of due process of law during the last fifty years.

Haines, Charles G., "Judicial Review of Acts of Congress and the Need for Constitutional Reform," 45 *Yale Law Journal* (1936) 816; also I *Selected Essays* 844.

A critical examination of the operation of judicial review in recent years which concludes with a consideration of certain possible reform steps.

Hutcheson, Joseph C., "The Judgment Intuitive: The Function of the 'Hunch' in Judicial Decision," 14 *Cornell Law Quarterly* (April 1929) 274.

A brilliant, witty description of certain nonlegal considerations that sometimes influence a judge in his decisions.

Powell, Thomas Reed, "The Judiciality of Minimum Wage Legislation," 37 *Harvard Law Review* (1924) 545; also *Selected Essays,* I, 553 and II, 716.

A powerful attack upon the decision of the Supreme Court in the *Adkins* case by a scholar who knows no peer in the critical analysis of specific Supreme Court decisions.

Warren, Charles, "The New 'Liberty' under the Fourteenth Amendment," 39 *Harvard Law Review* (1926) 431; also II *Selected Essays* 237.

An examination of the increasing tendency of the Supreme Court to protect civil liberties against state encroachment under the Fourteenth Amendment. The author criticizes this tendency.

Index

Abbott, Edith, quoted, 209
Adkins v. Children's Hospital, 154–
57, 191, 207, 255
Anderson v. Dunn, 283
Apex Hosiery Co. v. Leader, 3–17,
21, 22
Ashwander v. T.V.A., 187–88, 201

Bailey v. Drexel Furniture Co., 194
Bailey v. United States, 112–13
Barron v. Baltimore, 176
Beard, Charles A., 64, 245; Eco-
nomic Interpretation of Constitu-
tion, quoted, 40, 48; on eco-
nomic motivation, 39; Founding
Fathers on judicial review, 45–46,
48–49; Supreme Court and Con-
stitution, quoted, 46, 48–49, 50
Beard, Charles A. and Mary R.,
Rise of American Civilization,
quoted, 39, 259
Beveridge, A. J., Life of John Mar-
shall, quoted, 103–4, 237–38
Bill of Rights, 88, 175–76, 177, 178,
181
Black, Chief Justice, quoted, 283–84
Black, Justice, 173, 248; opinion in
Chambers v. Florida, 182–83
Blackstone, quoted, 14
Borah, Senator, 266

Boudin, L. B., Government by
Judiciary, 46
Brandeis, Justice, 154, 166, 179, 180,
201, 232–33, 239–40, 244–45, 248,
255; dissents in Oklahoma Ice
case, 169; opinion in Ashwander
v. T.V.A., 187–88
Brooks v. United States, 112
Bryan, William Jennings, 259
Bunting v. Oregon, 152–53
Business affected with a public in-
terest, 161–71
Butler, Justice, 154, 182, 231–32,
247, 256; dissents in Near v.
Minnesota, 180

Caminetti v. United States, 113
Cardozo, Benjamin, 240, 244, 248;
Nature of the Judicial Process,
quoted, 19–20, 234, 235–36, 289–
90
Carter v. Carter Coal Co., 123–24,
129, 187, 196–97
Certiorari, 10–11
Chamberlain, John, American Stakes,
26, quoted, 28
Chambers v. Florida, 182–83
Champion v. Ames, 107–8, 110–11
Chase, Chief Justice, 252, 254
Chase, Justice Samuel, 262

Checks and balances, principle of, 91–94
Chicago & Grand Trunk Ry. Co. v. Wellman, 186
Chicago, Milwaukee & St. Paul Ry. Co. v. Minnesota 147–48
Child labor regulation, 108–12, 114–15, 133, 209
Choate, Joseph H., 30
Circuit court of appeals, 10, 227–28
Clark Distilling Co. v. Western Maryland Ry. Co., 208
Clarke, John H., 190n, 240
Clifford, Justice, 242, 266
Coke, Sir Edward, quoted, 41–42
Coleman v. Miller, 198–99
Commerce power, 82, 83–84, 99–138; as basis for control of local enterprise, 115–30; as basis for federal police power, 107–15; interpreted: in *Darby Co.* case, 131–35, in *Gibbons* case, 102–4, in *Jones & Laughlin* case, 124–30, in *Knight Co.* case, 104–6, in *Schechter* case, 116–23
Common law, influence on statutes, 16–18; on married women's property, 31–32; origin of, 13–14; relation to equity, 15; as superior law, 23–24
Constitution, United States, amendment of, 274–77; as instrument and symbol, 95–98
Constitutional Convention. *See* Founding Fathers
Corwin, Edward S., "Constitution as Instrument and Symbol," 183, quoted, 46–47, 54–56; Founding Fathers on judicial review, 46–47; "Judicial Review," quoted, 69
Council of revision, 44–45
Cushman, Robert E., *Leading Constitutional Decisions,* quoted, 103, 177; "Problem of Independent

Regulatory Commissions," quoted, 228–29

Davidson v. New Orleans, 145
Dicey, A. V., *Law and Public Opinion in England,* quoted, 16, 33–34; on married women's property law, 31–33, 246
District court, 9–10
Douglas, Justice, 247, 248
Dr. Bonham's Case, 41–42
Dred Scott v. Sandford, 188, 201, 208, 258, 264, 267, 285, 286
Due process of law, 139–83; and civil liberties, 173–83; evolution of, 143–49; and police power, 140–43; and price fixing, 161–71; and wages and hours legislation, 150–61
Duval, Justice, 241–42

Eakin v. Raub, 63–64
Eastman, Joseph, 225
Edgerton, H. W., "Incidence of Judicial Control," quoted, 281–82
Elliot, J., *Debates,* 52
Ellsworth, Oliver, quoted, 52
Equity, 14–15, 32–33
Evans, L. B., *Leading Cases on Constitutional Law,* quoted, 13–14
Ewing, Cortez A. M., *Judges of Supreme Court,* 250–51
Ex parte McCardle, 265

Fair Labor Standards Act, 131–35, 159–60, 218
Fairman, Charles, *Mr. Justice Miller,* quoted, 242, 252; "The Retirement of Federal Judges," 34–35, 273
Federal Trade Commission, 228–29
Federalism, principle of, 80–87
Federalist, The, quoted, 51
Field, Justice, 236, 254, 273; dis-

sents in *Slaughter-House Cases*, 146

Fletcher v. *Peck*, 57n, 189, 194

Foster-Fountain Packing Co. v. *Haydel*, 195

Founding Fathers, 275; attitude toward judicial review, 41–56, 71; economic motivation of, 39; on separation of powers, 91

Frank, Jerome, *Law and the Modern Mind*, quoted, 233–34

Frankfurter, Felix, 149, 247; on due process of law, 142–43; *Law and Politics*, quoted, 79, 236, 241, 244, 290–91; *Mr. Justice Holmes*, quoted, 233; "Supreme Court, United States," quoted, 260

Frothingham v. *Mellon*, 202

Fuller, Chief Justice, 247

Gibbons v. *Ogden*, 102–4, 105

Gibson, Justice, 63–64

Gitlow v. *New York*, 179–80

Haines, Charles G., 280; *American Doctrine of Judicial Supremacy*, quoted, 2, 23–24, 49, 70, 237, 238, 270, 286

Hale, Mathew, 163

Hale, Senator, 264

Hamilton, Alexander, quoted, 51

Hamilton v. *Kentucky Distilleries Co.*, 193

Hammer v. *Dagenhart*, 108–12, 114–15, 133, 134, 194–95, 209

Hand, Learned, 234

Harding, Warren G., 240, 253, 269

Harlan, Justice, 179, 179n, 181, 200; dissents in: *Knight Co.* case, 105, *Lochner* case, 152; opinion in *Champion* v. *Ames*, 107

Hart, Henry M., "Business of Supreme Court, 1937, 1938," quoted, 230

Hipolite Egg Co. v. *United States*, 111

Hoadly, Bishop, quoted, 20

Hoke v. *United States*, 111

Holden v. *Hardy*, 150–51

Holmes, Justice, 180, 190, 193, 201, 232–33, 238, 244, 245, 248; *Collected Legal Papers*, quoted, 31, 35, 282, 287; dissents in: *Adkins* case, 156, *Hammer* v. *Dagenhart*, 109, *Lochner* case, 95, 149, 151–52, *Tyson* v. *Banton*, 166–68; on due process of law, 171–72; on separation of powers, 220–21

Hughes, Chief Justice, 221, 248, 254, 256; dissents in *Apex* case, 6; opinions in: *Jones & Laughlin* case, 128, *Near* v. *Minnesota*, 180, *Schechter* case, 118–21, *Shreveport Case*, 121; *Supreme Court of United States*, quoted, 20, 159, 273

Hutcheson, Joseph C., "The Judgment Intuitive," quoted, 235

Hylton v. *United States*, 186

Implied power, principle of, 75–76, 83–87, 88

Injunction, 14–15

Interstate commerce. See Commerce power

Jackson, Robert, *Struggle for Judicial Supremacy*, 173–74, quoted, 35, 206, 243, 285, 289

Jacobson v. *Massachusetts*, 90, 200

Johnson, Justice, 283

Judges, age of, 250–51, 272; appointment of, 11, 237–44, 251–53, 269–70, 271–72; impeachment of, 261–63; recall of, 274; removal of for bad behavior, 263; retirement of, 272–73; training of, 247–50

"Judges' Bill," 249

Judicial conservatism, 33–35

Judicial legislation, 20–21, 211, 212–21

Judicial review, conspiracy theory of, 51–52; courts which exercise, 205–6; criticism of, 257–77, 284–87; defense of, 279–84, 289–90; defined, 23–24, 210; delay in exercise of, 201–2; early precedents for, 41–44; frequency of exercise, 204–5, 210–11; influence of on Congress, 207–8; limitations of, 184–203; in *Marbury* case, 57–71; normal function theory of, 50; of administrative rulings, 209–30; in Philadelphia Convention, 44–47; Sir Edward Coke on, 41–42

Judicial temperament, 244–45

Jurisdiction, of circuit court of appeals, 10; control of by Congress, 264–66; of district court, 9–10; of federal courts, 8–9; of Supreme Court, 10–11

Kales, A. M., "New Methods in Due Process Cases," quoted, 172

Kent, Chancellor, 233–34

Kidnaping legislation, 112–13

La Follette, Senator, 268

Limited government, principle of, 87–90

Lincoln, Abraham, 269, quoted, 258

Lochner v. *New York*, 95, 149, 151–52

Logan-Walter Bill, 223–24

Lurton, Justice, 238–39

MacLeish, Archibald, quoted, 245

Mann Act, 111, 113

Marbury v. *Madison*, 57–71, 78, 185, 189, 204, 281; background of, 58–59; evaluation of, 67–71; Marshall's opinion in, 59–63

Marshall, Chief Justice, 56, 85, 86n, 135, 236, 237–38, 253, 257, 260, 262; evaluation of *Marbury* opinion, 67–71; opinions in: *Barron* v. *Baltimore*, 176, *Fletcher* v. *Peck*, 189, 194, *Gibbons* case, 102–4, 137, *Marbury* case, 59–63, *McCulloch* case, 72, 74–77, 97–98, 275–76; in Virginia Convention, 52

Martin, Luther, quoted, 45

Maternity Act, 202

Mathews, Justice, 247

McCulloch v. *Maryland*, 72–78, 83, 88, 97–98, 275–76; background of, 72–74; Marshall's opinion in, 72, 74–77

McLaughlin, Andrew C., *Constitutional History of United States*, quoted, 48, 58; "Marbury v. Madison Again," quoted, 70

McLean, Justice, 252, 254

McReynolds, Justice, 170, 180, 182, 240, 245, 255; dissents in *Jones & Laughlin* case, 129

Miller, Justice, 173, 177–78, 236, 242, 252, 254; on due process of law, 145, 164

Morehead v. *Tipaldo*, 157–59

Mulford v. *Smith*, 85

Muller v. *Oregon*, 152

Munn v. *Illinois*, 162–64

Murphy, Justice, 255

Myers v. *United States*, 93–94, 201

N.L.R.B. v. *Fansteel Metallurgical Corp.*, 214–16

N.L.R.B. v. *Jones & Laughlin Steel Corp.*, 124–30

National Industrial Recovery Act, 116–17, 286

National Labor Relations Act, 124–26, 214–16, 217, 221, 286

National Labor Relations Board, 92, 127, 211, 221–22, 225, 226–27

National Motor Vehicle Theft Act, 99–100, 112
Near v. *Minnesota*, 180
Nebbia v. *New York*, 169–71, 172
New State Ice Co. v. *Liebmann*, 169

O'Mahoney, Senator, 266–67
Otis, James, quoted, 42

Partial invalidation, 195–97
Peckham, Justice, opinion in *Lochner* case, 151
Pepper, George Wharton, quoted, 30–31
Pitney, Justice, 179
Police power, 89–90, 139–43, 170
Political questions, 197–99
Pollock v. *Farmers' Loan & Trust Co.*, 186, 196, 208, 259
Pound, Roscoe, quoted, 17
Powell, Thomas Reed, quoted, 130, 157, 193
Powell v. *Alabama*, 182
Pressure groups, 26–30; influence on courts, 29–33, 284–85
Pringle, Henry F., *Life and Times of William Howard Taft*, quoted, 242, 253

Rathbun v. *United States*, 94
Reciprocal Tariff Act, 202
Ribnik v. *McBride*, 168–69, 207
Roberts, Justice, 173, 180, 247; opinions in: *Butler* case, 79, 190–92, *Nebbia* case, 170, 172
Roosevelt, Franklin D., 207, 240, 243, 249; Court reform plan, 126, 130, 257, 269, 271, 273; on *Schechter* decision, 64–65
Roosevelt, Theodore, 238–39, 244, 280

Santa Cruz Fruit Packing Co. v. *N.L.R.B.*, 124n, 129n
Schechter Poultry Corp. v. *United States*, 116–23, 126–27

Schlesinger, Arthur, *New Viewpoints in American History*, quoted, 49–50
Separation of powers, principle of, 90–95
Sharpless v. *Mayor of Philadelphia*, 283–84
Sherman Act, 4, 5, 6, 12–13, 17, 21, 104–6, 212–14, 217
Shreveport Case, 120–22, 134
Sinking Fund Cases, 189
Slaughter-House Cases, 145, 146, 164, 177–78
Springer v. *Philippine Islands*, 220–21
Stafford v. *Wallace*, 118–20
Standard Oil Co. v. *United States*, 212, 213, 217
Stare decisis, 18–19
State courts, 11–12
Statutory law, 13
Stettler v. *O'Hara*, 153–54
Stone, Justice, 161, 169, 180, 240, 247, 248; dissents in: *Ribnik* v. *McBride*, 168, *Tyson* v. *Banton*, 168; opinions in: *Apex* case, 3, 7, 8, *Butler* case, 67, 192, *Darby Co.* case, 133–35, 160, *United States* v. *Morgan*, 222
Sutherland, Justice, 154, 180, 231–32, 248; opinions in: *Adkins* case, 155, 191, *Carter* case, 124, *Ribnik* v. *McBride*, 168, *Tyson* v. *Banton*, 166, 191
Swayne, Justice, 252

Taft, Chief Justice, 236, 252–53, 254, 256, 269; quoted, 240–41, 242–43; dissents in *Adkins* case, 156; opinion in *Brooks* v. *United States*, 112
Taney, Chief Justice, 86, 236, 252
Trevett v. *Weeden*, 43–44
Tyson v. *Banton*, 166–68, 191

United States v. *Butler,* 67, 79, 85, 190–92

United States v. *Darby Lumber Co.,* 131–35, 159–60

United States v. *Delaware & Hudson Co.,* 188

United States v. *Doremus,* 193–94

United States v. *E. C. Knight Co.,* 104–6

United States v. *Morgan,* 222

Van Devanter, Justice, 180

Wages and Hours Act. *See* Fair Labor Standards Act

Wagner Act. *See* National Labor Relations Act

Waite, Chief Justice, opinion in *Munn* v. *Illinois,* 162–63

Warren, Charles, *Congress, Constitution and Supreme Court,* quoted, 280–81; *Supreme Court in United States History,* quoted, 106

Washington, George, quoted, 38–39, 39–40

West Coast Hotel Co. v. *Parrish,* 159

Wheeler, Senator, 268

Wilson, James, quoted, 45

Wilson, Woodrow, 239–40

Writs of Assistance Case, 42